$10.⁰⁰

To my dear
friend
Marshal Karp
with happy
Five Island
Memories
Best
Harry Rasky
Toronto · Feb 19/82

NOBODY SWINGS ON SUNDAY

The Many Lives and Films of Harry Rasky

by

Harry Rasky

Collier Macmillan Canada, Ltd.

Collier Macmillan Canada, Ltd.
1125B Leslie Street
Don Mills, Ontario M3C 2K2

Editor: Sarah Swartz Consultant Services

Design: Taylor/Sprules

Canadian Cataloguing in Publication Data

Rasky, Harry, 1928-
    Nobody swings on Sunday

ISBN 0-02-990660-1

1. Rasky, Harry, 1928-   2. Moving picture
producers and directors – Canada – Biography.
I. Title

PN1998.A3R37   791.43′023′0924   C80-094781-9

1 2 3 4 5 6 84 83 82 81 80
Printed and bound in Canada

TO
ARLENE, HOLLY AND ADAM

"They change their clime, not their
disposition, who run beyond the sea."
(Horace, Epistle 1)

"Perhaps it is true
One needs to bleed to write poetry.
One must be a little of every man—
Surely Shakespeare's recipe:
Who used the human race to write his diary."
(from *To Tell The Truth* by Paul Roche)

Contents

PREFACE   *vii*

PART I

CHAPTER ONE	St. Clair Avenue West	*3*
CHAPTER TWO	My Mother's Kirkland Lake Kimono	*21*
CHAPTER THREE	A Voice for Lorne Greene	*31*
CHAPTER FOUR	Europe and an Interview with the Queen of England	*41*
CHAPTER FIVE	Ed Murrow Needs Me	*53*
CHAPTER SIX	Revolutions in Latin America/ Revelations in New York	*67*
CHAPTER SEVEN	Africa: *Rainbow of Darkness*	*77*
CHAPTER EIGHT	Heroes: *A little less Brando, please, Fidel*	*95*
CHAPTER NINE	The Nobel Prize: *I will live through my son, Martin Luther King Jr.*	*111*
CHAPTER TEN	Peanut Brittle from Lady Bird/ Vietnam Letters to Holly	*125*
CHAPTER ELEVEN	Hall of Kings: *How I came to be buried in the Abbey*	*145*
CHAPTER TWELVE	Upon This Rock: *Orson, don't breathe so hard on the Pieta*	*159*

PART II

CHAPTER THIRTEEN	The Chain	*171*
CHAPTER FOURTEEN	The Wit and World of G. Bernard Shaw	183
CHAPTER FIFTEEN	My Brother Tennessee	*195*
CHAPTER SIXTEEN	Next Year in Jerusalem	*213*
CHAPTER SEVENTEEN	Marc Chagall: *This film will help me live longer, not less*	229
CHAPTER EIGHTEEN	Arthur Miller on Home Ground	247

AFTER WORDS   *257*

Preface

Wandering around in my life are Fidel and Tennessee and Lady Bird and Marc Chagall. I don't think I entered their lives the same way. But something happened. There were interviews, film crews, frustrations, contacts, interchanges. And out of it we changed, the world altered a bit and I perhaps a great deal. This is an account of the lives of some famous people as I have known them. It is also a personal journey to my own beginnings, then till now.

There is the danger of putting to paper a memoir of times past. My friend, Tennessee Williams, wrote one and later had to suggest it was something he did at the wrong time. But what is the right time to recall? Once I knew briefly the great satirical film director, Preston Sturges, who confided at my New York apartment, "You know, I have just been to the doctor and he tells me I will live forever. I have begun my autobiography, *The Events Leading To My Death.*" It proved to be a great title but not a great idea. Two months and a couple of chapters later, the genius was dead. And now we will never know.

There is the question of who should join me in these pages. Some will say I have just dropped names. Perhaps. But let me mingle those whom you feel you know with those whom you will never see mentioned elsewhere. My own life journey has taken me to half the world's countries over half a century.

I feel I owe it to you to explain what has prompted me now to begin these mental wanderings. It has to do with the line of work which has taken up most of my time in recent years—films. The films, strangely, took on a biographical theme: the lives of world–famous people. Some of them might even be called definitive studies. With each passing study of a life, somehow my own life became more and more reflected in the subject material. Suddenly I was looking at a passing scene on film and there was I. It is important for me to examine why.

For instance, why was it that I saw myself in the pain and loneliness of Tennessee Williams? Why was it that in my most acclaimed film, *Homage to Chagall—The Colours of Love*, that Chagall's memories in his childhood synagogue listening to the prayers of his grandfather became my memory of my father? Why was it that in my film about playright Arthur Miller, when we toured his history in Brooklyn, his street became my street? How had we fused? Were they I and I they? Had I become too involved for my subjects? Had the consideration of myself as an artist forced me to make every film about myself, and were the subjects just an excuse to involve an audience? Perhaps by stating here and now my own story, this will become clear. To begin . . .

PART I

CHAPTER ONE

St. Clair Avenue West

S t. Clair Avenue has never left me. At Buckingham Palace in London, the White House in Washington and Oscar Night in Hollywood, that is the image of myself. Always there. Those cold Canadian winter nights over the store listening to the Bay streetcar whish through snow and slush, and those muggy August mornings with heat that actually hurt. The Bay car clanged by and some of me with it.

Later when I was asked which side of the street I was born on, I just answered, "Right on the tracks." It was not far from the truth. St. Clair Avenue West was a wide boulevard with great pretensions, heading nowhere. To the east it disappeared into something quite rich, which I later was to find was the northern limit of the WASP districts of Moore Park and Rosedale. To the west it became mud which ended up in the "Junction" in those early years. The Junction was where the rail-lines converged and the slaughterhouse of Canada Packers began. On a hot day the bacon rind fumes gave the air an unkosher odour. I swear I could taste bacon (God forbid) in my clothes.

The streets on either side of the St. Clair of my Toronto were decorated with names that gave the inhabitants of its lower middle class semi-detached grey buildings more than semi-detached aspirations. The park was Earlscourt. The public school, Regal Road. The street opposite, Ascot, and the local movie house, my local escape, Royal George. It was transplanted east-end London and grey Glasgow.

Somehow on St. Clair a band of Jews had decided to set up a merchant fort. The Scots and the English around us were like the attacking

Indians in an old-fashioned western. But our block, the 1200 block of St. Clair West, was as Jewish as Tel Aviv in July. How that happened, I don't know. Most of the immigrant Jews had huddled downtown, somewhere around Spadina and College, clustered as if ready for a Canadian pogrom.

The merchants were a mini-nation. You did not have to go far to find a cross-section of Europe in those Jews who shared that block. Every prejudice and pain had come with them. If Israel today is as diverse as the collection of attitudes on my block, it must be a constant argument. Not one of those merchants remains there today. But I can see them in my mind.

Let's start on the corner. The Waller family had no use for any of us. Old man Waller ran a hardware and gas pump. In those days gasoline was pumped right at curb-side, and what soaked on the roadway was merely washed down by hose at night. In retrospect, I don't know why Waller didn't blow us all up. Much later, after the Jews had departed, the store was obliterated when the Italians moved in and the Mafia apparently wiped out some inconvenient resident. But in our time, Mr. Waller looked down on the Yiddish-speaking neighbours. He had Palestine plans for himself and his kids, and mingling with us was worse than associating with gentiles. Somewhere in Israel today the Wallers have taken up residence and have Hebrew names. To us they stayed constant strangers in a strange land. Old man Waller chewed on the stubs of old cigars and the ashes seemed to blend right into his skin. He sat on a camp chair outside his store in summer, waiting for trucks to stop at the pump. I don't recall him ever speaking. He grunted if you entered his store for a bolt or screw. Ashes flew and he'd be off in his dream of Jerusalem. How could anyone imagine Jerusalem on St. Clair Avenue West?

Next door, with shelves to the ceiling, was the shop of Maylech Zolotovsky (later stylishly changed to Zolt), a Polish Jew with glittering gold teeth which seemed to flash more at the ladies than the men. Maylech was in what was then called "dry goods": skirts, slips, socks, etc.—a lot of etc. I have to laugh when I hear people today say, "You Jews all stick together." Each Jew on the block was his own island. And Maylech Zolt was a kingdom. Waller to the south of him was like an Arab army, and on the other side were the Anisman clan.

In terms of Maylech Zolt, the Anismans did not exist. How could they? They were also in the dry goods line. Competition. Competition right next door. Zolt had to stare across the wide avenue, watch the streetcars go by and try to imagine he had no neighbours. Mrs. Anisman had an extra problem. She was a widow with half a dozen kids. She was treated as if she had committed a crime, to live so brazenly without a husband. One of her children was Art, who was one of my childhood friends. Frequently he was chased by my mother with a broom. I never knew exactly why, except that he was half orphaned and for some reason was blamed for his family state.

Next were the Minks. They were in the millinery line. The Depression was a time when ladies wore hats. Make something of that if you will. I must admit I seldom saw any customers in the store, but regularly those bonnets in the window would change. Veils up and down, pink for Easter, grey for winter. Mrs. Mink was rather puffy cheeked. Her husband worked somewhere downtown in the garment shops and, therefore, was seldom seen.

The Minks were in hats and the Garaways next door in furs. I always thought there would have been a kind of justice if the Minks were in furs. But what's in a name? My impression is that the fur business was profitable, because the Garaways also had a large car in their garage. Mr. Garaway always seemed secretive and angry. That may have been because we played handball on his garage door.

Every Jewish block needs a socialist. The Levine family next to the Garaways filled the role. Another millinery shop, so you can imagine how they did with the Minks. Who needed a pogrom with all that instant hostility? Young Gilbert Levine went on to become a fiery labour leader.

We were separated from the Levines in my early years by the Ardreys. Now that has always seemed the final irony. The Ardrey family sold Christian literature. They were sizzling members of the Church of the Nazarene. Bibles and busts of Christ incongruously decorated their windows. As you can imagine, they did little indigenous business.

We lived at 1281 in what was called ''a cottage.'' That meant there was no basement and the house was made of wood. There was something frail about it. The store had been built over a large chestnut tree root. So stubborn had been the root that when the floor was built, rather than try to cut it out, the workmen merely sloped the floor. This was handy for playing marbles, as the coloured agates could roll with ease for an evening game while we waited for customers to pass through. To this day I don't recall another store with a sloping floor.

We'll get back to the family Rasky. For the moment let's continue up the street. Our next-door neighbour for all of my childhood was a certain Mr. Yung who had a Chinese laundry. He smiled a lot and naturally we never talked. I don't know if Mr. Yung ever spoke English, except to list the price of laundering shirts and sheets. He vanished behind clouds of steam in his back room until summoned by a bell on a blank counter. I always thought there was a strange, hidden hell back there, when he would appear in his apron and the clouds floated over his head.

He would smile, deliver a plain brown package and vanish again in the clouds.

Beyond the laundry stood the Church of the Nazarene, site of a former garage. From it blared Christian hymns, organ music and a call to Christ. Not too much business from our side of St. Clair. We always appreciated the Chinese laundry as a kind of no-man's land between the Jews on the block and the church. There was a gentleman's agreement that we would not protest the constant preaching if the church would make no comment about the chicken calls that used to break the morning street noises. In back of our store we kept a chicken coop of constantly changing chickens, brought in weekly for the ritual slaughter. But roosters never seemed to differentiate between country and town. They crowed as if to wake up the farm which was not there. So the church blared Christ-praising songs and the roosters announced the kosher chickens for sale.

There was a pause in the street beyond the church, an empty lot where once there had been a building destroyed by fire but never restored. Personal arson was popular during the Depression years, as businessmen decided to collect the insurance and run. Strangely, no one could recall what had stood there. But for us kids it was a perfect setting for kick-the-can and hide-and-go-seek and other rituals of growing up in the city.

The stores beyond get vague in memory. Of course there was the dress store of Leslie Feldman's mother. Leslie was part of my gang. And there was Lipshitz, the used furniture dealer. He sat like an Einstein amid the clutter of pots, pans and pianos. He was a growling free-thinker. There was Willer's fancy shop near the corner and Magani's Italian grocery on the corner. Later, when Italy entered the war on Germany's side, it broke Mr. Magani's heart that the local Scots and English started their own personal blockade. As if Magani himself were bombing Britain. You really didn't have to leave the block to find a world war.

St. Clair Avenue was so wide that to cross it was almost like entering another village. To be sure there were certain contacts. Snowbell had a jewellery store. It's still there. Clavir made suits. Lou Litwin of St. Clair Paint and Wallpaper carried paint cans on to a fortune. And we would visit the McQuoid Drug Store for five-cent ice cream cones and to check the temperature at the Ex-Lax thermometer outside. Beyond were the gentiles, and a Jewish boy wandering around was asking for trouble, or so it seemed.

One block south was McKay Street. This was the home of the remarkable McKay Street *shul,* the local synagogue that somehow held our band of diverse Jews together. The *shul* was always part of my life. I'm told that it was the first home of the Rasky family in Canada.

My family left Russia just after World War I. They had lived in a town near Kiev in the Ukraine, called Desha. They had owned a mill for the grinding of flour. The family name was Poberregesky, which I'm told means "beside the stream." They were modest capitalists, I suppose, in a revolutionary time—capitalist and Jewish. Naturally they lost all. This was especially difficult for my father because he had been raised to be the family scholar, a non-ordained rabbi. Each family allowed one son to be the carrier of the tradition, much as the Irish provide a child to the Church. The Revolution came and left the family to wander across Europe.

They must have been a strange group of wanderers. My grandmother, the Baba Bayla who had no teeth, my grandfather, a tall, elegant silent man, my parents and three or four young children. Ads for help were placed in overseas papers. A distant relative from Chicago sent boat fare and the group boarded a boat in Antwerp.

Ellis Island in New York is where the name split in two. My uncle became Pober and my father Rasky.

Our group continued on to Canada because my mother's sister, Aunt Lillie, had married a pedlar, Uncle Ben, who lived in the Junction. So what does a scholar do in a cold, wintry city where he knows no one and not even the language? My father, a short, powerful man with red beard and strong faith, offered himself out as the local religious person. He taught the kids Hebrew and sang. How he sang! He talked to God in the melodies of the suffering of the Jews. He put his family in the back room of the synagogue and there they lived, all of them, safe from the Cossacks and the pogroms and the gentiles, with no money but lots of time to pray.

Heat was provided by a pot-bellied stove. Since fuel was difficult to come by, the family scrounged around the neighbourhood. My grandmother noted that each morning a young boy toured the neighbourhood tossing papers, the *Mail and Empire*, in nearby doorways. How wonderful to have the paper to start the morning fire. How convenient. Except that the local readers became annoyed at their disappearing papers. A motorcycle policeman was sent to study the crime. He caught grandmother red-handed in her black robes. Since my grandmother never had learned a word of English, my oldest sister, Pearl, was sent to the police station to be translator and lawyer. They vanished down McKay Street in the side-car of the cop's motorcycle. Somewhere there was a kind judge who understood that the papers had not been stolen for resale, or even for reading. What would the Baba Bayla know about reading the *Mail and Empire*? She never did know how to read. She promised to give up petty crime, and peace returned to McKay Street.

It was decided that with so many mouths to feed, the most sensible thing was to buy food wholesale. Thus the store was planned on St. Clair to obtain apples by the barrel, tins by the dozen and milk by the gallon. My father was to take on the job of *shoychet*, the ritual butcher of poultry. Slaughter was only allowed by a holy man. Holy and poor and proud— that was my father. The store was our family.

The store set the pattern for all my early years. In all, there were five sons and three daughters. The family plan was quite simple. As soon as a child was able, he would pull parcels in a wagon to the local customers. As he grew, he would mount a bicycle with an oversized carrier and deliver beyond the local scene. Later on we would experiment with second-hand cars as delivery trucks.

On Monday and Tuesday, my father would visit the chicken market down on Baldwin and Spadina, and pick the hundred or so chickens he would resell during the week. Wednesday would begin the slaughter, and the chicken plucking would take place in the back shed. On Thursday we would deliver after school and into the night, carrying our kosher parcels to milk boxes on nearby Lauder Avenue and Glenholme and into the hushed luxury of Forest Hill Village. Friday night there was the quick change into our best second-hand clothes for Sabbath eve services at the McKay Street *shul*. Saturday, the Sabbath, I helped round up the local Jews for the *minyen*, the quorum of ten men needed for Jewish prayers. I think I got everyone on the block at least once, except for Waller who seemed to have no use for God, Jewish or otherwise. Palestine yes, but prayers no. Sunday was the day for collecting the accounts from those Thursday night deliveries.

Once on a Sunday, I was picked up by the police for breaking the Lord's Day Alliance. I don't know with whom the Lord was allied. But in Christian Canada and proper Toronto, I was a criminal for helping collect bills that would pay for the next week's supply of chickens. Indeed there was never enough profit to do anything but feed the 100 chickens and the ten Raskys and get us through school. It was no accident that the day my brother Norman, the youngest, had worked his way through dental college, the business disappeared—not sold, just vanished. The store had served its purpose. We had been educated, sent out into the foreign world. The singing on Saturday and the killing of chickens on Wednesday and bicycling up those snowy and sometimes sweaty streets were part of the educational process.

After the collection period on Sunday, there was the question of what to do in Toronto. Fear of the Lord was everywhere. At the Earlscourt Park there were tennis courts; no nets could be hung. There were sandboxes and swings; the swings were padlocked. Padlocked! Once, when I found one free and began swinging, a policeman in his bobby hat grabbed my shoulder. His words have never left me: "Nobody swings on Sunday!" Amen.

On summer days we visited the Toronto Islands, the sandbars which were a ferry ride across the harbour. We would swim in the polluted lake, listen to a band concert at Hanlan's Point, chew Cracker Jacks, our one weekly treat. I will never forget the journey home. My mother led the attack. If all eight kids hit the turnstiles simultaneously, the streetcar ticket operator was so confused that at least three got by free. Three times three cents, a saving of almost a dime.

My mother. My mother was a woman of incredible energy. I've often thought that if there were creative juices passed down the line in the family they came from her, despite her lack of any academic skills of reading or writing. But there was a way of expression, a way of sweeping phrases to support or condemn. She was a woman of large emotion. She could cry for two days non-stop, or express joy almost as if in levitation and flight. She embraced us all with varied passion, anger and love. Between childbirths she plucked and cleaned chickens, acted as hostess at the synagogue, and tried to find temporary release for us from the pavement existence of St. Clair Avenue West.

We were always tired from our work routine. Even today I can recall the addresses of our customers: Mrs. Cohen, 210 Glenholme; Mr. Wagman, 67 Westmount . . . I still dream of that bicycle route. Sometimes we would fall asleep in our classes at Regal Road Public School, only to be startled by Miss MacPherson, our teacher, and begin answering lessons in Yiddish. Miss MacPherson was not amused. We had to collect pictures of the British Royal Family. To this day I have a slight touch of Scottish in my dialect: we were all Presbyterians.

Mr. Foreman, my Hebrew teacher, used to break a dozen rulers a week on our heads and hands to make us learn the five books of Moses as the good Lord had obviously told Mr. Foreman we must. And I can still recite "Berayshish boroh Elohim . . . In the beginning God created . . ."

We slept three in a bed, crowded around a wood stove, and bathed in a wash basin. Our diet was composed largely of left-over chickens and apples bought wholesale by the barrel. I can still recall the lonely lost feeling of reaching into an apple barrel for the very last piece of fruit, and tumbling into it and crying my eyes out because no one knew where I was. And how many ways can you boil a chicken?

Occasionally there would be unusual treats. Down on the Lansdowne Road, just across from the cemetery which I always thought was a park, we were invited to a party every Christmas. The family's name was "Christian." And they had one lonely, skinny boy. He always struck me as a little sad. My father encouraged us to go because it meant a free meal. We did get the bonus of Christmas crackers; they went bang and there was a supply of candy. Mr. Christian manipulated himself on a board on wheels, a quadraplegic, a basket case from Verdun. It seemed odd to me to see this Christmas host wheel himself about on his platform. But it wasn't until a decade later that I discovered why we were the Christians' guests. They were the neighbourhood's only Negro family. They were being kind to the other minority. A child doesn't notice those things. Negro or white, they were the *goyim*, the gentiles, the enemy. Had they not torn the family from its Russian roots? Sometimes my father would flatter them with a *gutten goy*, a good gentile, but they were different. How could they know a Jewish heart?

Once I remember having a crush on a Marie Hamilton who lived on the Dufferin hill. She was the prettiest in the Regal Road class. There was something beautifully, simply sinful about the way my heart hurt when she passed. How I would have loved a valentine just once from her, the prettiest girl in the school! Perhaps I wouldn't have felt the shoes-with-holes rubbing against my stockings-with-holes at age ten. In later years I took Marie to a newspapermen's ball at the regal Royal York. The white pancake makeup destroyed years of illusion.

I dwell on this Jewish thing because it has always been there, and I have found on my world travels that it is like belonging to the world's largest private club. The *mezuzah* on my neck has brought dinner invitations from accented Jews of Scotland and Scandinavia, and private greetings in Rome and Acapulco. If it has meant a kind of childish isolation, it has also brought an understanding of universal suffering and the most prized hand-me-down, learning.

My father had briefly studied Plato and other wisdom. But he remained convinced that no knowledge of any worth existed that could not be found in the Torah and the thousands of books of interpretation that had grown around it across the centuries. His profit and pleasure came in the hours he could steal away to read the works of the learned rabbis. Of course, there was also *Der Forward*, the Jewish paper that always arrived two days late from the Yiddish presses of New York. Even if it was the beginning of war, he would not accept it as fact until he was told first hand by *Der Forward*. Then it was so.

Constantly today we are being told that Toronto has changed, become more worldly. Maybe. There were acts of gallantry then, however, that were marks of a more courtly time.

Take the case of the Baba Bayla. After her husband had coughed his way into his grave and been buried in the distant cemetery of St. Clair Avenue East (West for living, East for dying), she would find her way from the old folks home on Cecil Street by streetcar alone to the store. She carried a note because, even if she had learned to say the address in English, she might not have been understandable because her teeth had long gone and her voice always seemed filtered through a bowl of borscht. It sounded of beets and cabbage and sour salt. She would sweep into the car and sit beside the conductor in her black, floor-length robes, testing her dark wig to be sure it had not fallen askew. She kept her dignity always, except for those awkward times when her bladder would not quite hold on cold nights waiting for the car's arrival. Strange puddles would form beside the elegant, doll-like lady in the dark skirts.

The conductors came to know her. She would sit silently, trusting to fate that she would be delivered. Even though we lived between the stops at Elmwood and Greenlaw, frequently the conductor would stop the car midway. The passengers would wait as he escorted Baba across the wide avenue. She would take his arm, as if being accompanied to a dance. She would smile her thanks, and through her gums would come sounds of distant Russia. When was it you last saw an act of such city tenderness?

Once planted in the rooms behind the store, she would insist that the children dance around her while she sang Russian songs. Feet would fly and, as a reward, there were those red sour-sweet candies shaped like raspberries. Even now when I see raspberries I think of her, and there is a little dancing in my heart.

It was a more personal time. The "copper" on the block would hand test each store as he went by, assuring the occupants of their safety. This was fine, except on Passover night when we all huddled together for the annual seder to recount the tales of the Jews' escape from Egypt. By tradition the door had to be left open for Elijah, the prophet who was supposed to come and drink the extra glass of wine. Inevitably, when the door was left open, a policeman arrived. He was no Jewish saviour. He scolded us for the inconvenience. When we tried the back door the cat, which survived off chicken remains, entered looking for some kindness. She was tossed out.

Of course, there was occasional crime. To the south of us were the Italians around Davenport and Dufferin Streets. Later they would take over the entire area. But then they clung to the edge of a church at the bottom of the hill. They were mostly latecomers, and in those years, the thirties, they took on the more menial jobs. They were hard working, but sometimes desperate. There was one young man, who looked remarkably like Victor Mature, who came to deliver parcels two days a week. The arrangement was that he would provide an old car with a rumble seat, borrowed from a brother-in-law. He was apparently newly married and already had a wife pregnant by four or five months, and the ten dollars he made was his entire income. He spoke no English, but we made do with sign language. He was a worried-looking man. We found out why.

Chickens had been disappearing. There was no way they could wander down St. Clair. It meant that someone had been stealing into the coop after dark and making off with them. My mother decided to lie in wait one night, and under a full Toronto winter moon, broom in hand, she caught the culprit. It was our Italian. What to do? Here he was, a noisy rooster under his heavy town coat. Caught in the act. Stealing chickens from our very mouths. *But yet . . .* who could call the police? He was, after all, a gentile and thus not trustworthy. *But yet . . .* he, too, was an immigrant. *But crime . . .* the curse of the commandments was involved, eye for an eye, etc. *But . . .* the police were the Cossacks in my father's memory. What did it have to do with them? *But yet . . .* every loaf of bread counted and food had been stolen. My father seemed to be weighing the words of his prayer books as he decided. He called the Italian mother-in-law.

Oy, did he get it! That woman, not much different from my own grandmother in size, came and pleaded his case. She had no idea that her son had been stealing. She took the very chicken he had stolen and slapped him across the face with it. I mean, a live chicken across the face must be the greatest insult a man can endure. And then again, across the back of the head. Oy! I can almost feel it now. The chicken let out a cackle. Imagine its thoughts, if it could think. Suddenly it was a weapon. The young Italian thief was in tears. How could he bring such disgrace to the woman he loved, to the child unborn. He was hungry; they had all been hungry. He had been trying to impress his in-laws. After all, what did an immigrant have to offer? The mother-in-law listened. My father listened. My mother, never parting with her broom, listened. And justice was done.

Never would he forget chickens. For each chicken stolen he would personally pluck 40 new ones—about five cents per chicken plucked. As an extra punishment, for one month he would be in charge of cleaning the coop, all those chicken droppings. (Let anyone who has a romantic notion about returning to nature and raising chickens first count the droppings.) And then to add insult to insult, there was a suspicion—no proof mind you, but a definite suspicion—that perhaps one chicken's worth of extras may have been spent on another woman. So along came the pregnant bride on those nightly deliveries. She sat beside him and wept. How could he have? More than a chicken had changed hands. I was sorry to see him go when the war came. Manpower became scarce as Canada dashed off to fight for king and country.

Among the chores assigned to me was delivering chickens to the Mount Sinai Hospital. No, not that big, handsome structure that confronts the General Hospital and the Sick Children's Hospital on University Avenue. Then it was on Yorkville, now Toronto's most fashionable shopping area. Then it was the darkest, and one of the poorest. The hospital was a brown building crowded with patients and the new crop of Jewish doctors who had managed to fit into the quota system. (Oh yes, there was a system of so many Jews allowed into medical school.) My father had been assigned the contract for kosher chickens. This was, I must add, no big deal. Maybe 25 cents a chicken profit, and they all had to be carefully drawn and koshered. This process involved dipping them in salt for an hour or so, and then giving them a bath. They seldom had a chance to dry.

Twenty chickens were packed into a fruit bushel. I carried them on my hip to the streetcar stop and delivered them on the Bay car. Now this might have been all right except for the Avenue Road hill. You see, while the street was flat, all that water and salt would merely sit in the bottom of the bushel. But when the streetcar would tilt down the Avenue Road hill, the salt water would begin to flow down the aisle. Quietly flowed the salt water down the streetcar. I tried to read my history text as if I had never seen salt water. My treat was one Chocolate Crisp candy bar. Today one of those bars almost makes me weep salt-water tears. I think of those angry conductors.

My embarrassment was surpassed only on those days when we would run short of chickens and I would be dispatched to the poultry market on Kensington Avenue to bring home about four or five extra live ones. They were wrapped in the *Toronto Star* newspaper. I tried to make it look as if I were carrying opened-ended flower arrangements. But sometimes the chicken would announce its presence, and an angry Englishwoman sitting next to me would stare at me as if my stomach had rumbled. Sometimes a chicken might just decide to relieve itself. Try to look complacent with a wet chicken in your lap some day. And then there was the one that got away. It was a hot night, the windows were open, and for all I know it might still be heading north, following the migration of Jews up Bathurst Street.

Without question, there were a lot of chickens in my life. And no question: the colours of death and life of those thousands of chickens which passed our way worked their way into my thinking. Mine could never be a Wonder Bread world. And so, when later I saw the slaughterhouse colours of Chagall paintings, I suppose they were as natural to me as the life I lived then on St. Clair. And when Chagall told me how he dreamed of flying, I remembered how I used to gallop across the pavements, really trying to fly, to fly away from the cry of the dying chickens, from the life of endless deliveries, to pull myself away from the predictable routine, delivery-collection-delivery, the life and death of the

weekly quota of chickens. I could run, jump across the pavements, see
those autographed markings paved in '28, '29, '39. Running was easy.
Existing was not.

But swimming was free. Every Rasky is a swimmer. Toronto is
a city on a lake. In those Depression days the lake and the city were
closely bound, before concrete highways built barriers between the people
and the water.

Remember the free car? Who was that benevolent soul who arranged that? Several times a week a certain streetcar would make the
rounds and gather us up, us semi-slum kids. What the hell, we were all
that way, except for those who were beyond my childhood horizon. Those
free cars: across St. Clair, down Dovercourt, across King, swinging
around in front of the beaches of Lake Ontario. Huge barracks-like changing rooms, boys on one side, girls on the other, packed with brown-bag
sandwiches, always the same, peanut butter and jam. How many hot July
sandwiches did I eat? A quick dash into the lake, polluted even then, red
bathing suits that looked like assorted long underwear. The whistle blowing, and then a rush like hell to change back again, dash back into the
streetcar, and hang the bathing suits out to dry as we passed along Queen
and up Ossington to "Hail, hail, the gang's all here." We were rolling
sing-song sessions. "Pack up your troubles in your old kit bag and smile,
smile, smile." So who had a kit bag and what was it anyway?

On Sunday there was Sunnyside. Mostly that meant the pool,
sometimes called the tank. It was an Olympic-sized pool that was the
migrating place for all the immigrant kids. A nickel would get you entrance, a locker, use of the pool and access to the beach. And on that
brown, pebbled strip, social engagements for the week were planned. We
would lay our towels down next to young girls who pretended to be
sunbathing, and strike up a conversation. If things went especially well,
an offer would be made to share towels and even Cracker Jacks. And in
the event of a real strike, perhaps we might arrange for a walk on the
boardwalk later on. The wooden walkway ran the length of Sunnyside.
On one side of the street were amusements, naturally padlocked on Sunday, and on the other, the lake. Who could figure that on the other side
of the shoreline was something called America?

If the evening was promising, we would stay for the sing-along
with Jack Sobel at the live radio broadcast arena. A projector announced
the words on a huge screen, and the patriotic songs of World War I were
intoned by a soprano whose voice had been hibernating all those long,
winter nights. "Surely you're proud. Sing it aloud. There'll always be
an England." And Scottish sword dancers, little girls who hopped around
crossed swords. I never could figure out why they did that for radio, and
did a sweet, candy-cheeked girl ever lose a toe? "And now, the accordian

with a gypsy melody!'' And then the streetcar ride home to the hot rooms above the store.

Considering my later travels to 50 or 60 countries, it was extraordinary how exciting was the move from 1281 to 1283 St. Clair Avenue. The Ardreys were giving up. The Bible store next door was an obvious error. Not many crosses could be sold to Willer, Waller and Feldman. Perhaps there had been a quiet hope that a convert would be made somewhere along the line. If anything, it was the reverse. When Mandel delivered that rich cream cheese and that sweet halvah, how could a Christian kid resist even if the neighbours had not accepted Jesus. The Ardreys moved from this corrupting, heathen influence, perhaps to some Bible school closer to heaven.

But with a down payment of $500 borrowed from lawyer Marcus, my father arranged the $3,000 purchase of the building. At last, my own bed. In the early years in the *kaltruum* (the cold room), I could not recall whether I had urinated in the bed, or whether it was my brothers. It was all the same beneath the heavy chicken-feather, home-made comforter. And when one of us caught diphtheria, everyone went to the isolation hospital. The entire family was almost wiped out. But we survived. We survived in glory to march up the stairs of the Ardrey store. ''Onward Jewish soldiers. Onward as to war!'' With my mother, slightly hysterical at the mess left behind shouting, *''Hack mere nisht kine chunik''*—not so much noise—as we entered the Jerusalem next door. Imagine a furnace of our own, a real upstairs!

There was one moment of difficult religious discussion. Upstairs in the hallway leading to the double parlour where I was to sleep in a folding bed, was a metal sign hammered into the plaster wall: ''Jesus Saves!'' Pretty tough stuff for us newcomers. It seemed to me that half the wall came down with the sign. The temple toppled, the reverse side later to be made into a feeding trough for the chickens. Question: can a chicken eating off a ''Jesus Saves'' sign be truly kosher? God lived with us in many ways and not on tin.

There never was any hope that my father would accumulate any amount of money. Each customer had a different price. The Cohens paid the full amount, the Wagmans a little less. Old Mrs. Segal, widowed and on relief, made a token payment, but her pride still made her grumble. Wandering Jews with a good religious background were brought home for dinner, their beards pulled apart like half-chewed sandwiches as they enjoyed my mother's constant chicken soup. Eager young rabbis without a pulpit, like David Monson, found a temporary home.

The McKay Street *shul* could never afford a rabbi. My father never missed a service. How I longed to sleep in on those Saturday mornings when I was required to fill out the traditional number of ten for *minyen*. During the war they even started me at twelve instead of the compulsory bar-mitzvahed thirteen. (The Talmud allowed!)

And the voice. Even now I rock back and forth in the memory of that voice of my father. God just moved in with him. How full of longing it was for the storybook Jerusalem, for Jews that were free, free from pressures economic, political, social. Those melodies passed on from generation to generation. My father, Reb Leib (Leib means lion), who never learned to read music, had long ago committed the words to memory, so he could sing with his eyes closed, his face always tilted upwards. Surely God hovered over McKay Street in personal attendance, now serious, now smiling at a melody that caught his ear. The awful and beautiful Hebrew God was, of course, an old, old man with long whiskers, grown tired from arguing with His people, with naive Abraham, with cunning Isaac, with wrestling Jacob, and especially with His Moses. What an arguer! And what's this blasphemous thing about a Son. We were all His sons. The women were behind a separating wall, nudging from the rear, daughters of Zion.

The men would pound their chests to beat out the sins. They would argue over inflection of sound. Who could pray the loudest? And after the prayers, there would be sweet biscuits and shmaltz herring and home-made wine from Niagara grapes, stirred into fire in caskets in our basement. Good fellowship and song: *"Loz mir alle, alle namen trinkin a glazzela vine."* Let us all, let us all drink a glass of wine in honour of the scholar. With herring, yet. Except on Yom Kippur, holiest of holies. The crying for forgiveness. I guess the gentiles on the block must have figured those Jews had a lot to be forgiven for—killing Christ and all that.

As part of the ritual, twice in the ceremony my father would fall to his knees to pray for the assembled sins of the congregation. Two Rasky brothers would always be given the honour of lifting him up. So we had to stay inside during the long sessions of Hebrew chanting, while other kids tossed filbert nuts in a game on the faded lawn. Once I was missing. I now confess I vanished to the Casino Burlesque Theatre on Queen Street to see three, count them, three striptease acts—and on the Day of Atonement. I think God is still after me for that one.

When the service was over, there was my father, all that energy delivered to God in prayer and song, and fasting from the *Kol Nidre* prayer and the ritual blowing of the *shofar*. The ordeal over, we walked silently down McKay and onto Greenlaw toward St. Clair.

"Nu?" he asked after a time.

"Nu, what?" I answered, still caught up in the majesty and passion of the tones of prayer and the ram's horn piercing my brain with its notes caught in God's arms above us. "So, what?"

"So, how was I?"

So, even with God, maybe especially with God, you've got to have some humour.

"If God had a son, how come he never had a wife?" To the Nazarenes trying to convert us on occasion, we threw the question. "You are too young to understand!" came the answer. Born again? It was so hard the first time, please. Not now, again. Sunday nights, the service from the Church of the Nazarene blared out on loudspeakers. Thank God we had Jack Benny.

Sex was never mentioned in home or school. But we caught a glimpse, a look, if not a feel of female. Sure, there were a couple of Jewish girls on the block. But they were like sisters. And, naturally, sisters were not for feeling. Expeditions were mounted into the dangerous gentile world beyond the barriers of our fortress isolation. The call of the wild came with the first growth of baby whiskers. Those little breasts, bulging from soft, woollen sweaters. Sometimes in the talk of the street it was called "a handful." How to search and find and finally hold "a handful?"

There were various possibilities. During the summers, the Jews who had found a little money also tried to find a place in the sun. This meant congested summer cottages at Lake Simcoe, 50 miles away, at the resorts known as Belle Ewart and Jackson's Point. We would hitchhike up the long Yonge Street highway, sleep on the hard, brown beach, and chase some of the young Jewish girls. And if there was the opportunity to catch them alone, the answer would always be, "What made you think I was that sort of girl?" "Full moon and empty arms." The dancing was hard on those young aching testicles. Out there was the forbidden fruit.

Beaches in the east end of the city in far-off places beyond what was called the Danforth. The challenge was to get by the signs that spelled out the rule, "restricted." To pass by without a look of guilt was like stealing green apples. How to look nonchalant when you know your nose might be just a little too long. A skilled observer might just cause that nose to be bloodied. The girls' gum chewing was hard to take, and the conversation—well, was there any? One did get to hold a female body slightly closer, but the "handfuls" were hard to find. How were we to know that Presbyterians, too, had rules, and what was a Presbyterian anyhow?

Sure it was early adventure, wanting to know what was out there. Was it true, as my parents believed, that the world of non-Jews was violent, that penetration outside meant asking for battle? But the mind would not relent, and the young body was travelling under a full wind of desire. Mostly the results were dreary. At the Palais Royal down on the lakefront, it was soldiers first, and what chance did early puberty provide? The Central YMCA held tea dances. The records were scratchy and so were the girls lined against the wall like tattered books in a dark library.

The movie house was the escape. I danced with Fred Astaire. I dared with Paul Muni. I memorized that speech in *Emile Zola* defending Dreyfus, and I was Dreyfus, too. And do you remember when Muni and I discovered pasteurization? And Edward G. turned good guy to wipe out the plague, or something, in *The Magic Bullet?* We did that together, and later when I actually sat and had dinner with Eddy G. in Hollywood, I couldn't tell him. But it was all okay because even then it was rumoured he was really a Jew posing as a gangster—he had a Jewish heart.

It's been said that Jews look after their own. In a way it was true about the organizations that shaped those early years. The Baba Bayla, as I've noted, lived out her last years at the Jewish old folks home. It was established long before "senior citizens" became a fashionable phrase. And she danced her last dance there, right on her final day.

For teenagers there was something called the AZA, which was part of a youth organization of B'nai B'rith. It meant parading around Dundas and Spadina in uniform: shirts with large letters sewn on. It was a time when Shopsy was called "Shopsowitz," and his delicatessen was in constant competition with a dozen others around, and the garlic from the pastrami followed you down the street.

Camp B'nai B'rith was the summer salvation. Ten days for ten dollars or so. You just had to be wanting and free of lice. One year we passed the first test, but not the second. Off came the hair, all of it. We were shaved like concentration camp victims. But we got our ten days at camp. "Oh, what do we do with the drunken counsellor, what do we do with the drunken counsellor early in the morning." And similar songs around a campfire at Lake Couchiching. There was talk of how one counsellor had actually been to Spain. Had he killed a man? And why? What was a civil war anyhow, and what did it have to do with these Jewish kids, huddled around the site of an old Indian graveyard?

There I learned one August night from my counsellor, Lou Applebaum, about theatre. My first role. It was a dramatic sketch around the writing of the *Moonlight Sonata*. And guess who got to be Beethoven, the first of my many other lives? How at home I was on that camp stage! And even though the music was being played by a record, I knew I had composed it. I talked to the stars that night because I knew I had found a way to join them, or at least be a little closer.

There was the constant question of escape. What would be the road out of St. Clair Avenue? None of us was interested in turning the chicken-grocery trade into a supermarket. We were all by nature not merchants. My only real knowledge about the outside world came from the films at the Royal George or the Oakwood cinemas. They were the stuff of dreams. I fashioned imaginary worlds based on the plots. But my fantasies seemed forever unreachable. I would sneak in the exit and sometimes watch a film three times, and dream myself right into the action of the screen.

Sometime during my high school years at Oakwood Collegiate, I discovered a vital fact: that if you were covering an event for the school paper, you were treated somewhat specially. You did not have to wait in line. There was a city-wide paper called the *Canadian High News,* edited by a man named Knowlton Nash. I visited the downtown office and Knowlton issued me a "press card." My world changed. I crossed boundaries that seemed till then impenetrable. I also involved myself with the paper's Saturday afternoon radio show on CFRB. My two worlds of fact and fantasy were beginning to take shape.

As soon as I attended the University of Toronto, I quickly registered at the *Varsity* paper and became involved in the UC Follies, the annual college variety show. I felt I had arrived, even if it was in the family pick-up truck, delivering the parcels of chickens on the way. I was ready for fame and fortune and my first real, outside-the-family job.

CHAPTER TWO

My Mother's Kirkland Lake Kimono

Perhaps as a defence against those grey snows of the cutting winter, "foreigners" were always suspect. Born though I was in Toronto, I would still always be a foreigner to those who thought that Canada was merely an extension of England. Out of college, ready to conquer the world, one by one the rejection letters arrived. In Toronto itself there could be no jobs. If the word "restricted" no longer appeared in the want ads, it still had not been removed from the minds. Go fight it.

"You see? If only you had become a lawyer, a doctor." Yes, it was a scold. My mother told me. My father told me. But I had been stubborn and now it was time to go.

"No, it is final. The boy cannot go among strangers without a kimono." My mother issued her order to my father and there was no arguing with her. I was going to make my own way in the world, taking my first job after graduating from the University of Toronto, and obviously I couldn't be living in a strange city without a bathrobe. I had answered an ad in the Toronto *Globe and Mail* which seemed to fit me well: "Wanted, reporter, young, industrious, $32.50 a week, apply *Northern Daily News*, Kirkland Lake, Ontario." My one offer. Roy Thomson, later Lord Thomson of Fleet, would hire anyone who worked cheap.

And now it was time to decide what to take with me. I owned two suits, two shirts, underwear, socks, one pair of shoes, and that was it. Three years of college had given me a degree in philosophy and English and a pile of textbooks. But I had neither profession nor bathrobe.

The garment was selected at Clavir's Department Store, a plaid robe of the MacIntosh clan, my first adventure in luxurious living. Mr. Clavir, a regular customer at my father's grocery store, kindly marked it down from $15 to $12.50. He swore he was not making a cent on the sale, but since it was to be my first robe for my first visit to another city, he would allow it to go at the bargain price. "A Jewish boy should always look neat." It was red and orange and blue and green, and although I didn't feel quite right about a Jewish boy wearing a Scottish plaid, the excitement of the purchase killed my prejudice.

My mother's hand trembled a little as she packed the robe neatly in the suitcase borrowed from my Aunt Minny. I was the seventh of her eight children, and one by one we had taken off, tried a new life away from the apartment above the grocery store. She had that quality common to Jewish mothers, the certainty that once away from home a son would be lost. Who would care for his needs like her? After all, who knows a son like his mother? "In this world a mother must suffer." And that was all she said as I left.

The trip by train, 400 miles north on the Ontario Northland Railroad, presented a new world to me: my first experience aboard a sleeping berth. It was difficult to look sophisticated among all the men who, I thought, certainly must have been seasoned travellers. What to do with my shoes after I undressed bothered me most. I noticed some pairs of shoes in the aisle. But since I owned only the one pair, I thought better of taking a chance on losing them. I couldn't arrive at my first job shoeless. Finally I tucked them beside my pillow, confident that it was the proper thing to do. The night was sleepless, uncomfortable and lonely. I stared at my new bathrobe and craved the moment when I first would use it. I thought of taking a stroll to the men's room, but the embarrassment of leaving an upper berth at 4 a.m. to relieve myself was more than I cared to face. And where were the stairs? Eventually, surrounded by my robe and shoes, I slept. I dreamt of Ingrid Bergman. I danced with her in my dreams.

Swastika was my stop. It's a tiny lumber town which prided itself on the fact that it refused to be blackmailed into changing its name to Winston during the war. It quite correctly announced that the swastika was an Indian symbol long before Hitler discovered its possibilities. A sign at the tired, orange, wooden station announced simply, "To hell with Hitler; we found the swastika first." Although the townsfolk had nothing personal against Winston Churchill, they found no need to adopt his first name. It was an action typical of the rugged frontier attitude of the lumber and gold and mining men of the Canadian north: "To hell with the people from the big cities; we got here first."

And my attitude as I looked around me at a withered mill, a wrinkled general store, two greyed houses on a hill, rock and sparse vegetation was, "My God, what have I done." But it was too late and too far to return. Bad day at Black Rock.

The vintage bus that was taking me to my first job, my new home, lurched and rumbled around granite bends where a road had been hacked out of the woods but never quite completed. My fellow passengers were school children making the four-mile ride from Swastika to Kirkland Lake. As each one boarded, the driver delivered a morning greeting. "How's your mom, Elsie?" "Morning, Bess, your brother Jack back from Timmins?"

As we neared Kirkland Lake, population 15,000, a city jutting out of the rock, slapped together during the gold rush of the twenties, I heard for the first time the sound that was to follow me long after I left the mining country. It was the deep rumble of the mills which hummed all day and night, as if you were in a room of constantly buzzing air conditioners and electric fans. I wanted to put my ear to the ground to listen for the sound of men cutting at rock, or coughing, or talking in the earth. Apart from the sound, the city's main street, Government Road, had the look of many small highway-side villages and towns: men's and women's shops, half a dozen hotels with the word "Bar" indicated in yellow or red neon, the sidewalk sitters, old men who chewed over the past, sometimes in conversation and sometimes only in looks of past memory.

The office of the *Northern Daily News* was in a red brick building on the edge of the Wright-Hargreaves property. My official greeter was Alvin Rakoff, a young college graduate like myself who fancied himself a writer and decided being a newspaperman was the way to show it. "Put your bag down and I'll take you to meet 'The Menace,' " he said with a smile of enthusiasm and sarcasm.

"The Menace?"

"The Menace is our pet name for Paddy Quin, the city editor. You'll find out."

The Menace sat hunched over a desk decorated with months of press releases, magazines, newspapers and the day's wire copy. A green plastic eyeshade pulled past an array of ginger hair and settled neatly at nose level. His white shirt was grey and frayed at the collar, sleeve and pocket, and it was topped with a black vest which showed equal indications of the owner's long absence from a laundry. "This is Harry Rasky, Paddy. He's the new man." Al made the brief introduction and Paddy shifted slightly in his chair, turned a well-wined face to me and said, "You're another college man, I hear."

The skin on his face was pulled tightly and all seemed to collect on the left side, as if he were squinting and sneering at once. His narrow eyes, one a little more open than the other, always reminded me of watermelon pits. His craggy face reminded me of a half-opened tin of sardines. "Yes. I have a Bachelor degree from Varsity."

"Another college man. Jeezus, why can't they send me a reporter. Never met a college brat who could spell yet. And now I've got Peter and Paul. Jeezus, only ten more disciples to go." He coughed a laugh at his own humour that sounded like a rusty bedspring being stimulated, and he punctuated it by spitting into a garbage tin full of news copy.

With this brief introduction to my new boss, Al took me to my home for the months to come, a combination rooming house and hotel on the city's main street. It was a three-storey brick building composed of single rooms, long green corridors and communal baths, which was owned by a practical Pole named Pat Sawchuck. Like many men in Kirkland Lake, he had sped to the gold rush area in the days of the first strikes. He had traded grub for shares in new mines, and had built his rooming house with the profits. Now the rush was over, the adolescent excitement of wild times was past, the city had settled down to middle-aged growth and decay, and Pat Sawchuck had found that there was no place else to call home.

My room was tiny, but at the time it seemed quite luxurious. With eight children in the family, this was the first time I actually had a room of my own. Carefully I hung my extra suit in the badly blemished wooden cabinet, and beside it I hung my new acquisition, my bathrobe. The $15 label still clung to the pocket and I decided not to remove it; not yet, at any rate. Quickly I undressed and put on my robe, examined myself in a mirror, and decided it was time now. I walked down the hall to the bathroom and studied each doorway as I passed. With an air of regal splendour, or at least the closest I could manage, I made the return journey. My first fashion show was a flop. No one saw me.

My years of training, working my way through college, driving a truck at night for my father so that I could learn English and philosophy and dream of adventure, climaxed in my first assignment, covering the weekly luncheon meeting of the Lions' Club. The club was largely made up of a group of middle-aged businessmen who began each meeting with a juvenile lion's roar and continued from there. "Let's hear that roar, Lions!" The insurance agents among them seemed to apply the most forced gaiety to the proceedings. "Doc" Long, the local druggist whispered to me, "Yep, an insurance man just can't have enough friends." Being a new man in town, I was like a virgin in a harem. I was handed three cards which spelled out Prudential, Mutual, Influential. And my lead paragraph began, "The local Lions roared through another meeting today . . ."

Paddy's eyes narrowed on the yellow copy paper, and the red veins on his nose, which already bulged into a clown's colour, seemed ready to burst. "Kee–rist, save me from smart aleck college boys." He was about to wind up for one of his Falstaffian loads of abuse which seemed to please him so much. "Those fat cats you intend to ridicule keep this paper going, you juvenile copy boy. Punk! What old virgin English teacher ever suggested you could write anything more than comments on toilet walls? Sit down and write something complimentary or grab the next train out of town."

And so I began, "In an extraordinary show of unanimous enthusiasm, the Kirkland Lake Lion's Club, now celebrating a decade of public service, voted to repaint the welcome sign at the city limits." My professional career had begun. Paddy was pleased, and his yellowed teeth glistened through the green eyeshade as he marked through the copy with a red pencil. I can recall thinking, "Oh, for a colour camera—a rainbow of colour at the city desk."

After work, Al and I had dinner at Chan's Empire Restaurant, the 75 cent roast beef sandwich special. I asked, "What about Paddy, doesn't he ever eat?"

"He never seems to make it, quite."

"What do you mean, *quite*?"

"Look, there he comes now."

Across the road I saw Paddy pacing a path towards the Kirkland Tavern. It was a walk I will never forget. Although his head was facing directly ahead, his body moved on an angle, his chest turned towards the wall. It was almost as if he were holding on to the buildings as he moved past them. Although it was a cold northern night, his shirt was open and his face was transfixed with a stare of almost lecherous delight.

In the Kirkland Tavern across the way, I saw the secret ritual of Paddy Quin. He sat at a table which held six bottles of Canadian beer. This was in preparation for the dinner closing of the pub. Canada, rich with the puritan traditions of Scottish Presbyterians, had strict no-drinking rules for meal times. A sober man would not sin. Paddy, over the years, had derived the mathematical formula of 15 minutes equals one beer. Since the closing was to last a long, dry hour and a half, he could remain nicely lubricated for the arid spell. No one could ever recall having seen Paddy set his narrow lips to food of a dry nature.

But next morning, Paddy was again painfully sober and sarcastic. "Hey, Joe College, there's a police report of a drowning up at a lake 30 miles from here. Go get it. And don't forget to show the cops your college degree so they'll know enough to call you sir." I sped 30 miles up a

snow-covered road with Keith Black, a photographer, and Maria Gra-
bovic, a young girl a year out of high school who fancied herself a
northern Dorothy Thompson.

To supplement my income, I was doing stringer work for the
Toronto Star and Maria was reporting for the *Toronto Telegram*. When
we arrived at the area of the drowning, we discovered that a whole
busload of school children had gone down through a crack in the frozen
ice. Ten were dead and another 12 had scampered to safety across the
frigid surface. All were being treated for shock. To us it sounded like
a great story for the Toronto dailies. We began a race for the nearest
phone two miles away. Since I was longer limbed, I could run faster than
Maria. And I don't think she ever forgave my getting to the only phone
in ten miles. But she wasn't interested in being beaten by a young college
boy. She paid the grocer in the general store next door to sing into his
phone, an extension of mine, while she sped by cab to the next town.
Between bars of "When Irish eyes are smiling" and "O Canada," I
managed to get the story through in time for the late editions.

The weeks passed quickly—meetings of the Lion's Club, Thurs-
days covering the courts with old Judge Siegfried McLeod presiding, a
few minor cave-ins, a slight romance with a mine manager's daughter,
a week in the Kirkland Lake hospital with pneumonia, a small part with
the local acting group, and a hundred routine assignments, each one
scrutinized with satanic glee by Paddy, who never seemed to run out of
terms of abuse.

On a July morning, the telephone started ringing early. Even
Captain Sturdy, our publisher, a retired British officer, jumped to attention
that morning. The most spectacular robbery in the history of the north
country had taken place at Larder Lake, about four miles south. Two
bandits had set their seaplane down outside the town, piled it full of gold
bricks awaiting shipment to North Bay, and skimmed across the water
for a clean take-off—the first hijacking by plane the north had ever
known. Paddy was at his best marshalling his troops into action, while
Captain Sturdy planned the grand strategy of manoeuvres. We were to
outflank our competition from the *North Bay Nugget*, the nearest city
daily, 100 miles away. And I was told that this was to be my biggest
assignment. I was to write the lead story.

And then the phone rang again. "Hello, Harry, this is Ed." It
was my brother calling from Toronto and his voice was quiet and troubled.
I shouted into the receiver, "I can't talk to you now, Ed; I'm going out
on my biggest story. I'll call you in a day or so. Give my regards to the
folks."

"Wait, for God's sake, wait!" His voice was almost hysterical
as he seemed about to cry. "You'd better come home right away. Ma
is very sick. I think you'd better come."

"Sure, sure. Okay. I'll be home as soon as I can get there." I turned to Paddy and said, "Count me out of the Larder Lake story. My mother is sick. I'm going home. Don't give me any of your Irish humour about being a mother's boy. I've got to go."

To my surprise, he said it was all right. There was not the slightest protest. But making the trip was not so easy. In order to arrive home that night, I learned that I would have to go 90 miles north aboard a mail train to an airfield at Porquis Junction, and then I would likely miss by five minutes the only plane that touched down in that part of the country. I called Trans-Canada Airlines frantically. "Give me a break, will you please? I've got to get to Toronto tonight to see my sick mother. I'm coming on board the Porquis Junction special, and it won't arrive until five minutes after your take-off time. Please, please hold the plane." They said they would.

I rushed to collect some things. I had a few minutes before train time. I decided I would buy my mother a gift. But what? I went to Sam Davis' clothing shop and asked him for the most expensive woman's bathrobe he had in the store. He showed me a blue silk robe. My mother had never owned anything of silk. Sam Davis said it would cost $45. I bought it.

Then by cab to Swastika, and on board the two-car mail special to Porquis Junction. I watched the green trees that pierced the granite swing by as the train slowly shuffled its way along. There were two passengers on board, a nun and a young girl of about twelve. The train seemed more like a trolley as it shook and clanked its way north. And each time it stopped to push off a mail bag at a small village, I nervously chewed at my knuckles and checked my watch. As it pulled into Porquis Junction, I could see the DC-3 across the field, its propellers feathering and tossing dust across the pasture nearby. I grabbed my bag and the parcel carrying my mother's bathrobe and ran across the strip. The airline stewardess standing at the open door of the plane urged me to be careful as I scampered up the stairs. I was panting hard as I slumped into my seat and the plane took off, and it wasn't until dusk, as I watched the engines cough out their tiny blowtorches of flame, that I realized that I had never been in a plane before.

I thought of the blue bathrobe that I kept on my lap, and the wonderful expression my mother would have on her face when she saw it. "Real silk," she would say. "What's the matter, suddenly because your mother is sick, you're a millionaire? What's the matter, you're not going to need the money for when you find the right girl and give me some grandchildren? A big sport I've got for a son. First he leaves me alone, and then he buys me a silk kimono!"

The static from the loudspeaker telling us we were arriving at Toronto's Malton Airport shook my thoughts. The city's sprinkle of street lights and neon spread out below. A limousine waited to take the passengers to the terminal in the city. I was squeezed into the back seat between two plump women who insisted on carrying on a conversation while I sat silently trying to think of how quickly I could get to a phone.

"Isn't Toronto nice in July," said the woman on my left.

Quiet! I shouted within me.

"Yes," answered the woman on my right, "everything is so nice and cheerful and alive."

Please, please, don't talk now, please!

I tried to pass the time thinking of Paddy and the boys at Larder Lake covering the hold-up story, but my mind kept shifting to the robe and my mother's reaction. I smiled, I think.

The driver of the limousine whistled as the vehicle sped down the highway, across the lakefront and through the traffic. I watched the lake boats through the window, and thought how lonely they looked lumbering through the bay. Suddenly the car lurched to a stop. We were at the depot.

Hurry . . . Come on . . . Calmly . . . calmly.

I ran to a telephone and dialed my home. My father answered.

Speak. "Dad, it's Harry. I'm home, Dad. I came on a plane. Boy! Wait till I tell you about my trip and what happened. I've got a surprise for Ma, and I'd like to go right away and show it to her. Where is she?"

There was a pause. *A silent pain . . . pain.*

"Dad! What's wrong? Dad, where's Ma? Please . . . please!"

"Well, I . . ." *A voice without words.*

He spoke slowly in Yiddish. "You'd better come here . . . come home. Your mother died an hour ago. She is not here anymore."

Nisht du? Not here, anymore. How was that possible? And what was death anyhow? There had never been time, time to talk to a mother who ran the store, who cared for the eight kids. Had the word "love" ever been used? Now, think upon it.

I thought as I headed for home that it would never be home again. There had been the day of the graduation last May. We had set out for the ceremony in the car and we had stopped along the way so she could spill out her guts. Cancer. How could I know what it was then? And death was beyond understanding. We had always been there, our group, the kids and ma and pa. How to understand? And even now I wonder if I ever knew this woman correctly. The cancer had already been there, and she had insisted on flying to visit my sister Rose in California, never revealing the illness. Sex and death were never discussed. And each morning after breakfast, my mother would go into the washroom and vomit out her breakfast and never reveal what was eating inside her, eating away her life. She carried a note on the plane, as my Baba had on the streetcar. Deliver her!

Who among us could do that now? This immigrant lady who lived on the edge of hysteria, shoved from Tzarist Russia to the bleakness of Canada, to live there, to die there. The funeral procession stopped as it moved its way past the McKay Street *shul,* home of us all. And there the door of the hearse opened briefly, so that according to Jewish tradition, her soul could fly out, fly out and be close to the God who hovered over the *shul,* who listened to my father's songs of praise.

At the Wilson Avenue cemetery, my brother Sam gasped as briefly the cover of the pine casket was removed so a scoop of dust could be added. "Did you see that?" he asked me, white with agony.

"No." No, no, I could not look at death, even in the face of my mother's. For me she was life. I never could accept her death. When later my father remarried, somehow I could not accept that woman serving the chicken soup. It was because I knew I could not accept the day my mother died. And even now, even now, I cannot tell you what happened to my mother's Kirkland Lake kimono. Or did it ever happen?

CHAPTER THREE

A Voice for
Lorne Greene

T hat summer of 1949 was a time for distant dreaming. I returned to Kirkland Lake covering the police beat, the courts and all kinds of local life. But I felt too far removed from the action. On the wires one day there was a report of a terrible disaster on the Great Lakes; a pleasure boat docked at Toronto harbour burned like an instant volcano. The *Noronic* became a graveyard for hundreds of people caught in panic. I asked Paddy if I could head south to cover it. He said no, but I went anyway. I began my story with great melodrama, "Today I walked through the valley of the shadow of death . . ." There were bodies everywhere, and I must admit that it was the thrill of life and death, more than the pain of it, that attracted me. The *Noronic* was the last of its kind.

I recall driving north again, stretched out as a passenger in a Volkswagen, making love to a girl reporter as we passed through North Bay. Not easy to do in a car that size. But we were part of the Hemingway generation. Hemingway was the greatest influence on young reporters and writers of the day. "Help me be a hero," we seemed to be saying. And she was Lady Brett.

It was obvious that I was not going to be able to make a world-wide reputation 400 miles north of nowhere. When the temperatures began to dip below zero, and when finally in early December it actually dug down to 40 below, I knew this splendid town caught in the frost was not for me. I had three different Christmas dinners honouring my departure. Of course Toronto would welcome me. I had my *Varsity* background and my *Northern Daily News* clippings. Ready or not, here I am, Toronto.

It was a cold New Year that announced 1950. The Toronto dailies had a select policy of hiring only a certain number of Jews. My number was not up. In those days, hard to accept now, there seemed to be Jewish quotas for everything. My father pleaded again, "Become a lawyer, a doctor, an insurance man. Give up this *narishkite*." Foolishness! But I couldn't.

The city was changing drastically in its makeup. Refugees from Europe were pouring in. Canada was the land of opportunity. The twentieth century was here, or so they said. Whereas American cities were experiencing urban decay, the old neighbourhoods of Toronto were being rejuvenated by industrious workers from Italy, Spain and Portugal. Fading houses were tarted up in purple and pink. My own locale of St. Clair was now almost totally Italian.

My father had moved to one of the side streets, the business gone. He kept busy with his involvement in the *shul,* and occasionally he would go to the market to visit his old haunts. One day a pleasant, middle-aged woman was pouring me chicken soup. My father said, "This is my new wife." The soup was not as good as in the old days. Nor was she.

To find employment I approached Richard L. Lewis, editor of the *Canadian Broadcaster*. Lewis was one of these unsung heroes of this country. He was a one-man employment service for young kids looking for work. He took on the tone of the time and called them his "DP's," which stood for "damned proteges." He was an out-of-context Englishman who believed in the total blessings of private enterprise. He had a voice like sweet vinegar and he growled like the wicked witch of the north, but I think of him as one of the most gentle souls I have ever met. Lewis put me in touch with the owner of a struggling radio station, CHUM—"CHUM, your friendly station." It was operated by a patent medicine man to sell his products: Zambuck ointment, Haley's MO, a mix of religious music and miracle cures. The station was licensed to broadcast from dawn till dusk.

I was given the lofty title of news editor, which seemed remarkable because I had been a cub reporter a few weeks before. The job, with its grand title, consisted mostly of ripping paper from the news wire and handing it to various announcers to read. CHUM had an additional appeal: listeners could call in with local items and earn ten dollars.

In my spare time I began to play with sound. The mixture of voice and music could make its own kind of poetry. I took a recording of a radio documentary called "The Freedom Train," and added a local sequence. I experimented with sounds for the blind. I heard inner rhythms but wasn't yet aware of what it was I was trying to do.

One of my daily chores was to write a noon commentary, called "News Bylines." Each day I pontificated to the world. At the age of twenty-one, I was able to preach, "Today a man will kill his brother." Of course, that was China. But my humble commentary was in competition with the most popular program of its kind: Lorne Greene with the news on CKEY. Lorne was a young actor from Ottawa who had spent the latter part of the war as the "voice of doom," voicing the calamities of war for the Canadian Broadcasting Corporation, and also as the voice of the National Film Board's "Canada Carries On" series. It was the age of the March of Time. The boom sound was in and Lorne was, and is, the greatest of them all. He sounded like the power and the glory of life and death. He had many fans. He had moved to the local commercial outlet in Toronto, CKEY, to be profound twice a day. He had been through a number of underpaid ghost writers and the job came open again.

The owner of CKEY, Jack Kent Cooke, called me. I was flattered to be in demand. Jack was a natty man with eyes that crinkled so deeply that they just disappeared. He was one of the great salesmen of all time. "Mr. Rasky, you are very fortunate to be chosen to write the commentaries for the greatest news voice of all time. Mr. Rasky, your future is here. Just think of the thousands that will be waiting for what you have to say. Mr. Rasky, there is no limit to how far your ideas will reach." And so he flattered me into moving to CKEY for just ten dollars *less* than I made at CHUM. There are words for people like that.

I was planted down into a windowless office in the basement of a refurbished Victorian building on University Avenue. I worked my way through the volume of wire copy daily, trying to find a personal view of the day's events. Lorne would trot through 20 minutes before broadcast time, rework the exclamation marks, and read each commentary as if it were "To be or not to be." After each broadcast the switchboard would jam with fans calling in. Depending on the news of the day, some would weep or just merely say, "Oh, Mr. Greene, your words are just wonderful." The more glowing the praise, the worse I felt. But then again, I was not exactly Shakespeare. In retrospect, I regard that time as great training in writing for the human voice, and Lorne and I have maintained a fond friendship ever since, working together whenever possible.

Between daily broadcasts I would journey with the local radio prophet-disc jockey, Mickey Lester, to the lakefront, and he would pass on his cynical observations of the day. We would go across to his "island." He had rented the only cottage on one of the Toronto Islands, and he would throw rocks back at the city. He taught me a remaining love of music and art. Sometimes he would call me at night and just say, "Listen." And for ten minutes I would hear Mozart or Bach. I would say, "So?" He would respond, "Dumb bastard!" and hang up. Next day it would be Beethoven. He was a splendid teacher.

Lester's style on the air was as smooth as anyone's of his generation. "Hello m'friendly, take it easy and you'll live longer and end up a whole lot stronger." The voice would purr and the music was impeccable. But off the air Mickey dressed like a bag of dirty laundry. When he smiled, a gaping tooth reflected his lack of personal visual concern. He was like a Halloween pumpkin, smiling cynically in the night. Until Sylvia.

Now I pause just briefly here to talk of Sylvia, because his story came to life with her. She was a divorced model in her early thirties, I think, and Mickey was then in his forties. Sylvia had become a fan of the voice, and then later of the man. Lester left behind the memory of his early anger: somewhere there was a divorced wife, and a son who had become a priest in Montreal. But one day he arrived for our mid-afternoon tour of the island cabin, and there was a new tooth where there had been a blank space. His suits were pressed, his shirts laundered, and he took on a rakish, benevolent air. Mickey Lester was in love! Soon after, he moved from his one-room pile of books into a new apartment and was married. Tragically, Mickey developed cancer. He died, and within a short while Sylvia was gone, too. Mickey is one of the most pleasant memories of growing up. He added to my soul.

Sadly, radio was fading as a medium of importance. By the early fifties, television was sweeping the imagination of North America. This development came just at the time when I had begun to perfect my skill in radio documentary. Jack Kent Cooke was delighted to have me feeding his station drama-documentaries with no budget. The most important of these came on the death of King George VI. King George was the younger brother of Edward VIII, who had been the most dashing member of royalty in generations. George was, in a sense, the first great anti-hero. Just to talk was painful for this shy, reluctant king. When he died, I wove together a radio program involving the music, mood and commentary of the time, and mixed in voices of amateur actors in what became *George the Good,* my first serious documentary.

The appeal of the new visual medium was too great for me not to want to jump in. We had begun to watch programs coming through two channels from Buffalo. While most people were hooked by Uncle Milty or Howdy Doody, I came to know the man who was to become a distant hero, the first and greatest superstar of television, Edward R. Murrow. I listened to his radio commentaries and watched his weekly television documentary, "See It Now." And I decided that was for me.

There were rumblings about a television station to begin broadcasting in Toronto, to be run by the CBC. About this time, Lorne organized a seminar on television, importing some of the more profound media philosophers of the day. As a bonus to my job of cranking out the nightly news, I was allowed to attend free. I had become restless with my daily activities. To amuse myself I would send love signals in Lorne's news. If I were courting some young lady, I would write, "Listen in tonight at 7 p.m. and I'll talk to you on the radio," but Lorne would do the speaking. I am sure it is one of the few times valentines were integrated into the daily crises of the world.

I applied for a job at the CBC. To prove my enthusiasm, I sent myself to New York and toured all the top news and documentary units of the time. I had my first encounter with Murrow, face to face. He was as impressive in real life as he was on the tube. Sadly, his one weakness was chain-smoking, and all during our conversation he would reach into his bottom drawer, where I saw several cartons of cigarettes, and light up a new cigarette every few minutes. The smoke curled past that expressive furrowed brow. He looked almost as if he could not stand the pain of the world. I wanted to scream, "Stop it! Stop smoking! We need you." And we still do.

But let me tell you about that time in Canada. We who began television in Canada were the wonderful innocents. We had assembled in an old barracks building behind the radio offices of the Canadian Broadcasting Corporation at 354 Jarvis Street in Toronto. We came for different reasons. I just managed to squeeze on board, and later discovered that the word had been passed down: not too many Jews. This fact will be denied, but it is true.

The thriving force behind the experiment was a pixie-looking, complex balancer of intrigue and academic power called Stuart Griffiths. Griffiths had come from the CBC's international service, and before that there had been a definite link with beer-mug camaraderie of high German tradition. I always thought he would have felt at home in the turn-of-the-century, spiked-helmet society of *The Student Prince*. His chief producer was a bald actor of note and goodwill, Mavor Moore, who carried the weight of a famous matriarchal figure in his history. He was a generous friend. The line of producers and directors-in-training included a number of young men who dreamed of distant glory, some of whom have since found it: among them, Norman Jewison, who had a musical touch, and Arthur Hiller, who had a sound basis in the psychology of drama.

I was attached to Sydney Newman, an elder statesman already in his thirties, who had come by way of the Film Board and a learning history under John Grierson, the fiery Scot who began the Board. Sydney and I argued, but liked each other. The problem, really, was to contain my own enthusiasm. We had all been heroes in our past jobs, and a conflict of egos was inevitable.

It was decided to test the new outside broadcast unit. We would do two programs a day from the Canadian National Exhibition in advance of the formal opening. And a testing time it was! I can still recall Sydney screaming into the headset, "Harry, cue the elephant." But scream as he might, I couldn't get the elephant to budge. We experimented with famous names about town. Lorne Greene hosted a program or two. Another host was Nathan Cohen, the tough critic of the *Toronto Star*, whom I found to be a gentle man hiding behind a crusty exterior. Nathan later became host of a famous Canadian series about ideas called "Fighting Words." Nathan loved to seem like an iron buddha, but he really was, as they say, a pussy cat among friends.

I left the outside broadcast unit before the official opening date to join Gunnar Rugheimer in the TV news department. The department was myself and Gunnar, film cameraman Stanley Clinton, and the highly skilled film editor, Arla Saare. We were the beginning of what was to become an international news-gathering and production facility.

I soon found out about the power of television, with the escape and capture of the Boyd Gang. The Boyd Gang was a group of desperadoes who were considered the most dangerous men in Canada. They had suddenly escaped from the Don Jail in Toronto. We were sitting in an inner office at 354 Jarvis Street, tuned to our new toy, a police radio. The report flashed: the gang was headed for a farmhouse in north Toronto. Clinton grabbed his camera and we roared up the back streets of the city. On the way, the gears of my '51 powder blue Ford jammed; we drove the last several miles in first gear. As a result of our speed, we arrived at the location before the police. Clinton filmed the arrival of the police and the surrender of the gang.

The difficulty was that (1) we were not officially on the air yet, and (2) we could not process the film stock. But those were, as they say, the good old days. Who cared about such minor obstacles? The decision was made to go on the air and talk about what we had seen until the film negative was processed, and then telecast the negative with reversed polarity, so that black would become white. I think I sat and talked ad lib for two or three hours. I must admit I can't remember a thing I talked about. After hesitating, delaying and apologizing, the 100-foot roll of the capture of the Boyd Gang was finally broadcast. We had made history.

Next day on the street, many people stopped me and asked for an autograph. They had watched the news event. We were instant heroes, stars for a day. I got a weird feeling in my bones that day: if fame could come so quickly, how long would it last? If fame could be achieved by merely sitting and talking on the tube, what had we begun? What would television be in the future? But it was not the time to weigh such questions for long. I was in my twenties, the century had just passed its mid-way point, and life was all a pleasure.

The official opening came, and as has often been noted, when co-ordinating producer Murray Cherkhover called for the slide with the call letters announcing the arrival of the Toronto station, CBLT, it appeared upside down. We all laughed at the time.

The opening show was called "The Big Review," and then began my own program, "CBC Newsmagazine," which is still the longest running television program in North America. I produced over 100 films, 52 weeks of the year, for "CBC Newsmagazine." In that time I felt I tried every experiment in film and documentary, filming disasters, blessings, coronations, royal weddings, the healthy, the insane, the boom, the bust, life all around. With this program we discovered a country. Somehow the thin line of people hovering close to America knew little about each other. Men who had filmed weddings and bar mitzvahs were hired to follow the growing face of an obscure nation. And there were great events.

Down at the St. Lawrence Market on King Street in Toronto, in a building that had once housed the great concert queens of the stage and had now fallen into disrepair, the Salvation Army provided a hostel every night for the homeless. St. Lawrence Market also became the first rehearsal hall for a stubborn, tough lady from London, Celia Franca, who was determined to found a ballet company in the raw wilderness of the city. They smiled just a little when she christened it the National Ballet of Canada. I made the first films about it, contrasting the visual image of the slender slippers of the dancers with the battered shoes of the worn-out men.

And word came down one day that at a railway town called Stratford in Ontario, a slightly mad young local man had decided to plant a national theatre. With camera crew, we set out into the wilds, trying to find Stratford, which seemed to have no road signs pointing in its direction. The man, Tom Patterson, who looked even then like a daytime owl, said it had been a boyhood dream. And there was this Irish giant I filmed, Tyrone Guthrie, who proclaimed that a theatre would rise in Stratford. His voice was like the trumpets. And there, bicycling around, as if he had gotten lost on an English country road on a grand and humourous detour, was Alec Guinness, who played a Richard II that will never be forgotten. And Irene Worth, with poems for lips, smiled a leading-lady smile. We put it all on film, including the tent-raising.

This is not to say that everything attempted in those early broadcasts was either meaningful or successful. But there were magic moments. When the St. Lawrence Seaway was about to be built, I toured the farm villages and towns along the river, and felt the pain of dislocation of the farmers who were living out the ritual of continuity. Each oak and team of horses that would be displaced seemed to require a sense of mourning. Land would be flooded in the interests of "progress." An inland seaway would change the economy of the inland cities, so they said, but I wonder if what came to pass was worth those uprooted trees and lives.

Once I went by pilot boat on the St. Lawrence to film the story of the one-millionth immigrant to arrive in Canada since the end of the war. I rode the ship to the docks and saw the longing of the families who desperately looked for hope in the new land. I saw myself in them. We boarded the train for Toronto and the west, and I still remember the broken voice asking, "But where are the mountains? I don't see the mountains." I've often wondered since if that particular man of hope found his mountains in the New World.

There was another film, dedicated to the life of Churchill, which we merely assembled as a matter of course, and which later was to be most important in bringing me to New York. At that time it seemed just another part of the weekly work. Other variations on my program were to follow, and the format later developed into the CBS program, "60 Minutes," with a producer who followed me, Morley Safer.

But I was getting restless. One day, an extremely competent cameraman, Felix Lazarus, walked into my office seeking assignments in Europe or the Middle East. He was looking for odd jobs that would pay his way through the continent for six months or so. We talked at some length, and I found a few small films he might work on for me. "Anything else?" Felix asked at the door before leaving. "Yes," I said, "just one other thing. I'm going with you".

I walked next door and put in my resignation. There were underlying factors, of course. I was twenty-six and the CBC had suggested making me an executive. I saw myself growing paunchy and hazy in Her Majesty's Service. Also, in my private life I was going through a complex time. I had been spending a good deal of time with a female broadcaster of note who was ten years older than myself and the mother of a young child. She was interested in marriage. I just couldn't, at that stage of my existence, commit myself to anything or anybody. Run. Run with the wind. I saw those locked-up swings in my mind, the complacent grey of middle-class morality. I felt smothered. Run! Run!

CHAPTER FOUR

Europe
and an Interview
with the
Queen of England

It was difficult to explain to my father. "What," he questioned, "go to Europe? What for? It's a death camp, the burial ground of Jews. Never. I would never go back." He shook his head and he wept. I could not explain that I had to feel and learn and experience and become part of the universe. But now I think perhaps he really did know.

As well as the film assignments, I gathered commissions to write for the *Toronto Telegram* and assorted journals. As much as possible Felix and I tried to get free travel, and arranged for the use of a Morris Minor station wagon that was to be our home for the next six months.

Lesson number one: do not travel with anyone. Lesson number two: if you travel with anyone, do make sure it is not with a member of the same sex. Felix was a splendid cameraman. Felix was a nice fellow. Felix liked old graveyards. I liked young girls. Big problem.

That aside, it was one of the best and most free times of my life. Every morning there was the stimulus of waking up to new surroundings and a new adventure. We filmed, and I taped and broadcast and wrote. We started in the wintry darkness of West Germany. Each night I locked my rooms in Bonn or Dusseldorf with the shadow of old Nazi terror in my heart. There was a smell of pork fat that brought to mind Canada Packers and the childhood memory of the odour that permeated the air on those St. Clair Avenue nights. I looked at the middle-aged German with the certainty that he had stuffed my cousins into blazing furnaces of hate. It's a feeling that never left me.

Our journey took us to Paris for interviews with Mr. Europe, Jean Monet, who had a vision even then of a Europe that would never be without its petty hatreds and its unceasing class wars. There was time with the great CBC wartime correspondent, Matthew Halton, who loved to sip brandy and talk of the war and days that had passed. Down to the South of France through the Alps. I knocked on Picasso's door, but he did not answer. Too bad, I thought, and when I knocked on Chagall's door many years later, I knew why.

Through Italy and down to Naples, where we boarded an Israeli ship heading for Haifa. When Haifa came into sight, I marvelled at the magnificent temple viewed from the harbour. It was great to be a Jew returning to the temple of his past. But it turned out that the temple was a Christian Bahai shrine. In Israel nothing was what it seemed. Except Ben Gurion. I mark him down among the five greatest men I have personally encountered in my lifetime.

Israel was an overwhelming experience because it brought so many conflicting feelings to my young soul. There was a frontier-town rudeness to the place that made me question my connection to Israel, which I was told was my basic home. There was the jostling, the waiting, the heat, the anger. The state, less than a decade into new life, was groaning under the pressure of its own new growth, but I was too foolish to recognize in it the part of me that was there. The mixture of Europeans and Asians was too harsh to put into perspective. The sight of young girls on the roadside with their guns, hitchhiking across the parched land, was too improbable. Nothing made sense until Ben Gurion.

There was a long wait in Tel Aviv while a decision was made as to whether the interview would or would not take place. The officers in the foreign office always seemed too preoccupied with getting the country to function for just one more day. A Canadian film team seemed the least interesting diversion. Every day I walked from my herring-and-tomato breakfast to the office, and every day they said that word had not come. Finally I was told we could go to S'de Boker, a kibbutz in the Negev desert, to see the great man.

Perhaps it is a cliché to say that the Negev is a moonscape. We journeyed south from Tel Aviv past the disappearing groves, with a stop at Beersheba for cold soda water at a service station, into the emptiness of this dreamland of baked soil. At the door of the clapboard shack, I knocked, to be greeted by Mrs. Ben Gurion, Paula, a legend for her ability to be as direct as possible.

"What language do you speak?" she asked.

"Either English or Yiddish," I answered.

"No," she said, slamming the door, "Here we speak Hebrew." I knocked again. She answered again.

"So what is a young man like you doing in Israel?" She merely picked up the questioning.

"I'm visiting, making films. I live in Canada."

"No," she said. "You must stay. Marry here in Israel. We need Jews from North America. Not just talk." The door slammed a second time.

I knocked again. She answered again.

"When he wakes up, I'll tell him you're here. So come in, why stand in the sun. Sit!"

After I had waited an hour or so, he entered. He looked much smaller than I had imagined. His legendary hair moved like a halo, and the light from the open door caught his smile. He looked so much, I thought, like Sam Jaffe playing the high lama in *Lost Horizon*. He had a mystical air, a sense of hundreds of years caught up in each gesture. If the world is in search of gurus, here was the most sacred. Yet he was worldly.

We sat for several hours under the hot lights. I do not know exactly what he said, because the film and transcript have since been lost. But most of the time he focused on how the Jews and Arabs must live together, two historical nations in partnership, making the desert bloom. When he stared out the window and the glare reflected back the cruel bleakness of the crusted, beige-grey rock, I know he saw rose gardens and wheat fields. He talked of having recently read the Greek philosophers in the original language, and the need to accept the lessons of history. His mind drifted back and forth across centuries, coming to rest now and again like a bee carrying pollen from flower to flower, finding life in one period and then moving on to the next. He was a man for all time.

As for Mrs. Ben Gurion, she stormed into the room at one point carrying grey sheets. "Look," she said to no one in particular, "he wants to make the desert bloom and I have to do the laundry twice." At another point she burst in and sat down beside him as he talked of his distant dream. "Am I all right here?" Felix assured her that she was out of the picture. "What do you mean I'm out of the picture. I want to be in." And finally she made one last entrance, this time to say, "Okay, finished. It's finished. He must sleep." Ben Gurion gave us a last smile and said, "So what can I do? Abraham had two wives!"

Sometimes still I dream of that face. Somehow it slips into the faces of sculptures of Moses and those Sunday school drawings of God— sometimes mingling with my father.

My side trips in Israel produced conflicting emotions. In the Negev I marvelled at the excavations of ancient civilizations, where the desert had been made to produce. I toured with an agricultural expert who showed me how the steppe system of farming collected the rainwater, and thus vines had grown 2,000 years ago. The study had been used to provide the same system now. What did it all have to do with me, born in Canada of Russian immigrant parents, so far removed in my St. Clair Avenue life? I was not sure then, but today I treasure a tiny fragment of pottery I slipped into my pocket from that desert civilization. Who made it? What person had applied its fine lines? Was he or she somehow connected to my family tree, so far away in the desert mists of a past I could only imagine?

I stopped for a couple of days at Kissufim, a kibbutz along the border of the Gaza strip, to visit American and Canadian young people who had come to lead a life with a purpose. I recall how serious they seemed, and remember Dave Kirshner who had been a counsellor with me at Camp B'nai B'rith north of Toronto, during my college years. We shared memories. But then one morning there was firing from the Egyptian side, and Dave arrived with a machine gun and sweetly said, "Stay in your room and you won't get hurt." I tried to make light of it. "Come on, Dave, get off it. You remember me from the next cabin at the camp in Haliburton, right?"

"Don't go outside and you won't get hurt," he said with a new sternness.

"Suppose I just walk over the hill to where the Egyptians are. After all, I am a reporter," I said simply.

"They would kill you," he said, and added matter-of-factly, "If you survived, we might have to shoot."

It wasn't until then that I noticed something that had eluded me. When I knew Dave at camp, he used to entertain us with his beautiful skill at the piano. Since coming to Israel, he had lost a finger. He would not play again.

I again began my story, "Today I walked through the valley of the shadow of death . . ." So strange. My friends were suddenly afraid of me and I of them.

We visited another kibbutz where Felix had a sister. Ein Hashofett was a much more developed community, almost middle-class in its attitudes, despite the fact that its residents said they were all sworn socialists. God was not welcome and religion was vague.

Then there was Jerusalem. At that time I could not fathom what all the fuss was about. We visited the most imposing structure of the time, which turned out to be a YMCA constructed by wealthy American Southern Christians for the recreation of Arab children. We asked to go to the tower to "take a few shots." The director of the Y said, "Please, please. No shooting." We explained we meant to do our "shooting" with a camera.

Maybe it was then that I began to understand something of the passion that was to haunt me for almost two decades until I returned to make my own statement on film about the city, *Next Year in Jerusalem.* The Western Wall, the "Wailing Wall," was in Arab hands. I could see bearded Jews peering over barbed wire, longing to be close. Close to what? Stones. Why? How could stones cause such longing?

Whoever heard of Mandelbaum? Do you think that the famous Mandelbaum Gate was named after some great scribe? Maybe a gallant soldier? Perhaps a proud politician? No. Mandelbaum was simply the man who lived in the house where the barbed wire barrier began. The end of the '48 war was on his doorstep. There a gate was constructed, the city divided, and Mandelbaum was a hero without a house. So what was this to me? And how did Mandelbaum, or any of these other strange people, relate? After all, I was a young Canadian and they were baked into a land of desert and rudeness. But there was that look of silent longing. The bearded men, swaying in the summer heat, facing the Wall they could not touch. I could not touch. Somewhere in the sponge of memory, the impression of that scene stayed. I, too, swayed in that wind until I returned to say what I had to say.

Of course, it was that Hemingway time of life. Each of us who wanted to break away from where we were had briefed himself on that quick, short-sentence way of thinking. Somewhere in those last days of Israel a beard began. That would make me tough! Along the coastline of the boot of Italy as we headed north to Bologna with its boulevard of beauties laced into tight-fitting satins, in Venice with its rotting canals, each day I yearned more and more to confront my literary hero. Who had seen Hemingway, and would he and I arm wrestle when at last we had our confrontation?

Felix and I at last decided to cross the Alps, because I wanted adventure even if I had to cross the next mountain on foot. Finally we arrived in Paris, if not in triumph, at least with freedom. From the Pax Hotel on the Left Bank I was able to visit the sidewalk cafés and pretend to stroke my beard which wasn't quite there yet. It was half past the century and it was a time of dreaming of fame, if not necessarily fortune. We took time to make a short film for the National Film Board on a struggling painter named Riopelle who had received a spurt of publicity. He seemed grateful for the attention.

Each day I would try the Hemingway haunts: long, lingering lunches at the Café Deux Magots and the bar at the Ritz. I practised opening lines, "Dr. Hemingway, I presume." You know how well Spencer Tracy delivered it, so casual in the heart of Africa, in *Stanley and Livingstone*. Hemingway, I am here. But the summer of '55 was fading and Felix wanted home. One night I went down to the Seine, tossed a coin into it. I would return.

I set up camp in London. All these places, these world capitals so far from St. Clair Avenue, were movie sets to me. It was a never-ending double bill, a Saturday matinee at the Royal George in three dimensions. In London I met a young medical student at a jazz joint. He was from Oxford, and he recommended a bed-and-breakfast place at 30 Porchester Place for 25 shillings a night. The landlady, whom I will call Mrs. Doolittle because I have forgotten her real name, was the living embodiment of the British class system. A lower class snob complete, she welcomed me reluctantly as someone quite suspicious because of my European name, but if I had been recommended by someone from Oxford perhaps I knew somebody. She wore those flowered dresses which seem stolen from drapery. Breakfast was scrambled eggs, always a little too watery, and a copy of the *Express* to read. Her accomplice was always referred to as "Mr. Doolittle," but I suspected it was more an arrangement than a marriage. I was confined to a back room, since the large parlour was already booked.

I decided I would go to Spain. That was it. Perhaps at the bullfights I would meet Mr. Hemingway. My beard was now almost in place. Since Felix had gone home to mother, I decided I would find a female travelling companion. In those days it was not quite that simple. After all, this was Victoria's hometown. My friend, Victor Bloom, suggested that I advertise in, of course, the *Times*. Each day in the personal column, the most popular section, people were being asked to rescue wild animals, or give hope to natives in far-off places, or act as nurse to a retired colonel back from India. I needed a female fellow traveller.

I drove down to the *Times* and asked to place an ad. The clerk in his heavy, woollen, dark pin-striped suit barely looked up until he saw the wording: "Dashing young Canadian journalist requests female companion for travels in Spain." There was a long, Alec Guinness-like pause until he looked up at me with a glance of studied contempt. "Have you thought, sir, of trying the *Mirror* or the *Express*?"

"No," I said, trying to look as if I advertised for female companions all the time, "I want to have the sort of person who reads the *Times*."

"This, sir", he said, as if to dismiss me, "is not a mating service."

"But," I said, my argument weakening, "I see many requests for companions."

"Did you wish a nurse, sir?"

Little snotty bastard, I said to myself. I'll bet he's never travelled farther than Blackpool. "No, I want someone who can type, etcetera."

"I don't know about the etcetera, but if you wish a secretary, that is permissible".

Okay, why not. How many secretaries would be male anyhow? So, I advertised. The word "dashing" had to go as part of the compromise.

Mrs. Doolittle could not understand how it was that I began to receive hundreds of letters at 30 Porchester Place. Each morning I was awakened with, "Mr. Rasky the post for you again. Must be serious business." The serious business was conducting interviews. Mrs. Doolittle insisted that the door be left ajar. A rather elegant Australian girl helped me answer some of the letters after she confessed she was engaged and not available. I requested photographs. The mail kept piling up. There really wasn't time to go to Spain. I knew somehow Hemingway would approve. I had constant company and found out a great deal about the English.

I was wondering how I would earn enough to see me through the summer when a letter arrived among the daily mail from my brother Frank, who had taken on the editorship of a breezy magazine, *New Liberty*. He asked if I could find something new to say about the royal family. I sent a naive letter back: "I will interview the Queen."

That summer when everything seemed possible, with letters arriving daily and snapshots of hopeful companions of travel, why not an interview with Her Majesty? When I first mentioned the possibility around the London offices of the CBC, there was a knowing smile and the standard comment, "But it's not done, old boy, just not done." If I had listened then to that kind of advice, I would still be on St. Clair Avenue, plucking chickens.

I decided on a direct assault. I would just go to the palace and have a confrontation. One sunny morning I drove my station wagon to Buckingham Palace and parked it outside, just as they were changing the guard around 11 a.m. American tourists lined the sidewalk, snapping pictures of the wax-still guards. I saw curtains part just a little at an upper window in the palace; I think I saw Prince Charles and a nurse peeking out at the crowd below. I've always felt at such moments that someone might say, "Parcel delivery, rear entrance." So I tried to look twice as confident. "I've come about an interview with the Queen." It was hard not to smile as I said it. But who would question a brash 26-year-old who was using the *Times* to arrange his social life in London? Although the polite police stationed at the palace are used to responding to almost any comment, I could tell that this one hadn't been put forth before. And in England, the rule of thumb is the rule of the voice tone: mine was decidedly studied and matter-of-fact.

"Just a minute." He bowed just a bit as he rushed around the iron gate to the phone. In a minute he was back, quite apologetic. "I called the Queen's press secretary's secretary. She doesn't know what to do; so you had better speak to the press secretary. He's coming to the phone now."

"Commander Colville speaking." He sounded like a BBC announcer. He was, as I learned later, the Queen's press secretary, Commander Richard Colville, CVO, DSC, RN, and perhaps a few more initials that have pushed him up the royal scale since. "I see," he said to my request to see the Queen, without blinking a pause in the conversation. "You'd like to come into the palace. Sorry, I'm tied up today. Just looking at my schedule . . . Yes, tomorrow morning will be fine in the palace."

Next day I just drove right into the palace grounds and parked my tiny station wagon. I think it felt most proud. I walked down the wide beige corridor, lined with portraits of royal ancestors, many long forgotten. Commander Colville was a lean-looking, terse chap, with horn-rimmed glasses and the look of a military man, which he was. He could have been a banker or a lawyer or a pub keeper, in the *private* sector, of course. "What can I do for you?" I just flung it at him. "I have come to interview the Queen." There was a silence and a look of anger, moving close to admiration. "Why, it just isn't done."

"Why isn't it done?"

A touch of annoyance on his part, but as I was from the senior country of the Commonwealth, perhaps he felt that a little explanation was in order. I thought for sure he would ask for credentials, or merely call the guard. But this was London, and one did have to be polite. "You realize that I'm not a publicity officer. We are obviously not looking for publicity for the Queen. Just the opposite." He squelched a laugh at some joke he had thought of, but chose not to reveal.

He was interrupted by one of the two phones on his desk. "Yes, darling, yes darling. I'll be home for dinner." I remember thinking how quaint, even the Queen's secretaries have wives and families. He continued speaking to me, with just a little impatience. "If you submit some written questions, I will attempt to find answers. Meantime, if you wish to see her in action, as it were, I think I can arrange for you to attend the Queen's garden party next Thursday." He pressed a button on an intercom speaker on his desk. "Am I right in assuming we have one more ticket for next Thursday's garden party? Good. Would you bring it in please?" He handed it to me.

The ticket was a plain yellow card, about the size of a wedding invitation. It emphasized the fact that "this invitation cannot be transferred, and must be given up at the door," and suggested "afternoon or lounge dress." For me, lounge dress might just as well have been skirt and blouse or tails and topper. I had one suit and I was wearing it.

Before the date of the gala tea party, I dropped off a list of questions to the guard at the gate of the palace. I felt like a royal regular. But perhaps the most important event that summer occurred when the hall coin phone rang at 30 Porchester Place, and Mrs. Doolittle answered in her usual trying-to-sound-upper-class tone, "30 Porchester Place here." The voice at the other end responded, "Buckingham Palace here. Is Mr. Rasky free to speak to the Queen's Secretary." Mrs. Doolittle knocked on my door as if in a trance. "Mr. Rooosskkyy, it's the—sorry to disturb you, sir—I mean to say, it is . . . it's Buckingham Palace on the phone."

"Of course," I said. I flung by her, wearing that robe from St. Clair Avenue that had been my mother's gift. I noted that Mrs. Doolittle was still standing there, unable to move. I waited. "It's really quite private," I said, and waited till her kitchen door closed behind her. Knowing she would be listening, I spoke quite loudly. "Why, of course, Commander. Yes, I can be at the palace *again*. Yes, I would be most pleased to further discuss the questions for Her Majesty, the Queen." When the conversation was over, I stood there regally in my stocking feet. Mrs. Doolittle came out, looking as if she had just recognized Cinderella. "Mr. Rasky, Mr. Doolittle tells me that the front parlour room has come available and . . ."

"Well, I had been thinking of moving because of my desire for privacy. I am used to private quarters."

"We'd be most pleased if you would stay, and have guests day or night."

And that's how Mrs. Doolittle came to iron my one and only suit, as together we prepared for the Queen's garden party.

When the big day came, I was as nervous as the day I had attended my first dance. I decided to leave my station wagon behind, because I wanted to be able to jump in a cab and command, "Buckingham Palace, please, and step on it." Mrs. Doolittle wept as she waved me goodbye. I recognized the footman who had greeted me on my first visit to the palace. He was wearing a bright scarlet-and-blue livery. I was announced over the loudspeaker, just after the Lord Mayor of Lincoln, England. "Mr. Harry Rasky." (Take that, all you customers who kept me in the cold!) I took note of the surroundings. I swept up the giant staircase and entered the state apartments. I later learned they were designed by Queen Mary in the Regency style. There was some Heathcliff in my soul, and I did a small, unobstrusive Gene Kelly shuffle—a touch of *An American in Paris*.

The state reception room was more like what I had imagined a palace should look like. Red and gold, and sparkling chandeliers. Giant pictures in gold-leaf frames were scattered about the walls. I felt as if 100 royal ancestors were staring at me. Me without tails and topper. I didn't know any of them. I straightened my tie and walked into the garden. Now you couldn't really call the area behind the palace a garden. It's 40 acres of lawn, more like a golf course or cemetery, and just about as cozy. The only ones who looked at home were the swans, nonchalantly paddling about in an artificial pond. They looked well fed. Not so the guests.

Two bands under canvas tents oompahed "Greensleeves." At one end was a giant canvas awning, and under it a spread of tea, bread and butter, cookies, ice cream and punch (non alcoholic), catered by J. Lyons and Company, the corner teahouse man. (What a put-down! I wouldn't normally eat at a Lyons' teahouse on my own money.) The bread was as thin as English roast beef, the texture sawdust yummy. This was royal?

Lester Pearson came strolling by in what looked like a rented suit, too large for him. And the queen? Well, she paraded around as if walking a dog, while the fans in their medals and lace giggled like kids at a summer camp. It was an intimate group of about 7,000, give or take a few Africans, Asians, and assorted high commissioners and lord mayors, and quite a number who looked like refugees from a Salvation Army hostel. The Queen, the papers were to report, was wearing "a full-skirted, shantung dress, sprigged with moss roses, a white-petalled hat with a cluster of red flowers, and she carried a red bag." A wave here, a smile there, a word there, and she was gone. I had a distinct feeling I had been dumped into a parking lot.

When I returned to 30 Porchester Place and was greeted by my teary landlady, I felt I had to make it sound like, well, Disneyland. That's what she wanted to hear. In the British game of role-playing, one could not say that the Queen wore no clothes, or even that the royal stingy sandwiches were stale. It had to be caviar and perfume and a grand ball, but really, it was bread and butter.

I had occasion to visit the palace again several times, getting answers to the questions I had been asked to submit. During one call, while being led down the hall by the footman, I almost walked into the Duke of Edinburgh. I was on my way to the Chinese waiting room, a room transported, complete with wallpaper, from the most elegant of Chinese homes, when the footman came to a sudden stop. He stopped so quickly I almost fell over him. I looked over his shoulder and saw what had caused the abrupt halt. The Duke of Edinburgh had left his car in the centre courtyard and was coming into the palace. He was wearing a neat, light grey, single-breasted business suit, and still had on his large, green sunglasses.

Apparently he was just as startled to see me as I was him. He glanced at me, as if to say, "I wonder if I know that chap?" And I glanced back with "I've seen that chap before." I was struck by his patrician handsomeness as he began mounting the stairs to the private apartments above. He smiled down at me. I smiled up at him. He continued on, and I went to the Chinese waiting room. But, to be absolutely candid, that's just about the closest I've come to interviewing the Queen.

There is something further to say about that summer in London when I went to see the Queen. The lyrics of a nursery rhyme kept coming back to me: "I'm the king of the castle and you're the dirty rascal." It had been recited on those summer days at Earlscourt Park in Toronto, as we made castles in the sandbox (which was also locked up on Sundays). The desire to feel superior to someone else, maybe everyone else, to climb to the top of the hill, to be close to the Queen, the president, the boss, the guy in charge, has always seemed most natural to me. I was later to find it is basic to every drive, in the East as well as the West. It is vastly important when mixed with compassion, and dangerous when it just sits there all on its own, naked as desire.

In England, where accent is king, I had my first brush with the BBC. A radio documentary I had put together for the CBC, based on tapes I had recorded on my journey to Israel, was bought by the BBC features department. The first thing done was to remove my commentary—too colonial, too personal, too passionate—and substitute a British voice that made the longings of all those Moroccan Jews bound for Haifa sound no more urgent than calls for tickets at a soccer game.

To hell with it, I said. It was too late to go to Spain. I ran into an attractive young lady from Australia and we toured the lake country and the Scottish highlands. The countryside was like a poem in its hazy shades of green. And then it was time to go home, if I could find it.

CHAPTER FIVE

Ed Murrow
Needs Me

Was Thomas Wolfe right? You can't go home again? That home, that remembered place, that little-boy location is gone because the boy is gone. He is living in someone else.

Toronto seemed to have shrunk. It was like Alice in Wonderland: size distorted all. My father, that giant with the flaming red beard, Leib the lion, had become a small, almost frail person, waiting out life. He had moved to a brown duplex on Ascot, where once the Scots had kept up those invisible barriers. The stores on St. Clair had been absorbed into an Italian village. The whole area was turning the shades of Calabria and Sorrento and Sicily. They were good people, half a dozen families per lodging. They had escaped the open city that was post-war Italy, and the hunger had been replaced by the longing for home. The Italian women, in their dark displays of self, wept for the sunshine and the barren rocks of that home in the wintry, foreign streets of Ascot, Earlscourt and (please don't tell the Queen) even Regal Road. I had been displaced. I saw Madonnas made of chocolate and strawberry and spindly kids serving up pool balls in the stores of St. Clair. And I wondered who I was.

I tried a freelance life for awhile, serving briefly as associate editor of *Saturday Night* magazine, a journal with its roots in the too sparse ground of the Canadian past. Each night I timed my movements so I would hear the siren voice of Edward R. Murrow, broadcasting from New York on the local Buffalo outlet, WBEN, "Listen to Murrow tomorrow." Each night he saved the world for me. I wanted to be closer to where he was. That voice of urgency was calling me.

In Toronto I almost had to avert my glance. They were crushing away what had been. Superhighways plundered the places I had known. Sunnyside: going, going—gone. The bright hopes that had begun with Canadian TV were moving off south, and some who believed there would always be an England tried London. But the English class system, too reminiscent of early days waiting on hard benches at the Sick Children's Hospital for a handout of hope, convinced me that I must try the United States. I detoured to Los Angeles.

As a "film-maker"—that was my phrase—the obvious place for me was Hollywood. Or so I thought. I convinced the CBC that they needed a good radio documentary on Hollywood, and impressed a Canadian magazine with the need for cover stories on some stars. I arranged enough work to pay for my plane fare and headed west, full of confidence that I would be "discovered": a film-maker in the rough, realism in the raw, an embryonic Joseph L. Mankiewicz.

Hollywood held no surprises. Doors were wide open. I visited all five major studios, viewed a dozen films in production, interviewed two dozen film stars, ranging from Natalie Wood to Jimmy Stewart, and even got to dance with hour-glass shaped Sheree North at the Coconut Grove. Nothing was too much while I was interviewing, broadcasting, publicizing, but when I started talking job possibilities, a strange silence fell over any conversation. "Job" was a word that was apparently taboo.

Director Michael Curtiz, a veteran of 25 years and such films as *The Charge of the Light Brigade* and *Casablanca* (he really made *Casablanca*), summed it up in a voice as Hungarian as goulash, "Hollywood is a cruel city. It allows little room for friendship." But I did have one friend there, Arthur Hiller, the gentle Canadian who had made good in Hollywood. His agent at the time was B.D. Shamberg of the Shamberg-Gold Agency. Art suggested I talk to him, and I did. It was Friday, and Bud Shamberg said he could spare 15 minutes before taking off for a weekend at Palm Springs. That was the style. He was a young, fast-talking American whose sliding eyes gave the impression he was on the verge of completing a suitably shady deal.

"I have a film here on the life of Churchill·and another on some immigrants arriving in Canada. Both were special documentaries I wrote and produced in Canada," I offered.

"Documentaries!" he spat out the word. "What are those? This is Hollywood. Here documentary means flat lighting, a picture without a story. Sorry, go home, do some drama and come back in a couple of years."

Mr. Shamberg had a suggestion. An old college chum of his named Perry Wolfe was now producing shows for CBS in New York. He had done "Adventure" and was working on a series called "Air

Power,'' both documentaries. ''Why don't you look him up some time in New York?'' He grabbed his coat and rushed me to the door. ''Sorry,'' Shamberg said, as he locked the door from the outside. ''I'm late for a very important date.'' As he drove off in a shiny red convertible, he smiled. ''Get off those documentaries—flat lighting, no sex appeal.''

In New York in early March, 1956, I paced the floor of my pint-sized Algonquin Hotel room. I was on my way back to Toronto without a job, and New York seemed cold and unfriendly. I pushed my hand in my pocket to pull out the number of Mildred Kosoy, a Toronto girl studying music in New York, and a scrap of paper fell on the floor. On it was the name ''Perry Wolfe, CBS.'' I called.

''What, you're a friend of Bud Shamberg?'' I tried to explain on the phone that I really wasn't a friend. But the eager voice said, ''I'm just down the street. Come on over.''

At the offices of ''Air Power'' on 45th Street, Perry Wolfe, a would-be poet turned producer, looked up from the Moviola, a film editing machine, and said, ''Canada. Wonderful place for documentaries. National Film Board. Great. Andrew Allan. Superior. Love to see your Churchill show. Great. We need good guys here. I'll call the boss, Irv Gitlin, and his assistant, John Jefferson. I'm sure they'll like you. Canadian. Churchill. Great. Damn it. We need a fresh approach.''

I did not see Perry Wolfe again for years. But he had indeed arranged for appointments with Irv Gitlin, director of public affairs at CBS, and his assistant. I expected Madison Avenue sharpies in grey flannel suits. Jefferson, a six-foot-four gentleman with a kind, understanding smile, invited me out for a drink and spent most of the time talking about ''the good old days in Europe.'' An appointment with Gitlin meant a ride down in the elevator with him as he strode from one studio to another. ''Sounds great,'' he said. ''Keep in touch. Terrific.'' Next thing I knew I was out in the street, walking along Madison Avenue alone and ready to go home to Toronto and forget about it. But before I left, I dropped off two cans of film, one with the show on Churchill, one on the immigrants.

My last contact with the U.S. and the CBS was a gift I sent to John Jefferson: a tin of Schimmelpenninck cigars, slender Dutch cigars I smoked after I had been introduced to them by Clyde Gilmour, the Canadian movie critic. I had offered one to Jefferson in New York and had promised to send some along. I thought, even if he had no job for me, I did promise the cigars.

The months passed and New York became just another place to visit in my thinking. Then one day in late June while I was attending the Stratford Festival opening and writing an article about the prince of Canadian players, Chris Plummer, I received a call at the Queen's Hotel.

The desk clerk said, "It's New York." John Jefferson was on the line. "We are going to do a series here on American history and politics. It will run ten weeks, maybe more. We need a writer. What do you know about American history?" I hesitated. I knew as much as any informed Canadian. I had studied it along with the battles of Wolfe and Montcalm in high school, had taken a course in political science at the University of Toronto, and had covered the first Eisenhower election for CBC television. I steadied my hand on the phone. "Oh yes, I'm an expert."

"Good. Bill Weinstein, the producer, saw your Churchill show and liked it. You'll be hearing from our business affairs department. I can't talk money. Thanks for the Schimmelpennincks."

I received another call from a man who announced that he was Sal Iannucci, business affairs representative for CBS public affairs. He sounded like a tiger at the gates, barking each comment so loudly I felt he was in the room with me. "Just how long have you been an expert on American history? How much do you think you're worth to us? What do you know about American television? How much do you want?"

I chose a figure out of the air. "Oh, say, $400 a week." That's ridiculous, I thought to myself. I'm not worth it. "I'll call you later," he growled.

For the next three days in Toronto, phone calls from Iannucci echoed out of my Maitland Street apartment in Toronto. Once he had me down to $190 a week. And I confessed I knew nothing about business affairs. I was merely a Canadian wanting to work in New York for the challenge of it. "Don't be ridiculous," he confided in a rare moment of humanity. "I'm a CBS negotiator. If I can, I'll buy you for ten cents." And he meant it.

I couldn't eat or sleep. My life was changing or was it? Finally, I got a call from Iannucci. "Okay, here's the deal. You get $350 a week and start on July the 9th. That's our last offer." It took me one second to say, "All right. I'll be in New York." There was a chuckle at the other end of the line. The tiger relaxed. "Okay, and look me up when you come to town. We'll have a drink."

I expected the knife-in-your-back atmosphere of the novel, *The Great Man*. Instead I found gathered around me a dozen serious young men who, in another setting, might be university professors or businessmen. The head of the department, Irv Gitlin, had in fact been a university lecturer. He had made his name at CBS as producer of a literate half-hour series about research at U.S. universities, called "The Search." I expected a gay life of night clubs, and names dropped frequently in the columns of keyhold gossipers. I found instead that all my working colleagues lived either on Long Island or in Connecticut, and had to make trains to be with their families. It turned out that I was the only bachelor around, and the only one who lived in a penthouse.

But the Canadian approach to American history seemed to capture the imagination. My first show, on the history of American political parties, was requested by American universities as an educational aide, and later won a Freedom Foundation Award. Most of my American history, I admit, I learned quickly from an old university textbook, *Introduction to American Government*, by Ogg and Ray.

My series, "Bandwagon '56," concluded the day the Israelis boldly struck out at Egypt in the strange pocket war of the anxious hours of October, 1956. It was decided to get an old series, "UN in Action," back on the air in a hurry. Since I had visited the Middle East in my wanderings, I was quickly shifted to the role of associate producer. Two months later I was offered a five-year contract as producer, and I accepted.

New York was a romance. At that time it seemed like everything I had dreamed of on those cold St. Clair nights. New York and I danced together and I sang to it. Poets, songwriters and just plain people have sung odes, written essays and called out curses to the international giant that just happens to be on American soil. They have searched the city, trying to transcribe its vast spring beauty and its angry winter ugliness. They have tried to touch its pulse in Times Square, listened to its music around Washington Square, heard its silence around Gramercy Square; attempted to feel its texture of granite and steel and glass and humanity at Rockefeller Plaza, and all have succeeded; yet all have failed in a way.

The reason is simple: New York is not one city. To each man, it is something different: a home, a mistress, a chance, a hope, a lonely cell, a world of happiness—or none of these. Once the prose poet, E. B. White, summed it up:

> New York is the concentrate of art and commerce and sport
> and religion and entertainment and finance, bringing to a single
> compact arena the gladiator, the evangelist, the promoter, the
> actor, the trader and the merchant. It carries on its lapel the
> unexpungeable odour of the long past, so that no matter where
> you sit in New York you feel the vibrations of great times
> and tall deeds, of queer people and events and undertakings.

It is sad that the visitor tastes so little of it. The mountains of its buildings, the groans of its subways, the roars of its millions as they fast-step for home make even the bravest tourist cringe and hide in his hotel until night, then nervously grab a cab and head for the carnival that is Broadway. But for those willing to grasp this tiger by the tail, for those enthusiastic enough to try its back streets and its subtleties, there's a universe to explore.

I viewed my New York at night from a penthouse terrace half way between the new elegance of lower Fifth Avenue, with its brother-hood of too polite doormen (a tip of the hat and two bits to hail a cab), and the old decadence of the Bowery, with its lonely, lost lives clinging to the memories of heartbreak. ("Brother, can you spare a dime? I've just murdered my mother-in-law.") At night I might try the black-stock-inged world of nearby Greenwich Village or a walk through Washington Square, where retired men lived only in the past tense and played chess and checkers by lamplight or flashlight.

Along West Fourth Street, The Little Place offered spaghetti or veal parmigiano for about two dollars. It was so crowded that you felt you were part of one large Italian family, and you belonged. And across the street, the off-Broadway tabernacle, Circle in the Square, was reliving that sentimental mortality play of American life, *Our Town*. The Lime-light Coffee House around the corner presented espresso and fat cheese-and-garlic sandwiches, and a chance to meet a beatnik who didn't quite get on the road to San Francisco. On a hot summer Monday night, I spread a blanket on the Washington Square grass and listened to a chamber music concert, free of everyone except a huckstering Good Humour man from whom I made an occasional purchase.

And when spring caressed the city, there was a special joy in just walking up Fifth Avenue or down Madison at noon, as the faces of the hurrying men flickered past in occasional oases of sunlight, and the girls in their summer dresses paced a path that made the sidewalk sing. For lunch I might try Michel's on 53rd Street, where the *hors d'oeuvres* were a meal in themselves; or the San Marino, where the bouillabaisse was the best this side of Marseilles; or the Oak Room at the Plaza, which had a kind of panelled elegance imported from London (with a large import tax on the menu); or the Russian Tea Room, where you could speak Russian if you could handle it; or a Central Park bench for a chopped liver sandwich.

And at the Algonquin Hotel for an afternoon cocktail I just might, as I did, exchange ties with the great director, Preston Sturges, and sit for half-a-dozen half hours drinking in a beer and an old Hollywood story, and striking up a sing-song with the headwaiter if that were the passing mood. In the evening I might rush along West 51st Street to Le Berry, where the chicken was so soaked in wine sauce it had a kind of alcoholic splendour, and the snails were so rich in garlic you likely wouldn't be able to, or want to, talk to a friend for hours.

Any afternoon I might detour along 33rd Street just to feel the heat and humidity of the garment centre, dodging a pushcart of wedding dresses or a flock of summer suits careening across the sidewalk. Possibly I might hide for an hour at the Museum of Modern Art on 53rd Street, and try to decide once again how it was that Picasso put so much humour into a tragic canvas. The museum's free afternoon movies, all old, reminded me again that movies weren't better than ever. And its penthouse restaurant shredded the carrots so delicately into the salad, you felt they were composed by an impressionist.

It's possible, too, that I might fight the crosstown traffic and try to lunch at the delegate's diningroom at the United Nations and admire Ralph Bunche from afar, and then walk in the UN rose gardens, study the tugs' soft shifting up the East River, admire the stone sandwich of a building, and damn myself for being a member of a human race that might just remove such afternoons and such cities for all time in a mushroom cloud. The thought of a world without a New York somehow seemed too unreal. And then I might look at the great buildings, at the city of eight million, and sigh to myself, "Oh my, oh my." It seems now like such a romantic and innocent time that it is hard to pull it all into focus and accept that it ever was.

At work at CBS, we were truly a band of brothers. Some of the most talented people ever to be assembled together were there: producers Al Wasserman, Arthur Barron, Chuck Romine, Fred Freed, Bud Benjamin, Ike Kleinerman, Perry Wolfe and, of course, Fred W. Friendly and Murrow, who was a collossus, larger than life, carrying the universe on his brow. Sunday belonged to us. We had great, thoughtful programs such as "Look Up and Live," my own "UN in Action," "Camera Three," "Omnibus," "The Seven Lively Arts" and "20th Century." During the week they were experimenting with 90-minute drama under the tasteful eye of Hubbel Robinson. Broadcasting was a shout, a call, an announcement that we were there and that there were ideas to be discussed and great deeds to be dramatized. We were in love with the vitality of it all.

Even then Murrow was brooding, warning of the vacuum that was to come. I recall an evening at the Plaza Hotel when we were all being honoured with Sylvania Awards for "outstanding contribution to creative television technique," and I was caught up in the innocent glamour of the moment, having followed Mary Martin and Lee J. Cobb to the rostrum. Murrow twiddled the dial of the clock that was his prize and asked, "Instead of subsidizing prizes, why don't companies such as Sylvania sponsor more of our better programs."

Later Murrow was to make a speech to a group of broadcasters that was to upset his own position of power at CBS, and thus change the whole history of broadcasting.

Our history will be what we make it. And if there are any
historians about 50 or 100 years from now, and there should be
preserved the kinescopes for one week of all three networks,
they will there find recorded, in black and white or colour,
evidence of decadence, escapism and insulation from the realities
of the world in which we live. I invite your attention to the
television schedules of all networks between the hours of 8 p.m.
and 11 p.m., eastern time.

Here you will find only fleeting and spasmodic reference
to the fact that this nation is in mortal danger. There are, it
is true, occasional informative programs presented in that
intellectual ghetto of Sunday afternoons. But during the daily
peak viewing periods, television in the main insulates us from
the realities of the world in which we live. If this state of
affairs continues, we may alter an advertising slogan to read:
"Look Now. Pay Later." For surely we shall pay for using
this most powerful instrument of communication to insulate the
citizenry from the hard and demanding realities which must
be faced if we are to survive. I mean the word *survive* literally.

This instrument can teach, it can illuminate; yes, and
it can inspire. But it can do so only to the extent that humans
are determined to use it to those ends. Otherwise it is merely
wires and lights in a box. There is a great and perhaps decisive
battle to be fought against ignorance, intolerance and
indifference. This weapon of television could be useful.

Few listened. I was enjoying the mingling with the UN delegates.
I would stop by the lounge and argue with the Russians. "Someday we,
too, will have skinny women like you," they would shout, almost in
desperation. I would listen to my friend Golob from Yugoslavia rhap-
sodize about how, after an all-night session, he would stop on the 59th
Street bridge as the first light was coming up over the city, and look back
at the monument that was Manhattan. And I would have long terrace
parties with strolling musicians at 11 Waverly Place, and believe it was
a time that would never change. I was trying to reproduce those early
movies of glamorous Manhattan at the Royal George. Occasionally I
would succeed. There was Bobo Rockefeller on the terrace and William
Saroyan, who wore his heart on his sleeve. (Those eyes of compassion
that would give you the world if he owned it!) I held the kind of parties
once frequented by Katherine Hepburn and Cary Grant in Lubitsch com-
edies.

And the girls I knew ring round now like Matisse paintings. New
York was never without its evening escapades. The carnival of women

who passed through my apartment left an aftertaste of candyfloss, and the permanence of the relationships had the firmness of pink sawdust. Who were they? All their names sung in a rhyme—Jane, Joan, Susan, Judy. . . Jane, Joan, Susan, Judy—all their names sound like a train gathering steam, heading out to nowhere, with little rush to return. They were assorted women of assorted beauty, dancing through life because the American dream had not taught them how to walk. I caught them on the way to the psychiatrist's couch ("Zip me up, dear. I'm late for my one o'clock at the head shrinker's."), and coming back from the divorce circuit. ("He was just a boy. My husband was just a boy. There are no men in New York!")

Shall I itemize them here, the lonely ladies of second-generation America? The girls who could not go home because home was hideous, where the values had the accent of Eastern Europe but not its substance. Home was at the end of the "E" train under the remnants of the "el" in the Bronx—and the "el" was hell. Home was a cold-water flat on Seventh Street, where the garlic had stained the plaster and a mouse was an unwanted pet. Home was a wall-to-wall carpeted one room on the cold but proper East Side, with a duo of Siamese cats to keep away the awful silence of the long nights. Home was a two-room flat hidden in the Puerto Rican sector of the West Side, where windows, doors and drawers were locked and sealed by day and night.

I found them in the darkened parlours of cocktail parties. I stumbled on them at the plastic and chrome reception desks. Her story, always the same, always different. I have known you well, girl of mid-twentieth century America. It was hard enough to find a man, and much harder to find the woman in yourself. It took two to tango, but you always wanted to lead and hated yourself for that forward drive. Travel girl, travel, but in reverse. For you and me, honey, it was always the same: the urge, the surge, the act, sometimes the guilt. And when it was over, where were we?

It was a time for learning my own emotions, trying to shake the cold-room dust of St. Clair from memory, with mixed results. And each Sunday I produced a half hour for CBS, "UN in Action," watching my credit beamed out from UN headquarters to cities and towns of America. Later I was to discover that a weekly fan was a young lady in New Orleans who became my wife; so I was still sending messages by the airwaves.

It was a time when the UN still had hope. It was a time when the balance of nations gave us all hope. I studied the face of Dag Hammarskjold almost daily, wondering if he were man or superman. He was truly a man in an iron mask, his one expression showing no pleasure, no pain. (Oops! There goes a revolution. No comment.) He was the glass and brick of the building. But was there a heart anywhere? Only later, when he was bombed out of the sky over the Congo on one of his Pimpernell peace missions, was it discovered that he quietly wrote reflective poetry. I can recall one of his few public utterances:

> This organization grew out of the pain and turmoil of the last war. Common to us all and above all other convictions, stands the truth once expressed by a Swedish poet when he said that the greatest prayer of man does not ask for victory but for peace.

At the time there were others who were more accessible. Lester Pearson was a giant among men. Quietly ambling through the blank corridors, with his hand characteristically thrust in his pocket, his bow-tie like his smile, he was a welcome, clean wind. I watched him single-handedly create the salvation army, the UNED police force. He had that Canadian missionary zeal, inherited from family ties in early China. Had there been more like him, the UN would not have become the cold scold of endless rhetoric that has turned the slab building into a tomb.

On my Sunday morning program I acted as a kind of referee for the world's woes. Golda was not welcome in the same studio as the Egyptian foreign minister in those long ago pre-Sadat days. There was an actual fist fight when the opposing forces met head on in the Cyprus dispute. Krishna Menon of India was a semi-fox, speaking for the so-called unaligned. He had the countenance of the devil. Who could understand him?

Harry Truman stopped by one day for a half-hour dialogue. The cab driver who brought him was so excited at having carried the former President of the United States that he could not accept payment and stayed during the live broadcast to drive the ex-President back to the Carlyle Hotel. Truman would not accept our offer of a limousine. He looked straight into the camera and proclaimed, "The Russians—never have trusted the bastards and still don't. Their word isn't worth a tin ruble. Stalin was an absolute son-of-a-bitch." He enjoyed himself and I enjoyed him.

And then there was Eleanor Roosevelt, so plain yet so extraordinarily beautiful in her compassion for mankind. Adlai Stevenson said of her, "She would rather light candles than curse the darkness, and her glow has warmed the world." Several times she appeared on my program. She took long strides, even when old, as if a mist were moving. She contained the inner disappointment of her private life, and her face was both craggy and comforting. She would drift off in a dream between film takes and I would try to remind her where she was in her thoughts. She scolded me, "Young man, I know exactly where I am." And indeed she did.

Some people ask how I managed to feel comfortable with the world's great. At that time I merely superimposed someone from my childhood onto the famous face. So that Mrs. Roosevelt was not only first lady of the world, a title she deserved, but she was also Mrs. Etkins. Mrs. Etkins was the warm-hearted widow who lived across from the McKay Street *shul*. She was the keeper of the key. She was the one who found the *shabus-goy* to light the pot-bellied stove on Saturday mornings in those desperately cold winters, so that the ten praying men could talk to God without shivering too much. And Mrs. Etkins always had a kind word after the service, and perhaps an invitation for a *gluzela* tea and honey cake. She took care of the men in her world, as did Eleanor. So it was not so hard to nudge Mrs. Roosevelt and say, "Time for the next take." It was merely like waking Mrs. Etkins. She was a little grumpy, but it wasn't too long before the lines, those lines of oak, those lines of life, those lines of eternity, eased into a smile.

From Mrs. Roosevelt I got that prayer that I was to use later in a film about her. It was a simple prayer of peace from Saint Francis of Assisi.

> Lord, make me an instrument of Thy peace:
> Where there is hatred, let me sow love;
> Where there is injury, pardon;
> Where there is discord, union;
> Where there is doubt, faith;
> Where there is despair, hope;
> Where there is darkness, light;
>
> O Divine Master, grant that I may not so much seek
> to be consoled, as to console;
> To be understood, as to understand;
> To be loved, as to love;
> For it is in giving that we receive,
> It is in pardoning that we are pardoned,
> And it is in dying that we are born
> To Eternal Life.

John Crosby, who was then writing excellent TV criticism, called my weekly program "TV's controversial corner," when he was writing for the *New York Herald Tribune*. The program was one of the most quoted in the world. And I believed that I was doing some good by providing understanding. It was my hope.

When the UN was not in session, I moved over to a weekly show called "The Last Word," which was a meeting place of the great literary minds of the time, playing a guessing game about words and exchanging sparks of thought. Bergen Evans of Illinois and John Mason Brown, the courtly critic, were regulars, with guests such as Mary McCarthy and Archibald McLeish. Some became friends. And it is now hard to accept that such programs were available on a weekly basis on American commercial television.

Occasionally I would drift off into a special, such as my *Day Called "X,"* borrowed from an idea by Orson Welles, in which I used an entire city, Portland, Oregon, as my film playground. With Howard K. Smith, I introduced America to "The 49th State." With Eric Severeid, I found a holy man who actually had a haze of light around him as he spoke. It photographed like neon. As I recall, he was called the Sharayekarya of Puri. It was the only time I ever saw Severeid out-pontificated. Between the delegates, the literary gentlemen and the learned people, I seemed to have found an ideal home. Until I learned a corporation is not your mother. Never be confused.

The CBS monopoly on news was breaking. Murrow's speech was quietly pushing him off into the distance. Irving Gitlin, who had hired me, had left for a more lucrative position at NBC, and though a hurricane was coming, I thought it was just a slight wind. But, in fact, my own contract was terminated. I argued that I had given my soul to CBS.

They answered, "Fine. You have 30 days."

I had a five-year contract.

"The small print says 30 days notice."

I could sue.

"We employ 12 permanent attorneys. How many do you have?"

It was the time of the quiz scandals. "How do we know you haven't been giving questions to diplomats in advance of air time?"

But, but, but . . .

And so I went south, to give up film and TV forever, and to write a book or something.

CHAPTER SIX

Revolutions in Latin America/ Revelations in New York

I landed in Cuba just after Christmas. There was a weird calm about Havana. The tart of the Caribbean had running mascara. The soldiers of Batista moved like dream-walkers with their machine guns ready, but they looked strangely afraid for men with guns. The hotels in town were at half-mast. Tourists rattled around in them. But somehow decadence needs a crowd and there was none.

Since this was the right time, I decided to become a great novelist—not just a novelist but a great novelist. I decided to head out into the hills and find Hemingway. After all, I assumed he would greet me and pass on some advice, and maybe we might out-drink each other or whore around or find some common meeting of minds. I rented a car and gathered directions from the hotel clerk who advised against it. The countryside was in rebel hands, he said. But I drove out rather fearlessly and, in retrospect, rather recklessly. I drove along empty highways to the Hemingway house. The gardener seemed annoyed at the disturbance. Hemingway was not there and the gardener did not know when Señor Hemingway would be back. It was not a time for strangers, and if the bell were tolling, it was not tolling for me. Hemingway was not home. Havana seemed flat. Nothing would happen there, I predicted. So the day before New Year's I moved further south to Acapulco for excitement. When I arrived, I picked up the local paper: "Fidel Castro takes over Cuba, arrives in Havana in triumph." So much for predicting revolutions.

It was a time for looking around. I was fascinated by the beach boys. The beach boy is as indigenous to tropical resorts as blazing sunsets.

He is the rare human product of an uncivilized life. Born usually as the result of an illicit moment on a beach, his crib is a native hammock, his lullaby is sung by the waves, his mother's milk is sucked from the breast of a coconut, his school and father provider is the sea, and most important, his playground is the beach. I suppose it was the beach boys' "street sense" that got me. I related their tough beginnings to my own delivery-boy days. The great difference was that the beach kept them semi-nude, and the waves seemed to mold their bodies like mahogany Davids. And the ladies came to adore and be caressed, even if it meant paying a price. The heat seemed to bleach the brain of all thought, and only lust was left. I wrote about the beach boys and the women who came to Acapulco in search of their dreams.

I lived in a *hakaleta,* a little hut with a thatched roof and a built-in *aguna* that rushed below its rafters. I wrote each morning and then drove to the beaches in the afternoon, except on Sunday, the day of the bullfight, when I pretended I was Hemingway in Spain or Van Gogh. But there is a time for all. One day the phone rang as I was struggling with a not-too-good paragraph. John Kiermaier, who had replaced Gitlin at CBS in New York said, "All is forgiven. Come home." The trouble with paradise is that its restfulness makes you irritated. I had become angry at the sea and the sun.

In New York, I moved quickly to re-involve myself with CBS, only to discover it was a short-term romance. It was a little like trying to revive a relationship with the one great passion of your life. My new series was called "The Great Challenge," and it enabled me to find a television place for a young Canadian-born economist from Harvard, John Kenneth Galbraith. He and the governor of New York, Nelson Rockefeller, were my guests on the opening program. It was an opportunity to work again with Howard K. Smith, whom I had so much admired for his wartime reporting during the days when Murrow was king. Another guest was Fred W. Friendly, who tried to keep an aggressive air of optimism, but the fact was that his old colleague Murrow was on a leave of absence, sending back notes from obscure corners of the globe. Murrow was on a journey to the end.

Another great man, who had written a book called *Journey to the Beginning,* entered my life—Edgar Snow. Ed and I plotted a trip to China that would wake up the American public. Ed Snow was a man who haunts me still, because he had a kind of American openness like the Kansas he came from. His face was craggy and handsome in a Spencer Tracy kind of way. He was part of the era of the crusading journalist, the foreign correspondent who loved women and truth. It is to the lasting shame of the American networks, and a loss to millions of Americans, that Ed Snow was considered too controversial to be allowed on the public air. He had an affection and understanding for China that was out of step with the dogma of the time. He had discovered Mao for the western world, and *Red Star Over China* is still a classic work.

His attitude was expressed by a quotation that preceded his book, *The Other Side Of The River*. It said: "Men will not receive the truth from their enemies and it is very seldom offered to them by their friends; on this very account I have frankly uttered it." How similar that was to the quotation that hung over Murrow's desk: "It takes two to speak the truth—one to speak, and another to hear." That was from Thoreau, and both Murrow and Snow were in the Thoreau tradition, which came from the land. And every time they took a step on that land, the connection between them and the earth was like a promise to care, to take responsibility for all beings, to worry about the world. Maybe this is what my own father had tried to express in those relentless Saturday afternoon sessions studying the books of God's law and man's interpretation of them.

Ed would just show up at Waverly Place. Occasionally he was on a lecture tour. We would talk about events and passions. I never heard a complaint from him, except about his teeth, which were being ground away, perhaps from years of strange and sometimes inferior diets.

A few biographical notes: Ed Snow began his search for truth about China when he was twenty-two and working for Colonel Mc-Cormick's *Chicago Tribune*. He was the first person to penetrate a civil war blockade and interview and photograph Mao Tse-tung and Chou En-lai. That was 1936. Out of it came *Red Star Over China*. From it the world came to know Mao. It was published in Chinese before it came out in English. When America and China broke off relations, Ed Snow was the only American who kept contact. John Foster Dulles considered it some kind of sin to have Americans see what was happening among the millions of China. Snow fought and won. He wrote:

> The era of freedom of inquiry which separates China from the United States is not an absolute gulf, but a frontier; not something fixed, or permanent, not anything ordained by God, but a will in men's minds.

But he paid a price. During the McCarthy era his children were called names by his neighbours. He dared to write what he saw and he was called a communist. He was not. But he moved his family to

Switzerland to keep his children away from the hate-mongers. When later on I visited him there, he often wondered if he had done the correct thing. His Kansas roots were deep. Along with Ed Murrow he was one of journalism's granite rocks of strength.

It was as a result of an interview with Mao published in *Life* years later that the great new adventure began. Then dozens of U.S. technicians set up satellite feeds. Grey TV anchormen prepared for the long television march. And even the President of the United States of America said that it was alright to go to China, because he was going. But Ed Snow was not there with Nixon. He died in his exile in Switzerland. His doctors were Chinese, sent personally by Chou En-lai. And I mourn him still.

I did not go to China. I went to Panama. Even now that seems improbable. But there I was. When Irving Gitlin moved over to the National Broadcasting Corporation, he began to devise a series to oppose the quality of the Murrow-Friendly epics called "See It Now." This series was to become "NBC White Paper," which is a title I have never understood. I mean, how can you have a paper on an electronic medium? It was decided that because I had become a Latin American expert (see above about Cuba and Acapulco), and because I had studied Spanish at the United Nations and been diagnosed as *sympatico* by the Latins, and because Canadians were sort of from out there somewhere, I was the one to do what became *Panama—Danger Zone*, the third NBC white paper. It was a distinguished season that included Al Wasserman's classic *U-2 Affair* and Bob Young's warm *Sit-In*, the first major network program on the rising blacks.

Panama is a wet sponge of a country. Its humidity is so intense that you have the sense of wandering through a perpetual steam bath. And each day between May and December, there is a darkness at noon, as clouds blacken the sky. And the silent people wait for the storm that is almost inevitable. At that moment in time, I quickly learned, another kind of storm was threatening. It was 1960, the beginning of a new decade, and I was thirty-two and in search of adventure. I had left behind a remarkably warm-blooded Italian-American girl named Antoinette, who had decided that in a contest between Jesus and me, the Church would be harder to give up. And, of course, the *shul* on McKay Street travelled with me. So, if I did not return, who would care? My heart was crushed pasta.

We were in search of trouble. And I was playing the temporarily mad role of a soldier of fortune, armed with a camera. Briefly, this was the problem: the Republic of Panama is located at the crossroads of the hemisphere. It just seems to join everything in sight. It links North and South America, and divides the Atlantic and the Pacific Oceans. It is the bridge between the Caribbean, which is an extension of the Atlantic on the north, and the Pacific on the south.

The country itself would just fold up into the jungle, which seems to grow as you watch, except that it is sliced in two by the American-built Panama Canal. The canal zone—just five miles on either side of the canal—is not just a little bit of America. The situation is more like the British in India under the Raj, the white masters in a gin-and-tonic world surrounded by a banana civilization. A year before my visit, the trouble had begun when an ambitious, dapper local Panamanian, Aquilino Boyd, on the anniversary of Panama's independence, had forced his way into the canal zone to try and plant the Panamanian flag. He was greeted by fixed bayonets under the direction of the keeper of the canal, General Potter. And the question was: when the anniversary came round again would there be demonstrations and bloodshed? I was looking for a revolution, as was everyone else.

It would have been wonderful if everything could have been divided between the good guys and the bad, as Ronald Reagan suggested out in California. But the issue had rings within rings, prejudice upon prejudice. And, in fact, in that tiny spot of cleared jungle were all the problems of Latin America, enough for half a dozen books.

From my office at NBC, I had been in touch with someone who signed cables "EDTEDSCOTT, Panama." So when I arrived, I was greeted by a man who said, "I am Edward Scott. You may call me Ted. I am your man in Panama." His too-pudgy face carried evidence of a lifetime of fist fighting. He was dressed in white and wore a kind of sombrero, his shirt would not quite fit into his belt line (the waist long ago having taken the count of ten), and tucked into his belt was a pistol. "EDTEDSCOTT, you see, is just ten letters, the maximum for a cable address. And I will call you 'the young master.' "

His story was revealed quickly. He was from Australia, had kicked around and won temporary fame as a middle-weight boxer. He carried with him a photograph of those pugilistic days, which he showed me. "Look how the mighty have fallen." He had ended up in Havana, running the English-language paper and doing stringer work for NBC. In Havana he had been a kind of brawling, freewheeling journalist-at-large. Part of his support may have come from Batista, so when Fidel came in, the cable address of EDTEDSCOTT moved to Panama.

Scott regaled me with tales of Hemingway in Havana, and claimed that he, personally, could testify that Hemingway was a coward. He confided this as he drove me into the steamy town of Panama City, while all the time pointing out the swaying movements of the *muchachas,* the attractive, dark, teenage girls in their purple and yellow dresses. "Ready for the revolution, young master?" It was obvious that to him I was a too-young, too-enthusiastic, too-inexperienced young man from the city in the middle of a country ready to explode. "Ready," I said.

What made Panama unique was the canal, truly the eighth wonder of the world. It is a living relic, the same as it was the day it opened, except that the donkeys that pull the ships have been replaced by rail engines. The number of miles saved between New York and San Francisco by using the canal is eight thousand. The U.S. has operated the canal since Teddy Roosevelt created the country in 1914 in order to build the greatest ditch in the history of man. A graveyard of equipment was still rotting in the tall trees, evidence of those who had tried before and failed. Ferdinand de Lesseps, the Frenchman who built Suez, met with ruin and heartbreak when 22,000 men died during his attempt.

The legend among U.S. diplomats when the Americans began digging in 1904 was that each predecessor was shipped home in a coffin. Panama was a sinkhole of tropical fevers; they called it "the white man's grave." Colonel William Gorgas set out to eliminate the dreaded yellow fever, and each mosquito that his Gorgas Gangs killed cost the United States government about $10. But his work saved 70,000 lives. All this is important because it is one of the great Yankee stories of achievement, and a memory that would not go away just because the local leaders decided it was their territory.

And who were the locals anyway? Blacks from the islands of the Caribbean had been brought in to build the canal. The Spanish whites treated them as semi-slaves. The slums were among the worst I have ever seen. As we filmed, assistant cameraman Bob Landry would pass out bundles of candy to the squalid kids in their homes of despair and he became known as "candy Landry." And each night we would return to the luxury of the local Hilton to wash away the humidity of this unreal world. The oligarchs, as the leaders were called, heard the siren sound of Castro not far off, and worried about the importation of revolution. But revolution is almost always homemade.

While awaiting the big day, the day that was supposed to produce the blood in the streets, I tried to entertain myself. The press secretary of the president of Panama had become friendly, inviting me to meet the upper-class folks who were in charge. And they were charming, even if the slums slept in their eyes. One evening he called and said, "*Enrice,* come. We think the Cubans have come in, posing as entertainers." With armed guards we slipped into one of the shady night spots in search of spies. First came the juggling brothers. Were they hiding state secrets in their flying milk bottles? The crooner who looked like Desi Arnaz, was he singing secret songs? The comedian with his baggy pants, painted moustache and sad eyes, was he spreading propaganda? So far not a Castro-ite anywhere.

Then she appeared. The closing dance number. What I saw on stage was the most beautiful woman I have ever seen. Part Indian, part Negress, part Spanish, part Oriental. All the parts together made for Deenorah. The whole history of the Americas seemed to be in her exotic movements. The continents were in harmony with just a gesture. And the gestures seemed to be calling me.

"My friend," I said to the press secretary of the president of Panama, "since my arrival in your splendid republic you have said to me over and over again that anything in Panama I want is mine." He knew what was coming and why. But his pride would not allow for any diminishment in his offer. Revolutions have begun with less provocation. He embraced me. "My brother, she is yours."

And that is how, next day, the president of Panama had to do without his personal limousine and armed guard for awhile, as Deenorah was dispatched and the NBC film crew was given the day off and I learned so much more about the real, passionate secrets of Latin America. I can see her still.

I can still see, too, the view when cameraman Joe Vadala and I went in a helicopter to see both oceans at once. From 2,000 feet up, you can see them both: the Atlantic in the foreground, through Gatun Lake, then Gaillard Cut, to the Pacific in the distance. God put in a boundary and man erased it, at least temporarily.

When the day came for the potential riot, the new governor decreed that the Panamanian flag could fly. Perhaps it was the beginning of appeasement, and thus the beginning of the end of the canal as a U.S. possession. History will tell. But that day as we were ready for a minor war, for the first time in half a century the Panamanians were invited, in celebration of their own independence day, to parade through the U.S. canal zone.

Along Fourth of July Avenue, in front of the post office where the riots of the year before were centred, there was the first tentative rush of morning traffic. Panamanian National Guardsmen moved into position. But no American troops. The parade went past the palm-shaded, government-issued homes of the U.S. zone residents. It moved past the American Church, as apple pie as Iowa. The band played Panamanian Latin themes; the skirts of the *muchachas* swirled. Into a place called Shaler's Triangle where it would happen. I was down among the crowd, looking for machine guns, grenades, pistols, roving for battle. But then it was over. In contrast to the year before, not one placard, not one anti-American sign, not a single rock.

    And where was the brave EDTEDSCOTT, my mentor? I spotted
him in the safe distance atop a building, watching it all with binoculars.
"But where were you?" I asked. "All this piss-and-vinegar talk of
bravery and Hemingway and the pistol on your hip?"
    "Young master," he said, "the reason I am here, and not dead
on some dumb battlefield, is that I know when to retreat. If you wish to
be an old master, I advise you to learn the same."
    So much for the revolution that never was. To give the film style,
I searched for an old Panamanian folk song. I couldn't find one in this
made-to-measure country, so I wrote one. To this day you will hear sung
my "authentic" song, vocalized by Lord Kontiki, that begins:

    Panama, Panama,
    My lovin' Panama;
    Breaking point of the Americas,
    The Land divided and the world united.

    I watched the film from the lonely comfort of a bed at the Beth
Israel Hospital in New York, drinking champagne with a few of my
friends. It turned out that the battle was one of credit for the work, and
as it happened, I was the only casualty of the revolution that never took
place in Panama. Yes, there was a storm brewing over the Panama Canal,
but it turned out at the time to be within me.
    I recovered to begin another adventure. Now, Africa.

CHAPTER SEVEN
Africa:
Rainbow of Darkness

Leib the lion was wounded. Leib, my father, was dying.

It had never been his way to exchange small talk. A conversation by phone never began with "hello," but proceeded immediately to the subject. He would call my friend, Gerry Morris, and without introduction begin, "Gerry, why Harry no marry?" And when some kind of explanation was offered, he would hang up without comment. So now, when the leave-taking from life was coming close, there was no talk of it. He had been operated on at the Mount Sinai. A malignant growth was found and he was sealed up again, as if to hide the secret from God. There would be no small talk from the doctor about how long. Nothing was said.

In his simple musical dialogues with God, I always assumed that my father received his own answers. He complained not at all, except that he sprang out of bed when he awoke to discover some shrivelled old nurse caring for him. They say it was like a sprinter's leap, and he would not leave the bathroom until a young nurse replaced her.

After the hospital, he moved to an apartment somewhere, God knows where, in the flat, indistinguishable northern part of the city. When I first saw him there I felt he had somehow left that giant lion's body behind on St. Clair. The little man with the sad eyes and the grey-orange goatee bore little resemblance to the powerful one who had run the store, the *shul*, and who carried a hell of a wallop, which I recall from the time I once stole Dentyne chewing gum from the Power's supermarket at

St. Clair and Dufferin. He requested that we all gather. So I returned, and as many Raskys as were available assembled, and he sang a song: "Who wants to die when there is life to live." He placed a great white crown of a hat on his head, and he was all dressed in a flowing white robe, and he stretched out his arms and sang a duet with God. The voice cracked perhaps, but that sound . . . that sound. Casals and his cello were never more in harmony. And we knew he knew.

That summer of my father's physical decay, I undertook a voyage of discovery of my country of birth at the request of a dreamer businessman, Spencer W. Caldwell, who decided that Canada could use an independent television network, to be called CTV. Would I do the opening film? So I set out from coast to coast to find a country.

Out there in Halifax I filmed Barrington Street, a kind of crusty gentleman among streets, and the carved wooden ladies that look out to sea. In Montreal I took note of 282 banks, and those stone saints pretending to be on St. Peter's, and a special look to the French ladies, and the undercurrents of tension of two increasing solitudes. In Ottawa the imitation changing of the guard—it was pretend-we-are-at-Buckingham-Palace. Ottawa seemed to be a one-street town. In Winnipeg, Portage Avenue was like a wheat field in the middle of nowhere and everyone looked Ukranian. In Edmonton and Calgary, I knew I was in Texas. British Columbia left me with a fresh-as-cut-trees feeling, but seemed so similar to Portland and Seattle. Each place was pulling apart and not pushing together: a wide expanse, huddling against the winter, a country not quite there. But it had been a haven against the oppression of the Old World, and I would always be grateful to Canada.

I toyed by mail with marriage to a girl next door, partially so that my father would go peacefully into that great night. ("Why Harry no marry?") But I was restless and felt the roots of the past being wrenched from me. It was all painfully unsatisfactory.

An invitation came from Gordon Cullingham at the CBC. Try Africa! I was to explore a whole continent to produce six hours of radio documentary on the emerging nations—every country south of the Sahara—to become *The African Revolution*. I accepted, and we tossed a coin to see if I would begin east or west. East was heads and that would be it. Radio would be quiet, personal, talking to myself while talking to the many.

One last time I would go to the synagogue with my father. The high holy days with him one last time. Now the jaundice had turned him yellow. And I knew when he asked to leave in the middle of Yom Kippur services that these would be his last public prayers. It was not his home *shul*. A different *chazun*, cantor, was singing the ancient heroic melodies. My father was a tiny figure in the corner, just another old man, I suppose, to those who passed by. The power had drained from him. I knew when he said "Let us go," that he was talking to God as well as me.

The next day, Fanny, his last wife, was shaving him. The once fiery red beard dimmed to a corner of his face, and he went into the bathroom to try to have a bowel movement. He looked so tiny. I was leaving for the airport to begin my travels to Africa. I knew I would never see him again. But he seemed to want it that way. The wounded lion wanted to go off by himself and just disappear, to let his time come so that his body could go. Then the spirit of the old lion could run free, to hit those high, melancholy notes of song, to move with his ancient glory. What mere body could confine the *nishuma*, the soul, of the old lion? We did not say good-bye. Not then, not even then was there time for small talk.

On the way to the airport, my sister Pearl, who now would be the eldest, the head of the family, was trying to fathom the trip that was ahead. She asked, "So if you make it, if you get through those 25 countries in God-knows-where Africa and you make it back and you know all about it, who will you talk to?" You know something? I never did have an answer to that question, neither then nor now.

I kept a daily diary. Some of it was later destroyed in a fire at my New York apartment, set, I believe, by the FBI or the CIA, or some crazy Cubans. But there is enough left to give you the tone of the unique trip that proved, perhaps more than anything else, how foolishly confident I was that God would travel with me, care for me, and that if I trusted myself totally to the kindness of strangers I would survive. So far, I have.

No trip I have ever taken seemed to have the same feeling of immense distance from my beginnings. Once an expedition to Hamilton was sufficiently exciting and Buffalo on Saturday night was almost beyond hope. But now I would voyage to discover worlds that at that time few had encountered. The only text of the time was John Gunther's *Inside Africa*, and it had been almost a decade since his exploration. He began his book: "Africa is not in some respects a Dark Continent at all; it is flashing with vivid light." And that is what I found: a rainbow, a rainbow of darkness.

I made a short stop in London, and in a moment of panic even suggested to a girl I was later to know well, "Come to Africa!" But I knew it was a journey that I could make only on my own. I suppose in thinking about it now I knew my father was going beyond all physical borders, and I had to travel the greatest distance I could to find him or to escape. I'm not sure which. Perhaps I could not face death. I had not been there when my mother died. Was the last word important, as important as the total memory? Maybe I wanted to be totally unconnected, swinging, swinging as far as I could from the centre, from the beginning. But then Africa is, in a way, the beginning of us all. I would look, record, imagine, find a continent, and maybe find myself. For most of us, Africa is the heart of darkness, and I tried to find that heart.

By the time I had picked up 15 visas in London and Paris, and had hit Athens, I had been struck by a terrible head cold. I tried to rush up to the Acropolis, to see if Aristotle were in disembodied residence. I dosed myself with ouzo and retsina. I boarded the Ethiopian Airlines plane with my typewriter and tape-recorder, and as the plane crossed the Mediterranean to the dark night, lost among the stars, I was violently sick. I was sure that I would be dead before the first stop. The inside of the plane tumbled and turned, air was heavy on my head, and I screamed with the agony of being lost, without sense of balance or time. Oh my God! Then I vomited out everything in me that was Canada, America, Europe, the West, childhood, pain.

"Vanilla ice cream!" I said. The cool touch on my forehead, the amber hand of the Ethiopian stewardess as she caressed my forehead with a cold washcloth. I had passed out. And "vanilla ice cream" was my call when I awakened after having my tonsils removed in the charity section of the old Sick Children's Hospital on College Street in Toronto. Vanilla ice cream, my reward for tackling a continent. She smiled that soft smile reserved for crazy white men. "No vanilla, nothing," she said. "Sleep." And I slept, somehow cleansed, ready for Africa. The southern cross in the dark blue sky gave way to dawn over the moon-like vastness of the Ethiopian plateau.

In a way Africa taught me to see. Without a camera I was forced to become one, to see and feel everything new, to be born again with a new set of senses. An airport visual shot in my brain in Asmara, the first stop, as the plane fuelled: women in white flowing robes, dark silhouettes against the morning sky. Pink and violet flowers beside the tarred strip. Always, always in my films I have looked for the way in which flowers seek life, no matter what the hardship, like us all. And then on to Addis Ababa, the city I came to know. Everything was a film being unspooled. Driving into town, I immersed myself in the brilliant shades of colour, ladies and men in indigo gowns, carrying orange and yellow umbrellas. They were like dancers down the road. And the bright beating blue of the sky framing them all. I knew that I would never see colour in the same way again.

Ethiopia was the correct place to begin because it seemed closest to the start of life. It looked so much like the land the world forgot. Tucked away on a high plateau, it was a country the explorers chose to ignore, too difficult to conquer in the conquistador days of colonialism. If the Bible were happening now, that is where it would be happening.

At any rate, so it seemed 20 years ago, when the emperor was treated like God. Even when he bathed at night alone in his bathtub, I am sure he was convinced that he was, if not a divinity, then at least on first-name terms with Him.

I have always found that first impressions are the most lasting and perhaps the most accurate. So at the Ghayon Hotel I picked up the phone book and noted that it was no thicker than a news magazine and represented the whole country.

These were some of the listings:

- HIM the Empress
  Imperial Palace
  Representative
  Steward
  Cashier
- HIH the Crown Prince
  Palace
  Palace, direct line
- HIH the Duke of Harrar
- HIH Princess Tenagne
- Imperial pastry shop (Ex Lasanga)
  Churchill Road

I still have it. I kept that book, and have thought since what a handy tool it was to prepare an execution list. For when it all changed, these were the names of the oligarchy, who would meet the executioner, like those knitted into Madame Defarge's scarf. And if the phone book names represented a country of 20 million or so, who were the rest of the people out there? Let me tell you about one of them, because the experience speaks so much about the innocence of so many in Africa.

One evening I received a call in my hotel room. The voice was as frail as a flute note. "Mr. Harry," the voice pleaded, "could you come see me?" I asked who it was. It was the girl who operated the switchboard at the hotel. I said I would come out to the phone area. "No, no, Mr. Harry, you must come see me at home tonight. It is important. It is very important to me. I will leave a map. Follow the map. I will be waiting. Mr. Harry, do not forsake me!" I found it strange, but decided to go. The "Mr. Harry" made sense, as the Ethiopians transpose their names. But the "do not forsake me" seemed an unusual kind of request. Forsake her for what? Were the police after her? Was she involved in some kind of plot? At any rate, the girl needed help. And I felt I would react just as Hemingway would in these circumstances. Bravado.

So that night, following a road map that seemed to lead to a lost country, I went beyond the white-washed walls. Addis Ababa is a city that seems to disappear into its own hills. The walls were erected, I understand, so that visiting dignitaries would not be assaulted by the sights beyond. This was a city where the red-light district still used the red cross as its symbol, causing some confusion for those in need of transfusions, and for other medical emergencies. But finally I found the pink clay building somewhere I have long forgotton. To give you an idea of the confusion of the streets, once John Gunther said, "Addis looks as if it has been dropped piecemeal from an airplane carrying trash."

Now a little background here. In Ethiopia there are 100 races and tribes speaking approximately 70 languages with over 200 dialects. "Ethiopian" is a Greek word which means "people with burned faces." Ninety per cent or so are illiterate. A third are Moslem. Christianity came in the fourth century, introduced by two shipwrecked brothers from Tyre. One in every five Ethiopian males is a priest or monk, and most Ethiopians cannot read or write. Religion is life. So, when the delicate "burned face" creature greeted me and said, "Oh, Mr. Harry, I am in need of a blessing," although confused, I was not totally surprised. After all, what is one blessing more or less in a strange land. So I said, "You are blessed," smiled and prepared to leave.

"No, no, Mr. Harry," she said, with a voice that was velvet as the r's rolled off her lips. "No, Mr. Harry, you don't understand: a real blessing." As I stood there in a room lit by one 20-watt lamp behind a pink shade, she spread her arms like winged victory and began to peel off her clothes. I was stunned and waited for the next revelation.

"You see, Mr. Harry, I have been watching you come and go, and I note you have a red beard, and I know you are the colour of my Lord, and I think you to be the brother of Jesus."

What!

"Yes, Mr. Harry, I know you are with Him. You see, I learned this when I was younger. I was born a pagan. Then came the Christian missionaries. They told me about our Lord Jesus, and showed me how I could have a blessing from a disciple of Jesus. And if you are the brother of Jesus, surely you must know the best blessing. Come. Come with me, brother of Jesus."

She walked over to me, the light hitting that sparrow-like face, so thin and young, perhaps twenty, and weighing less than 100 pounds. She began to undress me. I was spellbound. It was a ritual. Carefully she took off my jacket, shirt and pants, and laid them out on a box that served as a dresser, and now also as an altar. Then she removed my underwear and took a wet towel and began to bathe me. She took my hand as if leading me to a dance. And she lay down beside me, dropping her robe. We were both naked. "Now, Mr. Harry, I will be blessed." And as we made innocent love, if that is what it was, she began to sing spirituals, hymns of the church, "Nearer my God to thee."

When it was all over, I smiled. "Oh, Mr. Harry," she said, "I think you to be a very good Christian."

"Sweet girl," I said quietly, "as it happens, I am not a Christian at all."

"But you blessed me. Surely, Mr. Harry, you are not a pagan?"

"No. In fact, I am something called Jewish."

"Oh, good, Mr. Harry, then I will be that thing, too."

"No, no, sweet angel. I think you have been through quite enough."

She looked puzzled as I dressed and left. And I do hope she did not feel that I had forsaken her. I have never forgotten her. I've wondered so often if she has forgiven me and all the other intruders who delivered such mixed blessings.

And then there was the incident at Ambo. Ambo is about a hundred miles south of Addis Ababa. I don't know if you will find it on a map, because in Ethiopia very little is documented. I was invited down as the weekend guest of Samson, grandson of the emperor. I had called him as a result of a mutual friend in New York. Samson had been to Columbia University and was an African torn between two cultures. He had that haunted Ethiopian look—the thin flaring nostrils and those almond eyes out of icons—but when he spoke it was with the jazz talk of Harlem.

Samson's home in Ambo was like a Palm Springs retreat, super modern, built on the edge of a natural mineral pond. Considering the fact that Samson had invited about 50 guests, all young and more or less related, it seemed extraordinary that his house had only one bedroom. Around the house, tents had been set up. It all had the look of the film setting of Laurence Olivier's *Henry V*, except for the modern house. And in the house, which was totally wired for sound, Frank Sinatra records filled the rooms like sex juice. It was non-stop Sinatra and non-stop champagne, which was supplied in a seemingly endless fountain. Samson's date was an American Peace Corps black from New York. She was darker in colour than he. You know, the Ethiopian ruling class was fond of saying that they were the true whites. We westerners were pink. So much for the colour plan.

Samson decided that everyone should go swimming. In Ethiopia, one doesn't refuse the host's requests. So, bubbling with alcohol, we all went for a romp in the natural waters of Ambo. Now, as it happens, one of Samson's favourite cousins was married to a voluptuous Greek girl. She spilled out of her bikini, and appeared to be doing sensuous Greek dances in the water. Her body was an attraction of curved surfaces,

somehow magnified by the water. Samson began playfully. Little bits
of almost teenage horseplay. A touch here, a hold there. A race across
the water and then an embrace.

As we dried ourselves on the shore beneath the full moon and the
Sinatra lyric, "Take all of me"—Sinatra's voice like an American drum
among the African drums—Samson announced, "I have decided. She
will spend the night with me." You should have seen his regal gesture,
a kind of off-with-their-heads movement, and he pointed to his cousin.
We laughed. A party game. But the cousin did not laugh. The Greek
wife did not laugh. He began to plead, "Not my wife, my cousin Samson,
be reasonable." Samson dismissed him and proclaimed to all, "It is time
for bed."

I had heard vaguely that Samson previously had been assigned
to the Ethiopian embassy in Stockholm, and was asked to leave because
a servant had been killed in an angry interchange involving Samson's
pistol. But the Sinatra lyrics were loud and calling, "A man must be a
man." I decided to be a peacemaker. "Samson," I said, "don't you
think the joke has gone far enough, playing at being emperor. Why don't
we just all forget about this. Let your cousin's wife go." Blessed be the
peacemaker, I thought. "This is not for you to be involved. This is a
family affair. I suggest you go to bed. Go directly to bed." He pointed
at me, his finger like a bayonet. But after all, we were all civilized, right?
Samson had been to Columbia in New York. But Sinatra was calling,
"I did it my way."

"Samson, come on we'll feel better in the morning. Too much
champagne. Can't we be sensible?" Even as I talked, I knew that my
tongue should have been tied. Samson snapped his finger. An armed
guard, an old man wearing a scarf across his face to keep off the desert
night air, rushed at me. He jammed a Sten gun in my stomach. He
awaited a final order. There was no question it would have come. Sinatra
was my guide: "Fools rush in where angels fear to tread."

"One last chance to go to bed—alive." Samson stared at me as
if in a trance. I had interrupted a ritual which had to be consummated.
Tribes and traditions were involved. My own Toronto Presbyterian-Jewish
sense of fair play was on the wrong continent. "He will escort you to
your tent. Sweet dreams, my guest." And so with the Sten gun in my
side, I walked drunkenly up the hill to my tent. Had I not, there is no
question you would not be reading this report now, not first hand anyhow.
Next morning I was treated like a leper. The Greek woman was back
with her husband, and everyone behaved as if I had been the troublemaker.

Since that night at Ambo I have read that virtually everyone there
was assassinated in the revolution that followed. Gone, all gone. The
oligarchs, the princes and princesses—like the Shah of Iran in more recent

times—all dismissed by history. But I remember, I still remember the last of the great earthly kings. He was Haile Selassie, King of Kings, Defender of the Faith, the Elect of God, the Conquering Lion of Judah. I remember that first day I saw him, looking as if he had just stepped out of the Bible. And, you know, he reminded me of my father.

On the waters of snake-infested Lake Zuwaye, 100 miles south across a rich plateau from Addis Ababa, fishermen crowned in garlands chanted tribal songs of welcome as they paddled round and round. They had been waiting since dawn. A dozen Coptic Christian priests had patiently stood since early morning in their splendid golden robes, clutching a giant silver cross and pounding a goat-hide drum as they swayed in religious song and dance. Around noon an advance party of bearers arrived to create a carpet of bows beneath the soft shade of a magnificent, umbrella-like tree. An hour later, two trucks carrying 100 Israeli-trained troops stormed to a stop. Each man was armed with a Sten gun. Then came half a dozen vehicles with portable tables, chairs, stoves, and the ingredients of a feast. The troops fanned out to search the woods for intruders. The cooks and servants rushed to ready a banquet. All this was in preparation for a casual luncheon for the world's last and most powerful emperor in one of the world's most primitive kingdoms.

Traffic had been stopped for hours on the one highway that heads south from Addis Ababa, for no man could precede the emperor. When he arrived at the lake in his specially built Mercedes station wagon, 50 vehicles followed, clouded in the dust churned up by the wheels of the emperor's vehicle. All present splendidly bowed and kissed the earth as the short, 72-year-old absolute monarch, who looked like a magnificent mahogany gargoyle, took to his travelling throne beneath the shade tree for an afternoon snack.

The priests were dismissed and the fishermen allowed to entertain. After their wild calls and sweeping displays on the lake, the primitive fishermen were permitted to present the emperor with 1,000 fish and a live python. He accepted the gifts from the regal distance of about 100 feet, as if being offered a bouquet of flowers. He left, once again in a cloud of dust rising above the parched plateau, like a mirage of the past floating across the 20th century.

Haile Selassie seemed almost unreal. In a continent swept by the "wind of change," that had seen 30 countries born yesterday in an explosion of nationalism, he was, theoretically, the 225th consecutive ruler of a country that had known a kind of independence for 3,000 years, except for a brief period under Italian fascist occupation. Where other African leaders had fanatically declared the dogma of black nationalism, he had urged a conservative, moderate line. While other African leaders had crumbled to their political enemies, he had maintained his absolute rule for 45 years. In his own country of about 22 million people, he was worshipped as a god. He was as much myth as man.

To the outside world he was remembered as the tiny, dark man under a large umbrella, who in 1936 warned the world of the coming death of the League of Nations and the approach of World War II. He came out of the darkness of Africa to tell the League of the "systematic extermination of a nation by barbarous means," after Mussolini sent his tanks to Ethiopia to crush the tribesmen who fought bravely with spears. He told delegates grown sterile and stale, "It is international morality that is at stake. God and history will remember your judgement." The world remembered too late. He checked his crown in a British vault and waited for the brutal war to end. When the Italians were driven out, it was typical of his biblical judgement to warn his people not to take revenge. He knew the Italians could make a useful contribution to his country. In each town and village, a royal proclamation was signed by His Most Imperial Majesty which said: "Do not reward evil with evil. Do not commit any act of cruelty like those which the enemy committed against us."

When later I read about the coup that overthrew the government, I was not really surprised. But even then they did not dare to kill this rock of a man. He was retired to one of his palaces. And then he just faded away. Perhaps there was nothing left for him to live for; his son was an inept dud, his grandsons playboys of the southern world. His power was plucked from him. His voice was like my father's—gone. Once when we met I almost talked to him in Yiddish. I wonder if he would have answered.

Thinking back now to the whole African adventure, my approach was more talmudic than anything else. My father's training had given that gift to me. There were no ultimate answers, only questions that produced more questions. Could I find out whether all men were equal? For that matter, are any two equal? And what is equal? Can black and white mix? Was I free of prejudice? Certainly I began, or thought I did, almost totally on the black man's side. After all, he had been the oppressed. Colonists were all Colonel Blimps, were they not? And what right did they have in the natural kingdom of the black?

So when I first arrived in Nairobi, Kenya, I was quick to note that the question of race dominated the landing form. And the starched whites were ordering the black men around with English crumpet-toned cruelty. When we drove through the national park on the edge of the city and the blacks, ankle-deep in the mud, shoved with bare shoulders to release the white men's cars, I felt that perhaps I should be down there with them. Pushing my father's delivery car, stuck in the Canadian snow. But I did not move. And as the red earth hurled by and we came loose, I imagined the continent without any roads, before the white man paved his way and made his home there. And would there have been cities? I was grateful for the western hotel, even if all the world seemed to be sitting at suitably separate tables. Comfort was replacing compassion. The native waiters offered the smiles, but the British supplied the proper napkins. Make a choice: a world without smiles or one without napkins.

Shades of prejudice began to creep in after a few days of touring the beauty of East Africa. The first major leader I met in Africa was the extraordinary Yorkshireman, Michael Blundell, beet red and rugged as a tree root, who admitted, "We made a mistake thinking we could make this a white dominion. But as for me, I will die here. This is my country." Some, whites like him, loved each blade of African grass as if they had sown each seed, generation upon generation. It was *their* Africa. Then there were those who would have been happy to see Africa as a place for wild animals only. There was a Colonel Cowie who said he had no use for the "thugs who would take over." The problem, he said, was boredom: "The sports' results should read, 'England versus Pakistan, three to two at cricket; Kikuyu against Masai, six killings. Football results to follow.' "

Nairobi was stone dead at night. The one attempt at night life was the Equator Club, the "21" of Kenya. I was there one night when the black band was playing the soft, cool jazz of America, and I sat on the leopard-skin stools where once Hemingway and Ruark had sat. Tom Mboya entered, immaculate in his Savile Row suit and Hathaway shirt, trailed by a willow of a black girl and an entourage. The band played "I'm forever blowing bubbles," and you could see the distant dream of glory in his eye. He was a man-in-waiting in a country-in-waiting.

There is an old Kikuyu proverb, "When two elephants fight, it is the grass that suffers." It was assumed that when independence came there would be a blood-bath of tribe against tribe, with Mboya on one side and the old tiger Jomo Kenyatta on the other. But when that time came, and after Mboya sadly but conveniently died, Kenyatta, the most feared man in East Africa, became the first and most moderate leader of the independent Kenya. So the white journalists and the white settlers, second sons of other second sons who were fearful of the Mau Mau and a future of eating off paper plates because all black servants would vanish, were wrong. The tales of the Mau Mau and cannibals in the night were like the bubbles of that song—bubbles in the air.

I went to see Kenyatta and did, in fact, have a brief conversation with him. But it was a difficult time. We drove about 30 miles out of the city. The city outskirts were constructed much like those of New York, where first one goes through Spanish Harlem and then through Negro Harlem. Here we passed the European section, where one might think that all the Indians have girl children. They all wore school uniforms, school sweaters and blue and orange skirts. The standard of living lowered as we passed the poor working sections of the black man.

And finally out into the lush countryside: rich, red-black earth, purple and violet flowers, hills dotted with farms, hemp and coffee. Past a British army base and its neat, white children swinging and sliding in a pleasant English kindergarten. Past black women hauling lumber on their backs, with ropes that tied around their shaven skulls. Their ears were heavy with the burden of a dozen, brilliant coloured rings. Past Coca-Cola signs, and Standard Oil, and Shell and BP. Directions from two barefoot kids who said, "Look for the big fruit tree and that is where you will find Kenyatta's house." They gestured as if referring to God's house. Then up the mud road and into a compound. A bus unloaded natives in their primitive state. Women in scarlet and orange and yellow, all barefoot, and a dozen men in ill-fitting, western suits. A couple of tough, olive-uniformed young men, drinking beer and smoking and allowing no one in without a permit.

A chant began. It had a primitive but catchy melody, a chant of happiness when Kenyatta would bring *uhuru*—freedom. We waited outside. Our appointment was for 2 p.m., but it was almost 3 p.m. We were told he sleeps, the great man sleeps. They swayed and chanted and swayed, swayed from the hips and circulated their arms from the elbow, as if pushing a swing. And I was a camera filming visions for my mind, swinging in Africa.

We were about to leave when suddenly we were told we could come in. Kenyatta sat in a chair in his robe, nervously fingering his cane-head and coughing. His eyes watered; he was not well. "I did not want you to think I would not see you. I am not well." He looked old there, like Paul Robeson or "De Lawd" as we saw him in *Green Pastures*. And I thought that is what he must seem to his followers: "De Lawd" in the flesh. He seemed almost kindly.

That night in Nairobi, I went to the synagogue on the Kingsway, a modern building. Its service was rendered in the same way as services anywhere, but with the rabbi talking of Sodom and Gomorrah with a Manchester accent. We shook hands, wished each other *shalom* and a good *yom tov,* and went our separate ways. The restless Jew even there in Africa. Me, too. Was it that an older father figure like Kenyatta made me think of my own father, and I wanted to say a prayer for him? Perhaps I was mistaken. My father would live, live long.

When I returned to the lobby of the staid Norfolk Hotel, I noted that the gloomy grandfather clock never changed. It was always five to eight. But outside times were changing. New countries were being born and somewhere thousands of miles away an old man was dying.

In the scheme of things it was decided I would skip Uganda. What could happen there? It was then under the feudal control of the Kabaka, Edward William Frederick David Walugembe Mutebi Luwangula Mutesa, no less than a graduate of Cambridge and a Grenadier guard to boot. What could happen? Idi Amin could happen and did but that's another story.

My travels took me next to stifling, soaking Mombassa, which looked like a movie set for Bogart and Sidney Greenstreet, and then to Dar Es Salaam where "the light rains" were falling, causing a constant state of total humidity. I noted when I registered at the New African Hotel that the registry spelled out: "No private boys allowed. No dogs."

It was not long before I was pulled into the steady rain of conversation about race and independence that was going on everywhere. The whites at the bar told this story: When Nyerere arrived in London for a high-level conference, he was perfectly fitted in his Savile Row suit, immaculate shirt and tie, but he was wearing his hat upside down. When told of this by an aide, he said, "I'm not wearing it, I'm carrying it, you fool."

The only part of this story that could have validity is the last two words. Julius Nyerere, the first and only prime minister of Tanzania, has a fast mind that does not tolerate fools gladly. A chief's son, one of 25 children, he spoke to me without humility or arrogance when he said, "It is none of the West's business how Africans run their affairs. There was no excuse for colonialism, but it did allow me to inherit a country that speaks one language instead of 120." I often wonder about the quick man with the Adolf moustache, green sportshirt and open sandals. Of all the leaders I met, he is the only one still in power. So much for the natural evolution of democracy. White or black, I never did encounter a politician who believed anyone else could do it better.

Today I can't even find some of the countries I visited on a map. At that time there was a city called Blantyre in a country called Nyasaland, and that's where I went next to meet Dr. Hastings Banda, leader of the country the Church of Scotland built and then forgot about. In a crowd of worshippers, with the heat and humidity at 97 degrees fahrenheit, under a soaking palm tree, he waved his ragged wand and teased his crowd: "I don't mind if you pay four shillings instead of two. We can use it. Get your brothers and sisters and cousins to pay their fees." Since that time I think of him fondly as I watch the television hucksters of America raising millions on Sunday mornings. Charity begins, and too often ends, at the pulpit.

If Blantyre's poverty was like a fungus on the land, then the frontier opulence of Salisbury struck me as foreign as glass and chrome on a desert plateau. I found myself noting the November events at Salisbury's Miekels Hotel: "Alcoholics Anonymous every Friday, the Budgerigar and Cage Bird Society every second Tuesday, the Elvis Presley Fan Club at Eagle Star House, Friday at 7 p.m." So, who wouldn't expect a revolution? But that's another book.

I recorded hours of conversations, music, impressions, on tape and in my mind in Rhodesia and South Africa, and they are still there. But all of the impressions of prejudice, boring prejudice, were nothing compared with the inner emptiness that overcame me in Johannesburg. It came with a telegram on November 12th.

Cry, cry the beloved country. Each of us is a country. Can we not love each other more? "I'm afraid a little bad news" is the way the hall porter described a cable from Canada telling me that my father was dead. It was five to midnight, and I knew at that moment how great the distance was between me and the world that spawned me. No matter what I did, there was no way in the world of getting back for the funeral. So alone I looked for a way of distant mourning, confused by the barriers of time and space that did not allow me to know what hour it was when the mourning should begin. And in a distant land I did not know how to go about it. The learned rabbis did not allow for jet travel. I tried business as usual, with meetings and interviews, but could not laugh or concentrate or focus. Father, where are you? I flew to Cape Town but still the need, the private need, to wail, to weep, to follow the commandment, to reach back to tradition, to be again in my father's house so far away from home.

There was an incredulous look from the concierge when I explained I needed a place to pray. He suggested I try looking in the yellow pages. The only number that answered under the heading "Jewish" was the orphanage, a Jewish orphanage. Somehow I never thought Jews could be orphans. But there it was in Cape Town in the time of my becoming an orphan. I called. A concerned cockney voice: "Oh, yes, we must do something. Once my husband and I were in Canada, in a town in Saskatchewan about 200 miles from Regina. The people were kind."

A lady with a long nose and a kind face came in a station wagon. They had had their evening service. But now they would hold a special service for the dead. And boys of thirteen in sandals and leather short pants mourned with me. *"Boruch atoh Adonoy . . .* God who gives life and takes it, blessed be he.'' And afterward each boy came to shake my hand and offer sympathy and I could not hold back the tears. And I wept openly for my father and my life, and that which I did not and could not understand. *Boruch atoh Adonoy . . .*

I set out up the coast for Durban and the most remarkable man in Africa. I had been warned that I was officially refused permission to see him, Chief Albert Luthuli, winner of the Nobel Peace Prize. By rented car, always looking behind to see if I was being followed, I headed for a strange meeting at a place called Stanger. I passed black fields, bursting with sugar cane and vines for wine, the black men bent low in the afternoon heat. I was lost twice before I arrived in the back room of a bookkeeper named Mohammed. The chief wore a green shirt and a grey business suit. He had a slight growth of white beard and a laugh that made me tremble with pleasure and a look like a black Oriental.

He said quietly, but with full conviction, "Yes, like Nyerere, I agree this country is run by madmen and bullies. I feel no bitterness. Violence would be suicide." I have always noted among great men that it is the ones who care who ask *you* the questions. He had heard about my father and said he would pray, pray for his soul. About his country he said, "It is the oppressed man who determines the pace of change, not the oppressor. If we can gain our freedom without flow of blood, we will have gained a great achievement. But right is right, and we will succeed." Oh, the longing, the longing in his eyes. "Yes, I pray for my oppressor. I pray. Even when I was in jail I prayed for him." This man of men, how superior he seemed.

I don't know when I first realized that I was being followed. I would have to find an alternative way to leave that country with my treasure, the tapes of Luthuli, a saint who would die under strange circumstances. I was ashamed to be white. I've wondered often if my father and the saint met in a heavenly place reserved for men of God.

The end of the rainbow of darkness. All in all, I had lifted the bright veil of the dark continent and seen a little of it, but a great deal of myself. After my journey there were a few luxury days at the Dorchester Hotel in London, soaking in bubble baths, lounging in towels as soft as fur, indulging in crumpets and heavy creams and the trappings of so-called civilization. I was aware that I was back in the homeland of Stanley and Livingstone, the tiny island that had conquered so much of the African continent. Even as I sat there I felt the further shrinking of the old Empire, and could not quite imagine how it had been created the century before.

I had timed my return to be in England for Christmas, and it was as closed down as any Nigerian town frightened of an evil spirit.

Looking back now down the corridor of two decades, most of the leaders I have mentioned are gone: the emperor of Ethiopia displaced and dead of a broken empire and heart; many of the hotshot Oxford graduates of Nigeria deposed and destroyed; Nkruma, demi-god, toppled; Kenyatta, a victim of time, not revolution. New grass is growing in the Congo streets. Some leaders, then unknown, have risen to peaks of tyranny and fallen like decaying trees: Idi Amin lost in a cloud of madness, Jean-Bedel Bokassa I, the bloodthirsty, megalomaniac emperor of the Central African Republic, who spent $25 million for a coronation and then was deposed. Cities and countries have changed their names, but I wonder how much life really has changed for the African who hoped that independence meant equality.

When I condensed my recorded observations, 50 hours or so of raw material, to six hours, which I broadcast on the CBC, I found: (1) the South Africans banned me for being too liberal; (2) my liberal friends condemned me when I observed that black Africa would undergo a dark period of demagoguery not unlike Latin America. Had the end of imperialism come only for this?

And what was left of it all for me? I recall the story of the Congo tribe that had carvings going up their faces. Once a year they felt compelled to cross the river to attack the members of the same tribe who had carvings going down their faces. On alternate years the path was reversed. Every tribe has to feel superior to another group. And I wonder, really, if it was much different for my own group on St. Clair, attacked from all sides and attacking in their own way. So who was civilized? And as an African asked me in a jungle clearing, "The Nazis were a European tribe, weren't they?"

I had entered Africa alone with an open heart and hand. I came out on the other side, never once being hurt or hated. I accepted my brother, no matter what his colour because, after all, a rainbow of many colours is merely the way it looks to the eye for one given moment. The differences dissolve. To know that is a blessing. And I survived to prepare for another adventure.

My father lay buried in Canada, and in Africa, too—in all the Africas of my mind.

CHAPTER EIGHT

Heroes:

A little less Brando,
please, Fidel

S how me a hero and I will write you a tragedy. The words of F. Scott Fitzgerald were much on my mind in those years after my African adventure. Look at what became of them. Hemingway, in adulation of whom I had grown my beard, had proven EDTEDSCOTT at least partially right, and blown himself to bits at the thundering head of a shotgun. I can recall my broadcasting friend, Gordon Sinclair, who had known Hemingway from his *Toronto Star* days, tell me that during a last visit with him in Cuba, he seemed a man possessed by time and possessions.

Ed Murrow was struck down in a cloud of nicotine. His cigarettes caused a painful death from cancer. I can recall thinking in the church in New York the day of his funeral that we would all be less for his leave-taking of life. The network officials wept, but they were also relieved. That brow, furled at full force, was like a constant reminder of responsibility for the most powerful medium of all time. Media bravery was buried with him. And the Hemingway quotation, echoed from John Donne, rang in my ears: "Any man's death diminishes me, because I am involved in Mankind, and therefore never send to know for whom the bell tolls: it tolls for *thee*." CBS-TV interrupted a soap opera to mention Murrow's passing, and on CBS radio the announcement was followed by a cigarette commercial.

I tried my hand at some early film biographies on assignment from Hearst-Metrotone News. I went back into recent history in search of heroes and heroines. Each assignment provided me with techniques

I was to use in later films. The first of these films was called *Crown and Crisis,* and it was narrated by the superb Welsh voice of Emlyn Williams. I tried to explore the magic and mystery that was the crown of England. I blended voice and vision in a way that was new to me. I took a recording of King George VI, whose every word was a painful stutter, and laid the track over shots of children donning gas masks as bombs fell. He said, "In this grave hour—perhaps the most fateful in our history—I send to every household of my people, both at home and overseas, this message, spoken with the same depth of feeling for every one of you as if I were able to cross your threshold and speak to you myself." The effect of the halting eloquence of a king suffering through speech and the potential threat to the children is as poetic as anything one could achieve in a moment of film.

Crown and Crisis also marked my first attempt to use poetry as an ingredient of film. The theory was quite simple. Film is a kind of poetic vision and is measured in terms of length of shot in the same way as a line of verse is controlled. Together, I reasoned, the blend could be hugely magnified. And so Shakespeare came to write for me:

> This royal throne of kings, this scepter'd isle,
> This earth of majesty, this seat of Mars,
> This other Eden, demi-paradise.
> This fortress built by nature for herself
> Against infection and the hand of war;
> This happy breed of men, this little world,
> This precious stone set in the silver sea,
> This blessed plot, this earth, this realm, this England.

At that time I met a shy, beautiful girl in the elevator of my building and she became part of the next film and, more important, part of my life a year later as my wife. I wanted to capture the "shadow" of Eleanor Roosevelt, or as we would say, the *neshumah,* the spirit that had been the "first lady of the world." And my wife-to-be had that spirit—a mixture of shyness and strength. Arlene and I went to the snow-bound woods of Hyde Park with a film crew, and there with the interplay of light and the trees and the shadow of a figure which set patterns in the whiteness, I began using a concept that weaved its way into my visual style.

The third film was *Mahatma Ghandi: The Great Soul.* In terms of learning, there was much to find in the gentle and stubborn soul who hypnotized a generation. In this film I tried for the first time to use philosophic words with abstract visuals. So I was able to take his words about God and marry them to film shot in the gardens of the Museum of Modern Art, which included footage of Rodin statues. It was surprisingly effective. Then I added a narrative spoken by a saintly man who was to become one of the closest friends of my family, Sam Jaffe. In voice Sam was like a splendid wood instrument, and in delivery he truly became Ghandi. It became clear to me that I would like to work with great actors and make them a part of great works. But no one was quite ready for that, so I began to travel again.

My voyage of discovery was to profoundly influence and clarify my own vision of life. What happens when old traditions are swept away, when ancient faiths are deposed and new gods are worshipped? I wanted to sample the new "classless" societies that were communist, see them in action on both sides of the Atlantic.

But first I would stop in Hydra. It became my island. It's a barren bit of rock set off the coast of Greece, where each stone seems to be a link with the past. It's dotted with hungry trees, some 4,000 Greeks whose faces are like granite splinters and several dozen foreign artists and writers who have gone there to confront themselves on a personal battlefield without pretense or alibi. It was then a place of no appointments to keep, no subways to catch, no radio or television to divert, and a cost of living that made life liveable. There, in the stark light of the Mediterranean sun, a man had to produce or go under. He had to face the sometimes startling truth about himself, or hide in the shadow of failure.

I came to know the Montreal poet, Leonard Cohen. Leonard was a pale, frail, handsome young man, intense and open, friendly and private. At night we went out to the cafés, listened to bazoukis and drank ouzo and retsina wine, and I would dance the great Greek dances to the applause of shattering glasses and tossed flowers—a man's world.

Leonard Cohen and his friends and I played at an existentionalist game. I had a theory that wherever I went was where the world was, and that when I left, the place and the people just vanished, ceased to be a reality. They were all in a kind of "Brigadoon." When I boarded the ferry to take me to Athens and beyond, Leonard and his small band of writers and poets were all sitting on the shore clinging to their chairs, assuring me that they still existed. And since 16 years later I decided to make a film with Leonard, I presume he survived.

The Yugoslavs had long been my favourites among the communists I met at the United Nations. I had little to change my prejudice.

Customs and immigration men at the glossy new airport in Belgrade were more polite than those at Malton in Toronto, or the gum-chewing chaps at New York's Idlewild. The airport was a modern, impressive entrance to Yugoslavia.

I was greeted by Ignaty Golob, a former delegate to the United Nations who was a kind friend from New York. I felt there was something a little less certain in his tone now that he was back home. New York was still the greatest city, he said, but he was dedicated to his own Yugoslavia.

I couldn't help noticing at the Majestic Hotel, where I was staying, that the surroundings were the most capitalistic I have ever encountered: wallpaper of silver-blue satin and a fine, pink Turkish rug. There was little to do in the evening, and it seemed to me that the coffee bars were crammed full of young intellectuals. Across from me a young couple was dreamily enjoying the beginning of spring, perhaps plotting their own five-year plan. I said to my friend Golob, "It pleases me that young communists hold hands." Change human nature? Not a chance.

A great emptiness filled me the moment I landed in Budapest. I had flown in on a Polish Airlines plane surrounded by garlic-smelling men with leather coats and umbrella-like hats. It was an eerie feeling to be the only passenger deplaning, while all the others continued on to Warsaw. A rather seedy-looking immigration man seemed stunned to see me. In fact, almost everyone seemed surprised. During my stay in Hungary, I felt that the communist regime had done an excellent job of eliminating poverty. But in the process they had deadened the joy of life. Even the traditional gypsy music seemed muted in this world of sameness.

I had always thought of the "iron curtain" as a vague phrase invented by American propaganda. For me it became a real thing. Once I had entered this world with its immense experiment in human behaviour, I felt I had crossed a very real barrier. Nothing seemed the same. I felt cut off. I met students who were actually convinced that *The Daily Worker* represented the absolute authority on the Western World, and a lovely young girl who preferred to spend her summer in a factory rather than take a trip to Paris.

Sights I cannot forget: flower wreaths hitched to the front of streetcars carrying passengers to the cemetery. Old women in drab grey uniforms sweeping the streets, digging ditches. The metal red star incongruously perched on top of the magnificent cheesecake-like parliament buildings.

Thank heaven for the Hungarian humour. In Budapest, the Hungarians liked to display it with a story. There might be a tear in the telling, but they liked to explain their condition with a smile. During the 1956 revolution, or what is called the "counter-revolution," many Hungarians left to go to foreign lands such as Canada and the United States. Others chose more exotic surroundings. Some Hungarians who left returned, either out of homesickness, or just to visit relatives who stayed behind. According to a story, one Hungarian sees a friend who had left during the "unpleasantness," and asks him how some mutual friends have fared. "How about our friend, Mr. X. Where is he?"

"Didn't you know X is now a deep-sea fisherman off the coast of Australia?"

Then the Hungarian asks the visitor, "And how about our friend, Mr. Y? What became of him?"

"He is now a big-game hunter in the wilds of Kenya."

"And what became of our quiet friend, the little fellow with the glasses, the intellectual Mr. Z?"

"Oh," says the visitor, "our friend Mr. Z really is an adventurer. He believes in danger. He stayed in Hungary."

The Russians were a favourite topic of local humour. Hungarians told the story of a trip that Mr. and Mrs. Kruschev were making by train on their way to Russia from Berlin. The train stopped several times during the journey and each time Mrs. K. asked her husband, "Nikita, where are we now?" Each time he would put his hand out the window without looking. Each time he would bring it in, answering, "We are now still in Germany," or "We are passing through Poland," or "We are finally back in Russia."

"Nikita," said Mrs. Kruschev, "you are very clever. But tell me: how did you know without looking each time which country we were in?"

"It is simple, my dear," said Mr. K. "I knew we were in Germany because when I put my hand out, the people kissed it. I knew when we were in Poland because when my hand was out they spat on it. I knew when we were back in Russia because when I pulled back my arm from the train window my watch was gone."

I laughed. I observed. I found myself participating in a ritual that was a poignant reminder of the tribal wars of Europe. At dinner one evening at the Gellert Hotel, while listening to the sour notes of the gypsy violinist who stayed behind, one of the guests approached me. He said, "I have a sacred duty to perform and perhaps you can help me." He told me that he had been observing me struggling with German and was aware I had been speaking Yiddish. It was the eve of Passover. Would I attend a seder with him? The seder is the traditional family dinner that marks the exodus from Egypt by Moses, and has since come to represent all escapes from persecution.

Once there had been 800,000 Jews in Hungary. Now there were perhaps 100,000. Who could know? In theory there was religious freedom, but who dared to practise?

He was a wealthy Jew, now living in Argentina. He had returned to honour the memory of his family destroyed in the ovens of German concentration camps. I said I would be honoured to be at his seder. Could I, would I lead the prayers? I said I would try. Somewhere along the grey backstreets of the museum that was now Eastern Europe, I apologized to God for my ineptness with formal prayers and tried.

The seder was held in the livingroom of the home of his one remaining sister-in-law and what was left of her family. There were some 15 women and four men. Each woman had lost her husband and her sons. For them, this was the first service of its kind since the war. Time to gather again in an evening of the traditional prayers. None of the young present seemed involved. To them it was a strange ritual, not in keeping with the new teachings of Marx. The traditional four questions seemed odd. There was little of the fun of my own early seders. But I knew my father would have been proud of me. The older guests struggled over the old chants, remembering a phrase here, the suggestion of a tragic melody. Time has a way of deleting details.

The man from Argentina had provided the food. None of the Hungarian Jews could ever hope to provide such a feast. The state does not allow time off from work. A youth of thirty-one arrived late, apologizing for both himself and his wife. They were teachers, and it was his night in the mathematics class. The Jew from Argentina told me, "I promised I would make this service to honour my brother and all my family who died. I will bypass Germany on the way home, no matter how inconvenient. There is much to remember, too much to forget."

Back in New York, I worked on a number of films with a gallant Italian-American, John Secondari. The series had sweeping intentions and was called no less than *The Saga of Western Man*. We were trying to put together the places and people of American history. Secondari and his wife, Helen-Jean, were what you would call a husband-and-wife team. They were both extremely excitable, and working around them was stimulating, if sometimes nerve-wracking. I can recall that day during a music recording, sitting in a studio with a full symphony orchestra, looking through the control-room window. Helen-Jean was in tears. I have always thought TV is too tough for women. I went in to comfort her. "It's okay, Helen-Jean, they'll have it right soon. Don't get excited."

"You don't understand!" she shouted. "He's been shot. President Kennedy has been shot."

And I thought of F. Scott Fitzgerald again: "Show me a hero and I will write you a tragedy." But now the writing of the tragedy was for us all.

All these events seemed to be leading up to Fidel. The death of Kennedy left Castro the most visible leader in the hemisphere, and I wanted to compare his leftist way of life with eastern European communism. Secondari was anxious to include a sequence on the storming of the San Juan hill—a make-believe charge by Teddy Roosevelt—for his film called *1898*. I volunteered that, as I still had my treasured Canadian passport, I could get into Cuba, whereas the Americans could not. To verify this fact, I placed a long-distance call to the foreign office in Havana one evening. Despite the tensions of the Bay of Pigs and the Cuban missile crisis, and the fact that at the time even smoking a Cuban cigar was considered a sin in the U.S., by some strange quirk I was able to call direct. A woman answered and I asked, "Is it not true that as a Canadian I can enter Cuba?" There was a little static and I thought I heard a mambo in the background, but she did say *si*.

I convinced the deputy-head of ABC News, Jesse Zousmer, a Murrow alumnus, that if I were going to go I could also do a documentary on Cuba and perhaps an interview with Fidel, who had been elusive. He okayed the plan, and suggested I be joined by Lisa Howard, whom you might describe as the Barbara Walters of the day. I was anxious to go. I found a cameraman with a Canadian passport, Mike Lente, and was off on an expedition that was to leave some dead and some alive.

There was only one way to go to Cuba then—by way of Mexico City. Twice a week, a Bristol Brittania, even then a rather dated turbo-prop airliner, would make the passage. Mexico prided itself on being a revolutionary government, and maintaining relations with Castro was a question of diplomatic nuance. The Mexican government seemed to be about as revolutionary as Standard Oil. And there at the gates were mustachioed Latins, in neatly-pressed suits and neat little ties, photographing everyone who boarded with small cameras, obviously on loan from the CIA.

Now you have to understand about Mike. He told me on the plane, as his knuckles turned colour, that he and his wife had walked to the border in Hungary during the '56 uprising, carrying only one thing—a bottle of vodka to bribe a Russian if they were stopped. He escaped unharmed to the other side and they both got drunk on freedom in the West. This was his first trip back to a communist country, and he felt the very real peril that he might be shipped back. He was the entire crew. Just what I needed: a Hungarian refugee going into Havana.

When we arrived, we were fortunately greeted by a representative of the Canadian government. I thanked him and asked, "Do you meet all travellers like this?"

"No," he said, matter-of-factly, "but frankly it's easier than going down to the jail in the morning. It's a good thing that we heard about your coming. No camera crews are allowed at the moment." I explained about my call to the foreign ministry.

"Oh," he said, "the woman who answered said to come?"

"Yes."

He laughed. "That was the cleaning lady. She just happened to be going by and answered the phone. But they've decided to allow you to stay." So much for that mambo in the background. Mike trembled a bit. But we had arrived in Havana.

Havana had become a baked bread of a city. Once it had been the jet-setters' ultimate binge, all available for the yankee dollar: sex of every permutation and combination, gambling as wild as a deck full of jokers, drugs as accessible as in a nineteenth century Chinese opium den. The neon was still on, but it now blinked blankly. The emotional mercurial Cubans, once gay, were now grey. And memories of Latin women such as Deenorah, whom I had known so briefly in Panama, were shattered by the khaki-clad, buxom, gun-toting toughs astride the entrances to hotels, such as the once-raunchy Havana Hilton, now the Havana Libre, liberated by Marxist puritans and designated for eastern European technocrats. Bed sheets mended. Lust lost. Welcome, welcome, traveller, to the Havana Libre.

At once we began the "waiting for Fidel" game. He is the Scarlet Pimpernel of the red world. Members of the foreign office had no idea of his appointment schedule and, in fact, were never even sure where he spent his nights. It was rumoured that perhaps there was a lady somewhere. It had not been that long ago that he had been welcomed and adored in New York, the darling revolutionary in the dashing green uniform. I had sat at the Overseas Press Club as the women oohed and aahed as if Cary Grant were smiling. Murrow had had him person-to-person, complete with pyjamas, and Ed Sullivan had once put him on a really big "shew."

Reporting from Latin America has always been notoriously loose, if not downright dishonest; thus the grunts from the Bay of Pigs. There were a few exceptions such as Tad Szulc, who once wrote aptly, "Among Fidel Castro's incontrovertible gifts is the ability to cloud his course in confusion, like a squid emitting ink as it retreats to the deep." Somewhere in the deep of Havana was Fidel, and we had to find him. Meantime,

Mike bolted his door as protection from stray Hungarian secret police who might be having a Havana holiday.

The other player in this game was Lisa Howard. How do you talk about someone like her, especially when she is now gone? But to omit her would be like cheating a star of the needed billing. Lisa needed, needed much, and constantly. She was, as I understand it, a girl of some means, from the mid-West, married and remarried with a child, and living in a fashionable and expensive New York brownstone. Her blonde hair swivelled nervously from side to side, as did brown eyes that had the feeling in them of ancient stone statues.

But don't get the idea I didn't like her. I did. Lisa was a world unto herself in a world of men where she wanted to be treated like a lady. Once she had been a soap-opera star. In a way her life had become a soap opera. She had earned her reportorial stripes as a radio reporter at a local New York station. She gained fame by once cuddling up to Kruschev with a tape recorder during a state visit to New York, in such a way that almost no photo could be taken of the old bolshevik without her prominently in the background—no, scratch that—in the foreground. In an earlier trip to Cuba she had outflanked Fidel and conducted an interview, but the sound wasn't working. Now, by God, she would get Fidel for sure!

So, one nervous Hungarian cameraman, and one brash American lady reporter out for big game, and eventually a Cuban sound man who seemed to be listening on the headset to the Cuban secret police or minor league Cuban baseball, and me—all of us waiting for Fidel.

We heard Fidel was speaking to a crowd one night. We dashed to the theatre and went backstage. "Quick," I said to Mike, "get a reverse shot of Fidel from behind." Mike set the camera and handed it to me. "You're so brave. You do it." To my astonishment, I did. Fidel seemed to look up from his text to contemplate this mad *gringo* who stood behind him while his army of protectors stood guard with machine guns. He straightened his bullet-proof vest, went on with his harangue, and vanished.

"Just wait," said Lisa, flouncing her blonde hair, "I will get him." And I knew she would. Sure enough, a few days later, Juan, our driver, breathlessly broke into my room. "I think we should be ready." I don't know how he knew or from where his information came. He was one of those travellers' aids you find in many under-developed countries. Certainly he was once in charge of American businessmen out for a sordid weekend on the town, a kind of gentleman procurer. Since the revolution he had made himself available to the revolutionaries. But I always felt he missed the old days. He was out to please. When he heard about my obsession with Hemingway, he suggested that he had been Hemingway's personal chauffeur, and began to call me "Papa." He fed me long Cuban cigars, wrapped by his brother-in-law from the best hard-to-get Cuban tobacco, so fresh that the ends had to be chewed off and spat out in the best tradition of the cigar-smoking *aficionados*.

So with word of Fidel's whereabouts, we rushed downstairs with camera equipment. Lisa had somehow managed to have professional Magnum photographer Elliot Erwit allowed into Cuba as part of our group. She put him in the lead car as her personal cameraman, and sped off with the guards. Mike seemed relieved. I stood in the cloud of carbon smoke from the cheap Roumanian gasoline and shouted after her, "Lisa, wait for the film crew!" Somewhere, somehow, in the middle of a back road in Cuba, we caught up with Lisa. She had made the rendezvous with Fidel. "Isn't he wonderful," she gasped breathlessly while Elliot popped photos of Lisa leaning rather close to the bearded leader. "Lisa," I pleaded, "We're here to make a film, remember?"

"Oh, yes," she said, as if dropping an imaginary handkerchief for me to pick up, "you may join us." For the next hour Mike, nervously balancing himself on a machine gun, sat in the back, and I operated the sound in the front as we charged through the Cuban countryside. This was Fidel's domain. Yes, he was king, emperor and, of course, common man. In charge all the way. "Look, look! Look out the window," said Fidel as if examining his personal farm. "In January, in February, when the snow has covered most of the developed countries, you see our land— how green? There, alfalfa. Green, green. January, February, we have it eternally green. This is an advantage. Because with that green, you make milk, milk with that green." And Lisa nodded, somewhat adoringly.

Then we stopped at a farm. Fidel insisted we film the cattle. "We're transforming. We're going to transform a million cows from Sabu to Holstein, using insemination. Very pretty cows. They have them in the King ranch. Get the picture of the cows. You got the picture?" Then off again. To a worker's development. Into the kitchen, up with the baby to hold for photographers. "You see, lots of good. You get the picture of the beans?"

How similar, I felt, as he went from place to place in search of adulation, how similar to my tour in Ethiopia with the emperor. There is a common bond between absolute rulers, right or left. They will tell you how loved they are. And perhaps they are, but how does anyone really know without a voting process until it is too late. After all, Fidel had promised the people a rose garden and given them a red one instead. Who knows what they really felt?

That morning we finally learned the reason for the excursion. Fidel was upset. He announced along the way, "I think I will turn off the water at Guantanamo Bay." He proclaimed this with a vast gesture, chewing the words in his dark beard. I think that's when I heard myself say, "Come on, Fidel, a little less Brando, please." Who was the actor? How much acting was for us? Imagine having a country as a stage to play on that way.

Oh, yes—about the revolution—good had been done for the peasants. Illiteracy was being stamped out. The wealthy suburbs were being turned into housing for students. Medical care had been vastly improved. We even visited a farm for the rehabilitation of prostitutes, who seemed to miss the old days of glitter as they leaned over drab rows of Singer sewing machines, chanting the "Internationale." How well was it all working? At breakfast all that was available was ham sandwiches and banana juice. In the countryside in a restaurant, I saw a man stand on a table top in desperation at high noon in the middle of chicken country, pleading for scrambled eggs. So much for the efficiency of "direct democracy."

The revolution was being run nocturnally. We had an appointment to interview the man who, at that time, was strictly a second banana, Major Ernesto "Ché" Guevara. There was a joke at the time that when Fidel was handing out cabinet portfolios he asked, "Who here is an economist?" Ché's hand went up and Fidel said, "Well then, you will be minister of economics." Ché replied, too late, "I thought you asked who here is a communist?" We met Ché, at that time minister of industry, after midnight in an obscure office in a high-rise office building. Let me say now that Ché, although short of stature, may have been the single most beautiful-looking man I have ever seen. His eyes were quick and flashing, his smile wide and refreshing, his talk fast and intelligent. He reminded me somewhat of Tyrone Power in *Suez*, but of course with that scattered, famous beard. He was playing with Lisa, and she with him. In our meeting with him she seemed to be hitching up her belt as if at a pretend gunfight at the OK corral. The whole thing had something of the actor-actress duet about it.

All the time during the interview, which went on past dawn, I noted Ché breathing with what seemed to be great passion. It wasn't until later that I learned it was asthma. He was about as suited to mountain revolutions as a man in a wheelchair is to run the four-minute mile. But after all, what was an Argentinian revolutionary doing running the economy of a country in constant bankruptcy anyhow? When the interview was over, Ché, puffing on a superb cigar, asked Lisa if she would like to take some cigars back to America. She asked him how many boxes he had. "Only six," he said. "Six will be fine," she said, and handed the six boxes to Juan, who gasped, "I really don't know about this revolution."

In the days that followed, we filmed in and around the city. Lisa managed to corner a couple of *gusanos*, the Cuban word for worm— people who wanted out and were afraid to say so. We filmed them in silhouette, and I hope we did them no harm. I always had the feeling anyhow that the Cuban censor was out to lunch. When I tried using the hotel phone to place a call to New York, it never seemed to work at around noon.

It was arranged that there would be a long sit-down interview with Fidel before we left. But naturally we did not know when. Each midnight we would set up lights in Lisa's suite and wait. Finally toward the end of our month-long stay, one evening about 9 p.m., a drowsy soldier set up camp on a stool at the elevator in the hall. We knew that was it.

Half past midnight six guards appeared down the hall, and then the leader. Fidel is tall, good looking and seems at first sight like a likeable bear. When he entered the room, he began fumbling in his pockets. The machine-gun men tensed. But he was out of cigars. They studied me as I carefully handed him one of Juan's brother-in-law's specials. He bit off the end, lit it, took a deep, satisfying puff and asked, "Say, where did you get such a good cigar? I have trouble getting such a good Cuban cigar!" He laughed, so everyone laughed, and we did the film interview, the only extensive one ever conducted by Fidel in English. Because of recent events involving the Cubans and Africa, the Kennedy Assassination Committee, and the question of Fidel's credibility and what he was truly after, I am putting down exactly what he said, starting with Lisa's question about news of Cuban troops in Zanzibar.

FIDEL CASTRO:

Have you never seen the long distance between Cuba and Zanzibar? It is too far away to believe that our hand was in Zanzibar. We were surprised by the Zanzibar revolution, like the United States, too. You ask if sometimes somebody came from Zanzibar to visit Cuba? It's possible. I have no time to train anybody.

LISA HOWARD:

Well, your people then?

FIDEL CASTRO:

I have not any confirmation of that.

LISA HOWARD:

There have also been reports that South Africans are undergoing training in Cuba.

FIDEL CASTRO:

Why do you believe that a revolution can be made from another country? If it were possible, the United States government had made 100 counter-revolutions in Cuba. I don't understand how you believe it's so easy to make a revolution from Cuba, and is so impossible to make counter-revolutions from United States.

LISA HOWARD:

You said at one point after President Kennedy's death that you believed that under Kennedy it was going to be possible to normalize relations between Cuba and the United States. What leads you to believe that?

FIDEL CASTRO:

Kennedy, after three years as President of the United States, Kennedy had much more experience than he had at the beginning, and I think he had a better understanding of the world problems, and about Cuba. My opinion is that he was in the way of persuading himself of his mistakes about Cuba. And so . . . I do not want to make a speculation about that. But we had (*He turns to translator and says, "Come se dice dintomas?" Translator answers "symptoms."*) some evidence that some change was taking place in the mind of the government of the United States . . . a new situation . . . and we had evidence I do not want to speak about now. I think this is not the place to speak about that. (*I later confirmed this fact with various Kennedy men.*)

LISA HOWARD:

Dr. Castro, you have spoken often of your desire to normalize relations with the United States. You are a realist. What are you prepared to concede in order to bring about this normalization of relations?

FIDEL CASTRO:

You ask many things in a short time. Many problems you speak about. When you speak about peace, you are thinking of commercial business concessions. When we speak about peace, what we mean is really to live in peace. . . . You want to live in peace with Cuba, and Cuba in peace with United States? You ask me what are we decided to concede. I think that some concessions ought to be made for both parts, for United States and for Cuba. I think a peace *politico* means mutual concessions, dignity. I think that it is necessary to speak in this situation of dignity, for both countries—sovereignty, absolute sovereignty, for both countries—and to speak about our problems. For us it is not very difficult, because we have no cause that prevents us of living in peace with other nations.

Once the interview was over, Lisa asked that we all leave, and for an hour or so she was alone with Fidel. What happened in the privacy of the locked room I cannot tell you. And we will never know. After he had left, she came into my room and flung herself down on the bed. "Well," she said, "aren't you going to ask me?"

"Ask?" I studied her confident, almost virile look. "Ask what?"

"You know, whether he and I—you know. I will never tell."

In the days that followed we filmed jails, Fidel playing baseball, the cutting of the sugar cane, decreasing crops, a surprising mambo-filled beauty pageant. And then there was the uneasy moment of departure. We needed exit permits and some bureaucrat, trying to rule his own small empire, almost caused us to miss the only plane of the week. But we left. And what has become of us all after the Cuban adventure, because it was, after all, many years ago? Let us look at heroes and heroines.

Fidel, of course, outlasted everyone. Fifteen years later he took Barbara Walters on the same tour he took Lisa on, and he made the same speeches, more or less, but this time in Spanish because his English had slipped. The various plots by the CIA he complained of during our visit have since turned out to be true. He outlived them all.

Lisa, sadly, in a fight with Jesse Zousmer at ABC, was temporarily taken off the air after she publicly came out against the candidacy of Bobby Kennedy. She died of an overdose of pills, I think accidentally, but it made the front page of the *Herald Tribune* that day, which is also gone.

Dr. Ché got bored going to the office every midnight, and decided to fight a revolution in Bolivia, unfortunately in the mountains, the wrong place for asthma. He was gunned down, and the photos of that beautiful face riddled with bullets is a tragic remembrance of a brilliant man looking in the wrong place for excitement.

Jesse Zousmer died in a plane crash in Tokyo.

As for me, the program went on the air as "Cuba and Castro Today," and was remarkably edited by my friend Mavis Lyons. It was fair to all sides, I thought, but no one would sponsor it. During one of the commercial breaks, ABC slotted in a promo for Cuban "freedom fighters," who protested anyway. Subsequently, a mysterious fire broke out in my filing cabinet in New York. My Cuban notes were burned, but fortunately I kept carbons of those papers.

After the passage of so much time, I have often been asked what I think of Fidel today. I answer, with some irony I suppose, that he would be great to have as a friend if he were not a dictator. Of course there is more to it than that. Beware the messiah who knows for you and promises a tomorrow that may never come, whether he be a "born-again" communist or Christian. As for Cuba, yes, I know about the improvements in education, health and so on. But where is freedom?

My travels through the grey communist worlds of Yugoslavia and Hungary and the seedy side streets of Havana taught me that aside from health and the possibility to love and create, man's most valued item on earth is freedom. My experiences gave me an awareness that what I valued, making it from the poverty of St. Clair Avenue, was the freedom to be me. If I could be a hero to myself, then maybe I could be a hero to the world.

CHAPTER NINE
The Nobel Prize:
*I will live
through my son,
Martin Luther King Jr.*

"They call me the master of the obvious." This was my introduction to Walter Schwimmer when he called that first day from Illinois. His voice was a mixture of mid-west openness and big-city toughness. He had a Damon Runyon-like quality, with a heart as large as Chicago. In the parlance of the television world, Walter is a "packager," and although his name seldom makes news, he had justly earned the title of "the great innovator." He has also become my life-long friend as a result of what he had to offer.

Most of Walter's money has come from finding holes in the television screen. For instance, on Saturday and Sunday he noticed many men playing golf. Naturally he devised a way to carry golf on television when everyone else thought it was impossible; the program was "The World Series of Golf." He noted correctly that the country's most popular sport was bowling and put together a package called "Championship Bowling"—a natural. He loved to spend his evenings at bridge and thus came the obvious "Championship Bridge." One day, as I understand it, he and his associate, Art Pickens, were sitting around their offices thinking of what was the champion of all champions, and naturally one said to the other "the Nobel Prize!" And presumably Walter said, "Well, let's package the Nobel Prize."

Of all the obvious ideas in the world, the one most suited to television is the Nobel Prize. Here are the greatest minds of our time, living and available. Here is one of the great ceremonies, that even includes a king. One year Schwimmer found a way, and I did it for him. This is the story of the rise and fall of the Nobel Prize on commercial television.

Schwimmer found a sponsor, the Zenith Corporation, which seemed to want the "insignia of quality" to tie in with the prizes themselves. He found a network, ABC, which at that time was firmly planted at the number three spot, and was not against taking a chance if the money was right. They insisted on having someone who had worked for them in charge of the program, and that is how Walter found me. He located the most erudite host of the TV age, Alistair Cooke. Cooke was in limbo following the great success of the "Omnibus" series, now long dead, and it was before "Masterpiece Theatre" started running on PBS those endless English dramas from the bottom shelves of the public domain. Schwimmer then went to Sweden and convinced the head of the Nobel Foundation that only he could pull it off. With his honesty, he charmed the man who had to give his approval. So we became an official part of the Nobel Prize ceremonies for the year 1964.

Among the list of that year's Nobel Prize winners were scholars and scientists whose contributions to mankind have changed the world. They included the brilliant American professor, Dr. Charles H. Townes, and two Russians, Nikolai Basov and Aleksander Prokhorov, whose discovery of the laser principle made it possible to complete difficult eye surgery in 1,000th of a second, and some day would lead to the creation of a terrible death ray; Jean-Paul Sartre, who felt his philosophy would not allow him to accept $52,000 in prize money, even though he could not actually turn down the honour that went with it; a German scientist in Munich, Feodor Lynen, and a German Jew in Cambridge, Konrad Bloch, who shared the medicine award for their discoveries concerning the mechanism and regulation of cholesterol and fatty acid metabolism, discoveries that would help reduce heart disease; a remarkable English-woman, Mrs. Dorothy Crowfoot-Hodgkins, who became the first woman in years to walk off with the chemistry prize for her work on the atomic structure of biochemical substances such as vitamins, and thus would help reduce the hazards of anemia; and Martin Luther King, winner of the Peace Prize, whose stubborn belief that love is the strongest weapon against hate had changed the underdog status of the American Negro.

Since 1901, when the awards were first presented, the names of the men and women who have won the Nobel Prizes read like a roll call of all major achievements in the twentieth century. In the list of medical discoveries alone are names (sometimes not so well known) of men who have made life on our ever-shrinking planet more healthy and bountiful. A German scientist named Gerhard Domagk found sulfa in an experiment he was daring enough to try on his own daughter. Banting, a Canadian, discovered insulin and gave hope to millions of diabetics. Fleming, an Englishman, made penicillin a reality and years were added to the normal life span of most of us. Selman Waksman discovered streptomycin, and brought honour to the United States and a fuller life to humanity. All these men shared the prize left by a man once called "the merchant of death," who also became part of my film.

Alfred Nobel would have been delighted. The eccentric Swedish inventor and millionaire, whose invention of dynamite made mass death possible, but who also bequeathed to the world the gift of its most respected prize for peace, was a silent and unseen member of the royal audience of birth and brains assembled in Oslo and Stockholm on Thursday, December 10, 1964. What kind of man could build the greatest industrial complex of destruction, and leave as a legacy a will that specifically seeks to reward "those who, during the preceding year, shall have conferred the greatest benefit on mankind?" After weeks of pursuing this paradox, from Swedish and Norwegian officials and recently released private correspondence, there began to emerge a portrait of a patriarch of power.

From his oldest living descendent, his niece—the 82-year-old Dr. Marta Nobel-Oleinikoff, a magnificent dowager with a face marbled and lined with learning and living—came a personal remembrance of "Uncle Alfred." He was a lively but rather fragile, short, bearded man who came to call at Christmas time with generous gifts, including a mechanical ape that smoked cigarettes and puffed smoke into the nineteenth century air.

Nobel's father was also an inventor of sorts. Among his less practical achievements was a system devised by him for the Russian navy for the guiding of torpedoes by trained seals. When he died, he had a small bell attached to his tombstone with a string to his coffin, lest he should wake from death. The bell was never rung. Nobel's brothers got involved with his experiments. One of them died in a nitroglycerin explosion. Nobel himself was expelled from school for a time to work with his magic explosives aboard a barge outside Stockholm.

Until recently Nobel had been called "the man whom nobody knew." But at the Nobel Foundation at Sturegaten 14, in a mausoleum of a building, his secret papers were now open. He was, in fact, as a Norwegian official described him to me "a misanthrope and a philanthrope, a realist and a dreamer." Privately, he adored the poems of Shelley and wrote hundreds of his own. Publicly, he covered the world with factories manufacturing deadly explosives. He remained a rather austere bachelor until the end of his days, but carried on unusual, almost adolescent romances with at least two women. Despite his inventions, he grew in later years to be more and more of a pacifist; he called war "the horror of horrors and the greatest of all crimes." The final irony was that he believed that his inventions were so powerful that there would be a kind of balance of terror in the world and hence no more wars. (Atomic scientists please note.)

So suspicious was he of lawyers that when he drew up his will, he did it alone and in his own handwriting, and bequeathed his entire $9 million fortune to mankind. As Nils K. Stahle, the executive director of the Nobel Foundation and the man responsible for investing the funds, said to me, "It was one of the greatest fortunes of its time." It is the interest on the money that is used to reward the genius of today. In the magical balance of nature it is ironic that a fortune accumulated in the production of explosives should be left to those who devote their lives to human betterment.

At least some of the money might have gone another way. Partly because he lived in and loved Paris in his later years, and partly because of constant personal disappointments, Nobel wanted to do something for the lovely city, even if his idea was a rather macabre one. Along a boulevard that he was prepared to buy, he proposed to build a number of small, beautiful houses in which anyone at all could, free of charge, commit suicide in a respectable and painless manner, in the presence of doctors and lawyers who would take care of his body and last wishes. Fortunately for the world, the city of Paris turned down the offer.

In the grey and lonely outskirts of Stockholm, his grave is marked by a simple stone carrying only one word, the name "Nobel." To the world that has almost forgotten that the name Nobel once meant dynamite, there are periodic reminders. On the very day that the 1964 physics and chemistry awards were announced, at almost the exact hour, his original nitroglycerin plant, which had been in existence for 100 years in a small town in Sweden, blew up. Eight people died instantly and many others were wounded.

No question Nobel was a kind of fruit cake, but as fruit cakes go, his legacy was nourishment for the world. For one year, Walter Schwimmer and I more or less owned him. After the awards were announced we tracked down each recipient and filmed him. That is how I came to meet and commit to film a man who became a legend as well: Martin Luther King.

With film cameraman Andy Costikyan of Chicago and a sound man, we arrived in Atlanta to film King. We picked up a couple of southern lighting men and headed for the Ebenezer Baptist Church. That day King's father was preaching. His mood was exultant. The son of a southern preacher had been anointed by the world. Martin Luther King was to receive the world's greatest prize. Among the shouts of "Yeah, man," and "The Lord is with us," he preached: "I'm never going to die. I'm never going to die, because I will live through my son, Martin

Luther King Jr.'' Somehow, I felt that Sunday morning that he was tempting God.

Later when we joined King in his home for a fried chicken lunch, he seemed somewhat resentful of our presence. Perhaps it was merely that we were intruders into his world. I tried to make smalltalk, and told him of my meeting with Chief Luthuli some years earlier in Africa, but his responses were distant—sort of semi-thoughtful and uninterested. "Is that so?" and "You don't say." I had no sense of being close to this remarkable man.

Next day we met for a long sit-down interview. Around him were a number of hangers-on. I remember, in particular, a brash young man perspiring in the outer hall, anxious to get in the picture. He was Andrew Young, later to be Carter's controversial man at the United Nations. But then he stood and hoped. Everyone knew that the Nobel Prize would change many things.

The meaning of the award had already been tested. When J. Edgar Hoover decided to take off the stoic mask of FBI silence to accuse Martin Luther King of lying, even such a great institution as Hoover was faced with wide criticism. Recipients of the Nobel Peace Prize were considered by the general public to be contributors to justice in our society and therefore above suspicion.

King himself was well aware of this. Being a political as well as a spiritual animal, he knew that the award, aside from its immediate honour and $52,000 in cash, had raised him above the level of ordinary racial debate in the United States. It also had a profound effect on black leadership generally. The award automatically acted as a kind of nomination of King as king of the movement for black freedom. From now on he was something different.

Despite the fact that the world had acclaimed him, King's headquarters remained an unpretentious office in one of Atlanta's run-down Negro neighbourhoods. It was a weathered, yellow brick building at the crossroads of Auburn Avenue and Hilliard Street, close to the Atlanta Waiters' Club and the C & H Grill. Derelicts and drunks strayed by, paying little heed to the simple painted sign, "Southern Christian Leadership Conference, Martin Luther King Jr., President, Redeeming the Soul of America." His office was lined with books on the racial struggle, and over his desk was an autographed portrait of King and President Johnson. A wood divider covered a wash basin.

Not long ago I found a complete transcript of our talk. In view of events that followed, perhaps you should have an opportunity to examine it first hand. I cannot put in the dramatic pauses. I sense now in the transcript, a man who knew he would die a violent death. How ironic, I felt at the time, that his Christ-like complex, almost awaiting the crucifixion, was not unlike Fidel's feeling. But Fidel was surrounded by guns, King by Bibles.

RASKY:

> Well, Dr. King, where were you and what was your reaction when you learned that you had won the Nobel Peace Prize?

DR. KING:

> Well, I happened to have been in the hospital when I learned that I had won this prize. I was in the hospital for a general physical checkup, and to get a little rest. When I got the call from my wife, I had just awakened and it was all like a dream for a moment. But I soon discovered that it was real and, naturally, I was deeply moved to hear of this great honour.

RASKY:

> How will the Nobel Prize change your life if it hasn't changed it already?

DR. KING:

> Well, it has certainly changed it to a degree, because we have gotten many words of encouragement from many people that we hadn't heard from before. I think it has great international implications and it brings to our struggle an international dimension that it did not have before. I shouldn't say that it didn't have it, but at least it makes us conscious of the fact that we have the rolling tide of world opinion on our side as we engage in this great struggle in the United States. And I think the international aspect is probably the greatest aspect that comes to us at this time.

RASKY:

> How about nationally? Has it changed your position nationally as a result of winning this award?

DR. KING:

> Well, I think in a sense it gives real vindication to the whole non-violent program and the non-violent method of grappling with the problems of racial injustice in our country. Naturally, all along the way there have been those individuals who sought to criticize non-violence and even to ridicule this approach. But I think the Nobel Prize gives to the method and philosophy of non-violence a kind of understanding and a kind of respect that will certainly deepen my own commitment and I am sure will also cause other people to deepen their commitment, because as I have said, this prize is not merely an honour to me, personally; I think of it as something much larger. I see it as a tribute to the whole movement for racial justice in our country

and to its dedicated leaders. I think it is an award and a tribute
to the great courage, the discipline, the wise restraint of all
the individuals, both Negro and white persons, who have been
engaged in this struggle across the years.

RASKY:

In general terms, how would you describe your philosophy?

DR. KING:

Well, I would say that my basic philosophy, which grows out
of the non-violent tradition, is that a moral man cannot in good
conscience, cannot accept injustice and adjust to an evil system.
He must resist it; he has a moral obligation to resist evil. But
in resisting it, he must recognize that he stands on higher moral
ground when he will resist that unjust system non-violently,
so that he does not resist it with hatred, with engaging in physical
violence. In short, the individuals seek to achieve moral ends
through moral means. And I think this is what non-violence
is saying in the final analysis, that means and ends must cohere,
and that in order to bring about a just society and righteous
society, it is necessary to use just and righteous methods.

RASKY:

At what stage of your existence did you make the transference
from strictly a religious philosophy to one that involved the
work between races?

DR. KING:

I would say this came in my early teenage days. I was brought
up in the Church. My father happens to be a minister and has
pastored in Atlanta for a number of years. So I came up with a
great devotion to my religious background and my religious
upbringing. And naturally, being in a religious atmosphere, I
studied the Bible very thoroughly, and I came to see from
the Old Testament the greatness and the demand for justice as
expressed in the thinking of the eighth-century prophets like
Amos and Micha. From the New Testament I came to see the
great power of the ethic of love. Now as soon as I started
moving through society and working here and there as a teenager,
I came to see that if religion was relevant, these great insights
of the prophets and of Jesus Christ had to be transformed
into some kind of meaningful social action. It was at that time
that I started working, even though I was still in high school
and then later college, in the NAACP and other youth
organizations that were grappling with the problem of racial
injustice. This was a little before I decided to enter the ministry
myself. Even before that, I saw that if religion was to be

meaningful, it had to be active and meaningful and relevant in everyday life.

RASKY:

The basis of your thinking is the Christian tradition, but the method comes from Gandhi, who is a Hindu. Do you see a paradox in that?

DR. KING:

Not at all. The interesting thing is that Gandhi himself was the first to say that he was greatly influenced by the Sermon on the Mount, and I happen to feel that God reveals Himself in all the great religions of the world and that there is truth in all. Even though Gandhi was a Hindu, he was greatly influenced by the ethic of love. He said that when he first read the Sermon on the Mount, he was so deeply moved and saw that this expressed the kind of thinking and kind of ethical idealism that he wanted to serve as a guide of his life. I have been greatly influenced by Gandhi and I say often that I received the inspiration to carry on in the non-violent tradition from Jesus of Nazareth, and the operational technique from Mahatma Gandhi.

RASKY:

Some people say that non-violent action really doesn't work. In Gandhi's case he was killed and, in fact, by one of his own people. In South Africa, Chief Luthuli, another Nobel Prize winner, is a prisoner, and you yourself have been attacked, your home blown up. Doesn't it become a little depressing sometimes?

DR. KING:

Yes, it does, but one must understand one of the basic points, one of the basic precepts to non-violence; namely, that suffering can be a powerful force for social transformation. There is nothing in the non-violent activity that says that if you engage in non-violent activity that you will not be the recipient of violence, you will not be the recipient of suffering even. It doesn't say that you won't be the recipient of death. Indeed, it says that you must be willing to die for something that you believe. What it says is that you must always be the willing recipient, but you must never inflict violence upon your opponent. Through your suffering and your willingness to accept blows without retaliating, you, at that moment, find yourself working on the conscience of your opponent. You are exposing his moral defences. You are weakening his morale and you are disarming him, and at the same time working on the conscience so that even though one suffers in the process, it doesn't mean

that non-violence isn't working or that it isn't successful.
Because non-violence recognizes the need for suffering in order
to redeem the social situation.

RASKY:

How about its reaction on you. Do you sometimes hate your
oppressor?

DR. KING:

No. I think that we all go through these moments when we
become rather frustrated, and we are on the verge of becoming
angry, but there again non-violence at its best says that you
do not only avoid external physical violence but also internal
violence of spirit. You not only refuse to shoot your opponent,
you refuse to hate him. And I try day in and day out to live
with this basic point in the non-violent discipline. I say over
and over again to people that we must never allow anyone
to pull us so low as to make us hate them. Love is not only
injurious to the hated but it is injurious to the hater, because it
can bring about the kind of internal disintegration as many
psychiatrists are saying now. . . . Love is the supreme unifying
force of life. And I think that this is to the eternal credit of
the non-violent discipline that it recognizes this.

RASKY:

Gandhi in his life said that he believed in the beginning that
God is love and then he said as he grew older that love is God.
Do you agree with that?

DR. KING:

Well, I would certainly say that God is love. I would hesitate
to say love is God, because I think of God in personal terms,
which is not true of some other religions like Hinduism,
Buddhism, and some of the other religions of the East. They
think of God as the impersonal absolute, whereas I think of
God as the ground of all reality, but indeed a personal ground
of all reality, and this is where I differ. I would be the first
to say that God is love, and one cannot understand the greatness
of God unless he understands that deep in the nature of God
is the attribute of love as well as the attribute of justice. Certainly
when one loves, he does at that moment have the key that
opens the door to ultimate reality, and certainly one cannot
know God if he hates. So I absolutely agree with Gandhi when
he talks about God as love, as John says in the New Testament.

RASKY:

Do you yourself fear the possibility of violence that perhaps
someday you may be killed as Gandhi was?

DR. KING:

I don't think a man can be fully free until he conquers the fear of death, and I really feel that I have conquered this fear. We look at these things philosophically, but I don't have any fear of death. I realize that my life is a difficult one and I am going to have, and to continue to have, the dangerous experiences. I realize that there are many people who don't like us because of our determination to gain freedom and justice, and they are trying to hold on to the old order. But in a real sense, I don't think it is how long one lives, but how well one lives—not the quantity of one's life but the quality of one's life. And I think unearned suffering can be redemptive, for physical death is a price that I must pay to free millions of children and millions of my white brothers from a permanent psychological death and a permanent death of the spirit. Then I don't think anything can be more redemptive.

The interview was concluded on this magnificent note of spiritual triumph. Cameraman Costikyan and I congratulated each other on the tone and quality of the pulsating rhythms that had come from this man. Martin Luther King, the man who had been distant and almost indifferent in personal conversation, was inspired when sounding his themes of belief. I can recall thinking he was like a mighty *shofar,* the ram's horn on Rosh Hashonah in my father's *shul* calling to God, challenging God, rebuking man, warning man. It was both exalted and dangerous ground, I felt.

Our airborne mood collapsed hastily to the level of the streets when we folded our film tent and moved on. The two-local Atlanta electricians said, after packing their cables and plugs, "Well, do you want to have nigger food, or will we go to the other side of town and have white man's food?" So much for moving the masses.

It was a kind of warning of what was to come. At the ceremony in Stockholm, and at the separate one in Oslo that dark December day when the sun never rose, everything went with great dignity and precision. There was Martin Luther King listening to the refrain of *Porgy and Bess* before his studied and thoughtful speech. We trained our cameras on the recipients as they moved with grace to their own moments of triumph. Even the cameramen and I wore tie and tails. We worked all night to edit the tapes and rushed them back to New York for telecast. And miraculously, it all worked. The reviews were stunning.

Our victory celebration at Sardi's was interrupted by a phone call from Washington. James Reston had called to tell Alistair personally that it was the best TV program he had ever seen. Victory! Right? Wrong.

This is what happened. In Atlanta when King came on to get his prize, the TV sets went literally and ironically black. Someone had pulled the plug. Once King was off the air, the signal was resumed. Who did it? They claimed it was an accident. Yes, like an accident of birth or death. In the reforming south, Zenith, the sponsor, was notified by a dozen of its distributors that they were pulling out. So much for equality and liberty and the pursuit of happiness.

The ratings were not dazzling. Opposite the program the other networks had mounted Jackie Gleason, then in his boisterous prime, and over at NBC they ran the first telecast of *War and Peace*. I thought it was Tolstoy's revenge in a way, because they had passed him by for the literature prize in his time. But even so, one would think that somewhere there was a noble soul to put on the next year's Nobel Awards. Nope. Schwimmer took an option on it and paid me to stand by. I am still standing by.

One must really contemplate what is being denied the people of the world by the refusal of commercial U.S. networks to show these prizes and the men who win them. Just that one year, in science we had the invention of the laser and the meaning of cholesterol; in literature an honour to the greatest living French mind; and in peace the official consecration of Martin Luther King as a legend. One year. Think of the years we have missed. Think of the minds we have missed. Think of the people we have not known.

The company of those who had endured and excelled—the winners of the Nobel Prize—the message of King, and my disappointment with the number of TV viewers all were to have an effect on me and the films I was doing. I knew I had to find some other form of film for myself. The actuality events of the day seemed to eliminate themselves like calendar pages. The present-day prejudices seemed hard to control without the pedestal of the past.

Not that I was totally unprejudiced myself. I cannot say I had ever had negative feelings about blacks. But then I cannot say I had any commitment to their struggle either. I often wondered whether what I considered coldness on the part of Dr. King was merely that he knew I would never carry a banner in a march. I was an intruder in a way, a curiosity seeker both to his movement and the violence that I chose not to see. Can you ever really feel the pain of others? Without the blow, without the personal threat, can any of us really understand the suffering that others have experienced?

Psalm 24 asks: "Who shall ascend into the hill of the Lord?" And the answer is: "He that hath clean hands, and a pure heart; who hath not lifted up his soul unto vanity, nor sworn deceitfully." So, which of us would stand on that hill under those conditions? Which, if any?

I love the Bible. It drives me crazy. It brings me such peace to think that others have been driven crazy asking the same questions since there was a psalm, a song, a word, a man. It is a chain that links us all, you and me.

"Mark the perfect man, and behold the upright: for the end of that man is peace." So, there is no perfect man. So there can be no peace, only the search for peace—for myself.

CHAPTER TEN

Peanut Brittle from Lady Bird/Vietnam Letters to Holly

A film is a fragment of time. It is a statement of life. Because it is composed of images of the moment, its meaning may not become obvious until it is observed in tranquility. When the fragments are collected into the jig-saw puzzle that is to produce emotion, it can also be a vast learning experience for the viewer. For the film-maker it may offer insights into himself, not obvious at the time of shooting, but clear when measured in the intensity of a viewing theatre. All this is in the way of an introduction to the films I made in the mid-sixties, which were to reshape my existence. In a sense I was talking to myself through my work.

For instance, I began the year 1965 making a short film called *Thorn of Plenty*. The thorn referred to the sharp spur on the lemon, the plenty to the vast abundance of the fruit and vegetable crops of California. A third of all vegetables in North America come from there, and a third of the world's lemons. What did this have to do with me, a city boy? I was sent out by Tom Wolfe at ABC to film the story of the farm labourers. In a sense it was ground covered before, and quite magnificently, by Ed Murrow in the documentary *Harvest of Shame,* produced by the great David Lowe. The migrant workers had always been part of the shame of America, dating back to Steinbeck's haunting *Grapes of Wrath*.

I found little had changed, that Murrow's fine film had had little effect, and that men were still harvested like fruit but discarded like peeling. My concern were the *braceros,* the Mexican day-labourers brought into the dusty fields of Las Lomas. There was an attempt to substitute out-of-work Americans, but they seemed unwilling and unable to bend to the back-breaking task.

I followed the ritual of hiring: the worker, the grower, the government. And of course, I found the merchants of labour guilty as charged, misusing the migrant workers. There could be no other verdict, at least so it seemed to me. But truly, in the continuing drama of the harvest there was blame enough to go round. The film was narrated for me in the flat, rich, upper-class tones of Peter Jennings, in training as a news media idol. But it was the closing verse of a poem called "Nomad Harvesters" which I used to the script, that seemed to be speaking to me personally. It was the line, "rest never, ripen never," that haunted me. Each film was a moment of my life to be projected then placed on a rack, and I moved on—but to where?

When the film was concluded, I made the journey to Mexico City and visited the most magnificent museum in the world, the Museum Antropolgica, built like a giant altar to a proud past. I watched the faces of the peasants, the Indians, coming in barefoot from the hills of dust and despair. They had come as a kind of religious ritual in adoration of their own history, a history passed on from generation to generation. In looking at death they learned to face life, which is, of course, temporary, but they were sustained into eternity by continuity. I felt that someday I, too, had to make works that could last. But more immediately there was the question of my own personal continuity. For this, and for love, on March 20th, the first day of spring, I married. My meeting with my wife and our marriage has been a kind of miracle.

And how did I come to spend my honeymoon in the White House? John Secondari of ABC, with whom I had developed a pleasant relationship, called the day after the wedding to say that he would like me to direct the first lady of the United States. Ever since Johnson had taken over from Kennedy, there was an image problem for the first family. Kennedy had moved with easy grace. Johnson ambled with awkwardness. And Jackie had been the movie star of Washington. Her famous tour of the White House, directed by Franklin Schaffner (who went on to direct the film *Patton*), may have been one of the great media events of its time. The thin, elegant, fashion model-like first lady with her small, candy-cane voice took the American public through the once-secret rooms of its own first home. She became the darling of her time. Now there was

Lady Bird, an older woman brought in from the shadows. No one knew her. How could she compete with the "baby doll" who left the scene, but not the minds of the public? In movie terms, how could a character actress replace the leading lady? We had to help. It was decided that Lady Bird would do a tour of Washington, and I would direct.

There was one small point that stood between me and the contract. I was requested to shave my beard. Now perhaps you would not think that a particular hardship. But I had become attached to the thing, more than physically. I had grown it during my first Hemingway-striving days in Europe. When I looked in the mirror, the person I saw staring back was a man with a beard—me. I turned down the assignment at first. I also felt it was unfair to my new life, Arlene. She had been courted by, and married, a man with a beard.

But my agent, Harold Cohen, called back to say he had worked out a compromise. I asked how that was possible. A beard is either on or off. He argued that with the hippie generation still a sore point, the folks from Texas in the White House might be offended by a visitor with a scraggly beard. The beard would go but ABC, understanding the importance of the beard to me, would allow extra salary, so that after the filming was concluded I could go away to a Caribbean island and grow a brand-new beard at their expense. So off came the beard, and we moved to Washington to make a star of Lady Bird.

Entering the White House for the first time, every memory of my childhood walked in with me. We were a crowd. How many doorsteps I had waited on during those cold, snowy Canadian nights delivering my father's wares. How many back and side entrances I had gone through during those St. Clair Avenue years. Now it was my turn at the White House. It was something of a disappointment that everyone comes in through the side door. So where do the parcels get delivered? The proper checks had been done. I announced to the secret service man on the gate with a too loud voice: "Harry Rasky to see the first lady."

"Quite correct," he said.

"Quite," I replied which seemed strange to me even then. But after all, there I was: a bearded man without a beard going to visit the President's wife.

Mrs. Johnson was quite wonderful. Just that. She immediately made me feel at home, because frankly I did feel uncertain. I sat in the beauty of the yellow room, and admired this remarkable lady who had suddenly been thrust into the public domain. At first she was greatly resented by the public. With Jackie gone it was as if the wicked witch of the west had toppled Camelot. But her natural ways and grace would make her her own queen.

That day her daughters, Lucy and Lynda Bird, sat awkwardly in the background. It's strange what strikes you in uneasy moments. They were wearing bobby socks. Their white socks seemed incongruous in the room where Jefferson had held court and Lincoln had wept and Kennedy had paced. It was a full house in a ghostly way: all those presidents sitting there. I stroked my beard that did not exist, and was tempted to run.

In the weeks that followed I was able to move with ease in and out of the White House, finding different angles to give the great lady a kind of beauty to add to her natural strength. For instance, cameraman Bill Hartigan and I decided early on that technically we could enhance Lady Bird's looks by slightly throwing the foreground out of focus. Since her most striking feature was her hair, the point of focus was just beyond her forehead. This way her prominent nose did not dominate her looks. And she truly appreciated what we were doing. As spring gave way to summer, and the Washington humidity was as close as Panama at high noon, Mrs. Johnson would arrive for a day of filming with a plastic package of peanut brittle and say, "I think you all need some energy for the day." I never knew whether she stayed up long hours making it, whether she had her cook start the day with it, or if it were pre-packaged. But nonetheless, I was impressed with the fact that Lady Bird brought us candy.

The filming went smoothly, with the occasional humourous episode. For instance, Lady Bird had to have a wireless microphone stuffed down her brassiere, which made for some awkward diplomatic moments. The control for the sound stayed with a relay radio in the possession of the sound man, who turned out to be a character. He seemed to enjoy recording her conversations when she was called to the phone. So we had bits of "Yes, Lyndon, of course. No, Lyndon, I'll try not to be late for the state dinner." When the secret service found out, the sound man stayed under constant surveillance.

One day when we were working late at the Lincoln Monument— we were trying to get a certain kind of light on Lincoln—and she really was late, she went running down the stairs to a waiting limousine. The sound man went running after her. He owned the sound gear and was afraid he would lose his valuable mike. He began to try to retrieve it when he was surrounded by secret serviceman, grappling with him. He never forgot where he was again.

Perhaps the most awkward moment came when we decided to film Mrs. Johnson out on the river. Normally this would not have been a problem. But just around that time Daryl F. Zanuck was making *Tora! Tora! Tora!* and there had been a minor scandal about using navy personnel and ships for publicity. So it was ruled that we would hire a private boat for the outing. This was fine, except that there was only one available and it looked like a stand-by for the *African Queen*. What happened is best quoted from Mrs. Johnson's diary. (''Simone'' is her secretary; the character of ''Indian Joe'' is Sid Dobish, the rather regal assistant cameraman.)

Thursday, June 10
THE WHITE HOUSE

Today varied between being hilarious and serious.

At 10:30 I was to leave with the ABC crew to shoot film on the Potomac River, which meant Jean Louis for hair at 9:30 and make-up with Lillian Brown and getting geared up with my little microphone in pocket, and then to the river.

For the occasion John Secondari had engaged a boat—a quite elderly boat—that must have spent some part of its time hauling fish or even garbage. From the first moment of the day, we were ''snake-bit.'' Everything went wrong.

Always I am accompanied by my straw bag—necessary, ubiquitous container which carries sun oil, scarf, my own camera, maybe a big hat. Today we forgot it. The top deck of the boat was broiling hot.

It was hard to manoeuvre the boat to the locations where we had either the good view we wanted or the bad view we wanted of the banks. Everywhere we went we were directly under the air flight pattern from National Airport. Since this is the busiest airport in the United States, every one of us was ready to swear. Just as I got to the most earnest or poetic part of the script, ''roar. . .rr'' would go a jet overhead.

They had brought along a lunch, and we all sat below deck and ate while John Secondari, an accomplished raconteur, told us tales about filming near the Dead Sea in a daytime temperature of about 125 degrees. He also described a film he hopes to do of Cortez. (I wish he would bring the whole company by the ranch if he does it! I've grown very fond of them all.) I was their guest at lunch and they had a director's chair for me, with ''The First Lady'' inscribed on its back. This will be one of my prize possessions in my own little archives.

After lunch we went back to work, and pretty soon I began to have the feeling that something was going wrong and that nobody was anxious to tell me what it was. Finally it was inescapable. They had to tell me. We had been having engine trouble for some time. The boat had stopped dead now. We could not proceed. We could stay where we were and shoot the rest of the film with the boat drifting, in spite of the anchor, steadily toward the shore. We kept on doing takes— Simone dashing around like a kitten on a hot stove, the secret service talking on their little machines and conferring with each other and Simone and shaking their heads, as the boat drifted and drifted toward the shallow shoreline.

I noticed the police boat, which had been accompanying us at a distance, drawing nearer and hovering quite close. Finally, my secret service agent said, "We are just going to have to take you off. This thing is going to be grounded any minute. No, no, it's not dangerous." But it appeared this would result in a call for help to some kind of patrol, a lot of attention from the shore, and probably a ridiculous newspaper story if I were on board. But we didn't have much left to do of the script. John Secondari and Mr. Harry Rasky and my friend "Indian Joe"—all of them were so eager to do one more take. Over and over, we were doing small bits. Mr. Secondari was probably cursing under his breath, and I trying my best to keep a straight face while I said, over and over from the script: "Who knows, someday John Smith's sturgeons may return to their native home!"

A few minutes passed after the time that the secret service had wanted me to get on the other boat before the cameras stopped grinding, and I said farewell to my marooned friends, stepped into the police boat—it would hold only my secret service detail and Simone and me—and waved them goodbye from our glorious day on the river. We were soon back at the White House.

There was one detail that Lady Bird left out of her account. Just as the second motor of the old ship conked out in the middle of her last take, she looked at me as the director in charge and said, "Well, young man, what do we do now?" As the secret service boat gained ground and the ship sputtered its last, I said, "Why, ma'am, I guess we all just begin to sing 'There's No Business Like Show Business'."

On the final evening we had what would pass for the cast party, but it was a cast of one. Lady Bird invited everyone who had been involved in the filming for an evening with her. It was truly a surprise. She projected for us a silent film, which to my knowledge had never been seen before and has not been seen since, which involved her own early efforts as an amateur actress. While Lyndon was off to war, she took up acting as a part-time recreation, and someone filmed a sequence in which she played the wronged innocent lady from the country to a city slicker who was a Washington politician. It really was quite hilarious. During the screening she gave a running commentary which was witty and delightful. She concluded by saying, "You all have made me look beautiful and I wanted to entertain you for a night."

One day before we left town, we did stumble upon Lyndon. When he shook my hand, he stared me in the eye as if we were about to get involved in a horse trade, and his grip carried a threat. I really knew my hand had been shaken by a master. There was to have been an outdoor ceremony on the White House lawn to which several thousand people had been invited. But a brief shower had made the seats wet. While I stood next to him, he turned to his head of protocol and said, "I think we have lots of napkins around, couldn't you all go out and wipe the seats for the ladies?" But Lady Bird chimed in and it was decided that, in fact, it would be best to hold the affair inside.

So much for life at the White House. The rest you know: the girls in the bobby socks got married, had kids, divorced, disappeared. Lyndon—well we know about the war that beat this tough old guy. Lady Bird wrote in that diary: "I hope some day this crew will all come down to the ranch and see us." I never have, but someday I plan on knocking on the door or gate and saying, "I brought some peanut brittle for my star."

The film that came out of it all received rave reviews. This is how Jack Gould began his review in the *New York Times:*

> In a world dark with ominous headlines and ugliness, Mrs.
> Lyndon B. Johnson's television program last night was an island
> of beguiling beauty and loveliness. It was ever so much more
> than a tour of Washington; it was an enhancing interlude of
> serenity that healed and refreshed the spirit.

We were all collectively given the George Foster Peabody Award. And my beard, paid for by ABC, found its way back to my face at Rockefeller's Little Dix Bay in the Caribbean.

While in Washington, Arlene had an endless craving for dill pickles. It was obvious that soon we would be three. On December 20th that year, five days before Christmas, a child was born. She was sent home from the Roosevelt Hospital in a stocking. Her name is Holly Laura Rasky. In Yiddish and Hebrew she was named after my mother: Liebe Perl, the loved one.

The next month I took an assignment that could have ended my life and almost did. I had a great deal of time to think about the "sanctuary" that was the White House. The events, guided by its occupant of that time, profoundly changed the world and intruded into my own existence.

I went to Vietnam to make a film for ABC called *Operation Sea War—Vietnam*. I decided to dedicate what I found to Holly, still in her cradle. I wrote a series of letters to her, which appeared in the *Toronto Telegram* and were syndicated around the world by United Features in New York. At least part of what I experienced is best reflected by the actual letters, which were printed with a picture of Holly staring at the world. Here is what I felt as I tried to tell it then.

SAIGON, February 12, 1966
Dear Holly,
I have gone off to war. I have come here in search of knowledge about mankind and about myself. There are so many things to know. This is why I am here.
There are those who will tell you that those of our generation had the worst of it. We were hammered by the Depression and jabbed by World War II. But life had a simple, almost innocent focus. In the Depression you fought to eat and in the war you fought to survive. Hunger and Hitler were easy villains to identify. And after that war I remember the promises of peace. The lofty banners of the UN and all it could mean. We were all brothers, weren't we?
There were those at angry debates at the University of Toronto, who once tried to dent my student faith in man's basic desire for harmony.
There were the anthropologists who bluntly lectured that primitive tribes have always warred against each other. The historians recalled that every 25 years or so the so-called civilized tribes seemed to require war as a way of life.
I found a godliness in the non-violent philosophy of Gandhi. He died a violent death. I heard hope in the speeches of President Kennedy. The thud of his end will always haunt us.
And now this thing, this war that is not a war, this madness that I have come half way round the globe to live with.
A few advisors sent by Eisenhower a decade ago have become an army that somehow will alter all our lives, even

yours, Holly, not yet used to the absence of womb warmth. Holly, it all started with a couple of U.S. advisors and now it's called "escalation."

I brought you into the world, Holly. And now I want to find out what kind of world you may expect—full of hope or mushroom-clouded with fear.

I want to know if this is the beginning of World War III, or the end of a costly mistake of history. I am searching to find out why men seem to need war. (Do I dare say enjoy war?) I want to meet the Vietnamese. What must they feel after generations of death?

The only Orientals I've known well were those who operated a hand laundry next door to where I was born at 1281 St. Clair Ave. in Toronto. A certain Mr. Lee was most patient with our childish pranks as we rang his bell and ran out singing the rhyme, "Chinka-Chinka-Chinaman." I guess I never really knew him, and I hope he and all other Orientals will forgive me. Because, Holly, I am here and afraid. They tell me the drive into town from the airport could be mined. Several have died. Some just a few days ago. This is why this is being sent from the airport. But there is still so much to confide.

And how can I tell them I am not here to fight. Just to find out about this war and myself and all of us.

THE DAYS OF DEATH ON THE MEKONG RIVER
Dear Holly,

You are a child of this time, and this place is a part of our time. Now that it is dusk, there is the distant thunder of artillery. It is part of the frustration of this mad war that I can sit at a café in this delta city and enjoy a Vietnamese banquet and hear the voice of the guns as they chatter death.

I flew by helicopter to this Mekong Delta city. From 5,000 feet the green rice fields look like Holland Marsh or the Niagara peninsula. But there's war below because you see puffs of white cloud rise to the left.

The airport greeting was a kind of plaintive public relations, a sign that read: "Welcome to Vinh Long, home of the hard-working, dedicated flying soldier with a can-do attitude." I could see from the sky why this delta area is so important. There is enough in its soggy soil to feed a sub-continent. Few roads. A river that splinters into communist-controlled steams.

There is a U.S. adviser, a navy lieutenant, Ken Allison of Monterey, California, who has spent nine months here. The extent of his dedication is unquestionable. He is a daily target for the sniper. Part of his faith is based on a stylish Vietnamese commander, Tu T'in Hoa, a pipe-smoking sailor who seems to realize the weakness of his own side, but believes in his work. Tu T'in, like many a Vietnamese I have met, cannot remember a time when there was not a war here. The people have learned to live with it.

At night the sky explodes with light, rockets seeking out the Viet Cong movements. And the thunder of the guns. It is far away, I am told. Far away is five miles, the distance from Front Street to Eglinton Avenue in Toronto, Washington Square to Central Park West in New York.

There are some here, like a U.S. army sergeant who has been in the military for 25 years, who just can't live without action, even though he told me, ''Christ, I'm nervous every night.'' There are others, like Lt. Allison, who are here because they feel they are preaching a better way of life.

I met a young blonde school teacher who teaches English down the road, Sandra Williams of El Paso. She is a lonely figure in the officers' mess. A couple of months ago when she first arrived, her companion, a male teacher, went out to see the countryside. It seemed so peaceful. He was captured by some Viet Cong terrorists and beheaded, according to Vietnamese custom thus tearing the soul from the body for eternal damnation.

When I went back by helicopter towards Saigon, a machine gunner on either side, I listened in on the headset. They searched the fields with their muzzles, and on the headset the Armed Forces Radio was playing "Days of Wine and Roses." And days of death in the delta.

VIETNAM: NAVY JETS ROAR IN ALICE IN THUNDERLAND
Dear Holly,

If the Vietnam war seems unreal in the beleaguered city of Saigon, here at sea it is strictly Alice in Wonderland. I came by plane across the plateaus and mountains of Saigon. Again there was the peaceful-looking countryside. The pilot dipped his wings as we passed a bombing mission, and again the misty puffs of clouds. Here and there I could see the results of the scorch policy: pock-marked earth which will stay brown and cursed.

I buckled my seat and chest straps, breathed deeply, held my breath. There was the twang of the steel arresting wires that had caught us; then the plane trembled and settled. The wind on the giant deck was like a hot summer gust off Lake Ontario. It was hard to believe that I was at sea instead of on some land airstrip.

This is the *Kitty Hawk,* a vast floating arsenal. If the ship were turned on end, she would reach the 80th floor of the Empire State Building. There are 5,300 people on board, a small town of America afloat half-way round the world. And why is it Alice in Wonderland? Because most people, outside of the top officers, have never been to Vietnam. That is true, despite the fact that 24 hours daily and nightly pilots leave on missions to bomb targets in Vietnam.

The ship's publicity brochure (yes, it has that, too) tells me that the *Kitty Hawk* has a splendid hospital complete with operating room, a drug store, a barber shop (with 13 chairs), a shoe repair shop and three soda fountains. Sounds nice. If it had a pool and girls, it could be a cruise ship. But each night now, at 11:45 p.m., the red hangar lights open, and incredible air machines leave on missions of destruction in this incredible war.

How fantastic they are! The Phantom, twice the speed of sound; the Hawkeye, a travelling radar city; the Intruder, a flying IBM machine with bombs.

At night we go to the movies. Last night I sat with the admiral and watched *Who's Been Sleeping in My Bed.* And while Dear Martin chased young Miss Montgomery of "Bewitched" around the bed, the bombs were being loaded. And soft music played over the ship's own radio station. And a western was on the ship's own TV station. And the weapons were being mounted. And then in the red light of night the jets vaulted into the sky.

Holly, my child, I suggest that there is something monstrous about war, or perhaps just this war – because it is so unreal. Because here we are floating about in this calm tropical sea with Dean Martin in cinerama while bombs are being dropped. And now as I write this letter, the jets are being fired up. The prophets and the pundits will have to tell you if this is a just war or a good war or a bad war. I'm merely stating that I've arrived at the Mad Hatter's tea party, through Alice's looking glass.

The jets have gone off to drop their bombs, and you know, they look almost real.

THE VIETNAM GI'S SLOGAN: SORRY ABOUT THAT
Dear Holly,

Each man must fight his own war in his own way and have his own reasons. This I have found in my days aboard the *Kitty Hawk,* an aircraft carrier like a city at sea. The waters have been moderate to rough, the waves slapping smaller craft around us but seldom challenging the majesty of this proud ship. I have witnessed the foolish and the brave, met men dedicated and deplorable. But let others judge.

To celebrate the Chinese New Year truce, the entire strike force 77 of the Seventh Fleet did a water ballet. Twenty ships—carriers, cruisers and destroyers—posed for a picture portrait, while jets numbered the sky with a giant "77" overhead.

One admiral sent a message to another admiral, "From the Commodore of the Tonkin Gulf Yacht Club to the Chairman of the Board, a salute." Thirty thousand men engaged in a day of grandstand whimsy off the edge of the world dateline. There are times when you feel you are involved in a mammoth fantasy. The plan of the day lists the movie schedule (Elizabeth Taylor in *Cleopatra*). There is news of the *Kitty Hawk* softball team, and a warning to avoid the rush for flowers on Valentine's Day, and sometimes an almost Boy Scout atmosphere.

After a few days, a helicopter lifted me suddenly off the deck of the aircraft carrier *Kitty Hawk.* The proud but rusted destroyer, the *Hubbard,* had no place for us to land. So I had to be lowered by cable along with bags and film crew.

It was like going from a big city to a small town, from the giant carrier with its soda fountains to a "tin can" and a real sense of the sea. Fewer than 300 men aboard, but the food and hospitality left nothing to be desired.

Here, for the first time, I found a respectable debate going on. Junior officers were questioning some of the vast imponderables of this or any other war.

Next morning we waited as the sky clouded and brightened. There was news on the radio of a typhoon in the Taiwan Straits, and we, on the edge of it, bobbed about like a plaything in a bath. At 10 a.m., general quarters sounded, and the ship was alive with men rushing to battle stations, hastily donning bulletproof jackets and steel helmets. They were intense. But there was still something of the game about it. More of an exercise in precision than a morning of holocaust.

A small single-engine plane appeared over the nearby hills, and by radio the "spotter" called out locations. Lt. Stevens, in command in the combat room, called out the locations to the gunners. And the old ship rattled with its own force as the five-inch guns jolted. Amber smoke bellowed from the forward guns, occasionally puffing a perfect smoke ring in the sky. Just beyond the beach, puffs of white smoke drifted almost gracefully into the sky. The target had been hit. The spotter signalled buildings were afire. And once even added, "VC are in the open." The ship's rear guns blasted them as they ran into the thick of the jungle.

In all, 138 rounds were fired. The official toll: nine buildings destroyed, 17 afire, 15 damaged. Casualties: unknown number killed or injured. I don't know what the buildings were. Someone said they were huts. Someone else said it was a Viet Cong staging area. I don't know exactly what that means. I never saw the houses. I never saw the enemy. None of us did.

A Vietnamese technician travelling with me asked, "What were they shooting at?" I told him," I'm not sure. But it was a Viet Cong staging area."

He said, "How do you know?"

And I said, "They had a spotter who was working from intelligence reports."

"I was here under the French," he said. "I remember once such a shooting. There was a plane like that one that went round and round above us. I was not their enemy. Yet they missed my house by feet." He became seasick and stayed that way. It was a rough journey and maybe he would have been sick anyway.

As a result, lunch was an hour late. The usual prayer was said. And we all sat down. "What are you going to do after you get out of all this?" I asked the weapons officer.

"I've been accepted at the Union Seminary. I'm going to be a minister," he said.

The *U.S.S. Harry E. Hubbard* is a chipper ship. But that day at lunch, in pleasant company on a warm and windy sea, I thought that perhaps we had all been killers, including me. We had fired 138 rounds. And I may never know how many fatalities were caused by our exercise in firing from the sea.

A GRENADE ROLLS ACROSS MY FEET
    Dear Holly,
        It happened so quickly. There was a bomb at my feet,
and death rolled by. At the Saigon airport, where there have
been past incidents, I made ready to fly to Hong Kong on the
edge of China, to report further about the war in Vietnam.
With the casual, stone-faced matter-of-factness of a buddha, an
Air Vietnam stewardess, her blue robes flowing in the warm
afternoon breeze, announced that the plane had been cancelled.
We headed back to town and I said to my companion, Cmdr.
Bill Graves of Honolulu, "I don't like it. It's bad omen." The
hotel insisted my room had been rented, and I became the
reluctant room-mate of a Japanese technician.
        At the hotel, I spent time talking with Tien, a Vietnamese
who has a look of constant pain about him, even when he
laughs. He had been with me on the mission aboard the destroyer,
and expressed his anger then at what seemed to him to be
random killing.
        "Tien, okay, this is your war, your country. You tell
me. Do you want the Americans to leave here?" He looked
uncomfortable. He stuttered a nervous giggle, which seems to
be a form of oriental embarrassment about the naive, direct
questions of foreigners. "I cannot give you an easy answer. I
am not for the communists. I do not know the Viet Cong. Few
of us know them first hand. The Americans are better than
the French. Your soldiers do not take old ladies and young girls
for their pleasure. That is good. But I think the big bombing
is wrong."
        I tried the argument I had been given by the military.
"But the targets are closely chosen. Of course if there are Viet
Cong in a village and it is bombed, some innocent people
will die."
        "I tell you something," Tien said. "To kill a man who
comes at you with a gun, I can understand. But if they kill a
hundred Viet Cong and there are three, four or five or even one
innocent Vietnamese person—a woman, a child, someone who
is just there and not of this war—it is wrong. Wrong. Not
good."
        "The Americans say they want to help."
        "Yes, they want to help."
        "And if they leave?"
        "And if they leave, the government of South Vietnam
would not survive for one day."

"Then what?"

"Then maybe the Viet Cong would come."

"That would be bad, no?"

"I don't know. I don't know the Viet Cong. I know the government we have. It is not good. I don't know the Viet Cong."

I decided not to leave the hotel, to spend my last night safely. It was still dark when the phone rang to summon me to the airport.

A checkpoint at the airport notified us our taxi could not go beyond that point. It meant I had to transfer all my baggage and equipment. It was a nuisance, but I welcomed the precaution. I went through customs and settled down with a beer. I was not thirsty. But I didn't know what else to do. I tried to read the *Saigon Daily News*.

The plane was late, and I decided to check on the baggage. I watched a dozen soldiers parade across the tarmac on their way to the obscure front.

Then it happened. A Vietnamese policeman was shouting at me. And people were running. The Air Vietnam clerk who had been a study in boredom was screaming, holding her head. I looked at my feet. A hand grenade was rolling by, as casually as an unbalanced ball, like a brown tangerine off a kitchen table. A hand grenade, lethal and deadly, was rolling by my feet. Frankly I didn't have time to be afraid. I followed the others out of the terminal. American military policemen hurried in. Vietnamese policemen were buzzing incredibly on walkie-talkies. Jeeps full of soldiers stormed to a halt.

We waited. There were a dozen rumours. A Viet Cong workman had spilled the grenade out of a cleaning basket. An army colonel had dropped it. A GI back from the front had lost it. It sat there. A tiny ball of metal, enough to wipe out a dozen of us and tear the windows out.

Nothing happened. It did not explode. A jeep pulled up and a soldier took the bomb away. A waiter crawled back from under a table. The stone-like Vietnamese next to me stopped shrieking and smiled. We never found out how it got there.

The point of all of this, I think, is that death rolled by my feet and did not explode. So I am alive.

SAIGON'S UNFINISHED SYMPHONY OF TERROR
  Dear Holly,
        "There will be no victors in Vietnam. Only victims."
Someone said it and someone knew the meaning of this insult
to human civilization.
        I am on my way home. In Honolulu I stopped for a
moment to pay tribute at Pearl Harbour, and remember that
infamous Sunday morning now so long ago when America first
felt the urgent and fierce meaning of its link with the Orient.
Then Japan was the enemy. I was there a few weeks ago. How
ridiculous is war. The Japanese now are so friendly. And the
first morning of every month, the sirens sound at Pearl Harbour,
a mournful remembrance to be ready for any future. Asian
involvement. But America is involved, fully, sadly, completely.
        Hawaii was like Polynesian food, sweet and pungent.
Somehow the Sunday bikinis at Waikiki Beach seemed unreal
after the reality of where I have visited.
        Maybe if I had not been to Vietnam I would not feel
quite so haunted. Vietnam is not Korea, that isolated peninsula
that looked as if it were a battlefield before the fighting began.
Not even like the fields of Flanders I have seen, where memories
of mortar have eliminated trees and grass forever. The
Vietnamese, so fragile and fantasy-like, remind me of the
Christmas toys you shake and the snow comes down on a
Swiss village. They are small and fairy-like. If only I had not
seen the green fields, cut like an English lawn. If only I had
not heard the thunder of the artillery. If only I could have been
convinced by someone somewhere that the killing would some
day bring a meaningful peace to the gentle hills, the warm
beaches, and those lovely girls floating on the backs of
motorbikes and scooters and the families on a Sunday outing in
Saigon.
        Now the names in the news accounts will have personal
meaning. The kind of plane. The kind of pilot. No longer
statistics. Each one, I swear, dedicated to his own cause, no
matter how vague. And there is that matter of war itself. Pretty
heady stuff for a quick flight into fantasy. But I am convinced
it is deep and strong in the human character. I remember the
weapons officer on the destroyer. He talked of the exhilaration
of killing. He meant it. And now he will turn to God and the
Church. Too much exhilaration. Too much killing. I heard
many soldiers and seamen tell me, "This is my job. I am a
warrior."

This war—my war now, for I have been there—is a war without end. It is the unfinished symphony of terror. How will we remove the graveyard of metal that has been dropped on the doll people?

Holly, I've got to leave you a world. No adult should create a world dedicated to destroying its young. And yet I cannot see the end. So here, somewhere over the Pacific, coming home, I must finish my last letter with no more final solution than to say let us pray, and if we must, let us cry.

And so the letters to Holly concluded. There would be tears enough. And what was accomplished? Fifty thousand young American lives cut down. Millions of Vietnamese displaced, hundreds of thousands dead. A new agony on earth, the boat people. A demi-holocaust in Cambodia, an entire nation starving. America is mourning. Where were the days of wine and roses?

I have said that a motion picture is a fragment of time. Sadly, it can also be a lie. The film I went to Vietnam to make left me with a feeling of anger. The people around me at ABC had a John Wayne kind of product in mind. The script for the narrative began with sonorous sounds: "The South China Sea, key to the Orient, to Vietnam! To hold this sea the great powers of the world have given their treasure and their men, none more zealously than we." I protested, but no one seemed to be listening.

The half truths of the film told nothing. The great Canadian humourist, Stephen Leacock, once said, "The thing about a half truth compared with a whole truth is that it's like half a brick—it's easier to throw than a whole one."

I had watched the magenta plumes of smoke drifting from cannons on the South China Sea after the shells had killed, and had looked at them forming clouds as delicate as an Acapulco after-glow at sunset. I had actually sat and admired the colours. But I knew this had to be my last war, my only war, my departure from the ugliness created by man. I had to find the positive forces that made man lofty or I could not keep up my work in films.

I tried the other side. Maybe among the war protesters I would find meaning. I was hired to make a film with the leading poet of protest, Bob Dylan. I found to my amazement that I was considered part of the Establishment by the sad-eyed, confused singer. He refused to work with me and decided to make a film on his own. After an all-night screening session, attended by the Beatles, the superstars of the era, we decided a collaboration was impossible. Since I was handed a cheque for $5,000, I was able to remark to Dylan that if he made the film on his own it would never be seen. I was right. Dylan has since lost about a million dollars on his film, but found Jesus.

The times they were a-changin' and Dylan had composed the perfect lyrics for this brutal time in history. It was obvious that much would never be the same again. The authority of the old, represented so vividly in the White House I came to know, in the military I saw in Vietnam, could no longer hold society together. And the aimless young, so confident yet so uncertain, were truly just blowin' in the wind.

The past. Find beauty, find meaning in the past—this was clear to me. It was as if my father were whispering, "Listen . . . listen to the lyrics of history. Listen and maybe you can create your own song."

CHAPTER ELEVEN

Hall of Kings:

How I came to be buried in the Abbey

T here are Dickens and Kipling and there's me. Part of me is buried in Westminster Abbey. In the same way as Thomas Hardy is split up, with his body under the stones of the Abbey and his heart buried in the countryside he loved, giving rise to the rhyme, "I and my heart—we lie apart." So it came to pass that part of me would be there forever.

In most events you cannot find the exact point when things began. They more or less happen. But I can remember the moment for me. I had been in London and was to have an early dinner with a brilliant English actress of whom I was very fond, Billie Whitelaw. I went to pick her up backstage at the Old Vic after a matinee. There was to be an evening performance, so there was little time for dinner. I thought we would walk, but it began to rain. We found a cab and jumped in, not knowing where to go. As it spun by the old building, Billie called, "Stop the cab. We'll visit the Abbey." I objected. "I hate old churches."

"Dear Harry, this is different." Billie's voice seemed to carry all of England with it. I reluctantly went along. Because of the rain and the hour, the Abbey was almost deserted. A kind of chill followed me. Some will tell you it was the ghost we were later to meet. Others might suggest that, when the mind gets hot with inspiration, the air around pushes you like a sail. I started to get excited.

They were all there: the empire builders, the fathers of Western freedom, defenders of the faith, political giants, kings and queens, the men and women who gave lyrics to our language. I moved from tomb to tomb, encountering almost everyone I had ever heard about or been influenced by. (Hello, Chaucer! How are you, Milton?) Over there, the choir was beginning evensong, and the boys' voices were like the soothing sound of peace. By the time I had arrived at the grave of Browning, I knew I had found something special for me. This is his inscription:

Robert Browning—May 7th, 1812 to December 12th, 1889.
His wife, Elizabeth Barrett is buried in Florence, Italy, 1806—1861.

I thought, imagine what is suggested by a simple inscription, the drama and the romance of those lives. If only the inscriptions could speak. If only . . . well, why not? Suppose I had two of the great actors of the world there, at that very spot. One at either end of the tomb, enacting the words, beginning with "I love your verses with all my heart, and I love you too," and on and on. Would it work? Could I ask the mind to accept these spirits brought to life, not in costume, but timeless. I wanted to try. I knew then that I had found a form that all my professional history was preparing me for. (Many years later the *Los Angeles Times* was to call the form "Raskymentary" for want of some other description.) It would be drama and documentary mixed with the greatest ease and beauty. I caught my breath and said, "Yes, Billie, yes, everyone, this is different." What a cast of characters! What a stage! Now I had to figure out how to do it.

I must confess that the moment that the Abbey became a set in my mind, I knew that a film based on it would win an Emmy. I had no question about it. But I would need all my St. Clair Avenue street sense to pull it off. First I decided to make it a news event. How do you take one of the world's oldest churches and make it news? Well, as it happens, it was in the year 1066 that the church was built. The designer of the Bayeux tapestry included a large picture of the church. I argued that you couldn't let an event like that pass by without marking it—a 900-year-old news event. This was 1966.

This is the approach I sold to Elmer Lower, head of ABC News. He had once sent a telegram to me in Vietnam, "Bring back a bell ringer." What he meant, as it turned out, was bring back a very good film. I went to Tiffany's and bought Elmer a little gold bell for his desk, and with it I brought an outline for a film on the Abbey. I don't know if it was the bell or the outline, but he allotted enough money for me to go off to London and research a script.

Once in England I had to convince the powers of the Abbey to let me in with camera crews. There was great opposition to the idea. It was mid-summer and the busiest year since the coronation because of the 900th anniversary. I was rejected. Okay, try again. Somehow I made contact with Prince Philip's people. I argued it would be a great event for the Church of England. You should have heard me as an evangelist. Finally a couple of church officials leaned on the dean of Westminster, whose name was the unlikely Dean Abbott. And so word was passed down the line. A little prayer helped. I even agreed to one difficult condition without giving it proper consideration: filming was to take place only at night, and every day 1,000 folding chairs would be returned in place for the first dawn mass.

I began the chase for an on-camera host and narrator to give the language the right sound and to add some glamour. On the male side, I turned to all the various "sirs": Sir Alec Guinness, Sir Ralph Richardson, Sir Michael Redgrave, Sir John Gielgud, and even Sir Laurence Olivier, who responded politely, "I am afraid the complete absence of any time at my disposal makes it impossible for me to consider your most kind and thoughtful suggestion." I decided on James Mason, who turned out to be just the right mixture of style, composure, voice, authority and friendliness. It became the first of several collaborations with one of the world's greatest actors.

On the female side, the task was more complex. At first I went in a rather large way for Vanessa Redgrave. She had recently starred in a film called *Morgan,* in which she seemed to be the personification of grace and intelligence. She was having a big season in the West End doing *The Prime of Miss Jean Brodie*. I went backstage in pursuit. Alas, alack. How films can fool. The eyes—those watery deep eyes that had haunted me from the screen in *Morgan*—were in real life merely myopic. Her glasses were so thick I had the distinct impression that I was talking to her through a Coca-Cola bottle. And when I told her I had done a film with Fidel, I discovered that she didn't want to talk about acting or Mary, Queen of Scots. Revolution! She was obviously a fanatic. I have never forgotten that long, shocking backstage meeting. In fact, it went on so long that my car was hauled away to the police department. One good thing did come of it. Vanessa recommended her sister, Lynn, who had not yet done her famous *Georgy Girl*. For the second female part I had an acceptance from the fiery Irish first lady of the stage, Siobhan McKenna.

I remember when the lights were being hoisted into place that dark night in the Abbey. There was an eerie calm. I sat in the centre of the great church and watched 24 10-kilowatt lights hoisted into the dark upper cloisters where few men ever go. "It's mine, all mine," I can recall saying. I said a quiet Yiddish prayer, which may have seemed out of context, but I felt I had conquered something mighty when those lights rode off to the heights. I was the kid in command.

I hired some of the great minds of England to advise me. There was the poet, John Betjeman, who was an expert on old churches. From King's College came John Crow, a brilliant scholar of the English language. And from Dorset the gentle Lord David Cecil, who talked of having Queen Elizabeth's stockings still hanging at the family home—the first Queen Elizabeth, that is. His ancestor had been her most trusted aide. It was Lord David who told me in a pub that William Blake's famous hymn, "Jerusalem," was really quite lusty:

> Bring me my bow of burning gold
> Bring me my arrows of desire.

A lot of Sunday school ladies had been misled.

He also found for me an obscure poem by Thomas Hardy, which seemed to capture the essence of greatness in life. It has always been one of my favourite parts of the film.

> When the Present has latched its postern behind my tremulous stay
> And the May month flaps its glad green leaves like wings,
> Delicate-filmed as new-spun silk, will the neighbours say,
> 'He was a man who used to notice such things.'
> The dewfall hawk comes crossing the shades to alight
> Upon the wind-warped upland thorn, a gazer might think
> 'To him this must have been a familiar sight.'
> If I pass during some nocturnal blackness, mothy and warm,
> When the hedgehog travels furtively over the lawn,
> One may say, 'He strove that such innocent creatures should come to no harm,
> But he could do little for them; and now he is gone.'
> If, when hearing that I have been stilled at last, they stand at the door,
> Watching the full-starred heavens that winter sees,
> Will his thought rise on those who will meet my face no more,
> 'He was one who had an eye for such mysteries.'
> And will any say when my bell of quittance is heard in the gloom,
> And a crossing breeze cuts a pause in its outrollings,
> Till they rise again, as they were a new bell's boom,
> 'He hears it not now, but used to notice such things.'

A shooting script was finally put together, so we could begin this enormous task; take the crust of time, the wisdom of ages, the poetry of a people and commit it to film. Certainly the opening description read in lofty terms:

PROLOGUE

> *(The camera tilts down from the magnificent gothic arches of the nave. We zoom in towards the gold and royal red arches of the "screen." We follow through under the screen and roam the majesty of the ceiling in the choir, and in montage we see the setting of colour, pageantry and past, ending on the coronation of Queen Elizabeth II. The choir of Westminster Abbey sings Handel's "The sound is gone out" from the "Messiah.")*

JAMES MASON (*voice over*):

> It is a place for all seasons. For almost a millenium, it has enshrined the history of an island race . . . the beauty of its language.
>
> *(The camera zooms in on the magnificent rose window. Our theme reaches a note of triumph and the opening credits are superimposed: "Hall of Kings.")*

Hold it! Not quite so easy. There were questions that had to be asked and answered quickly. If England has provided us with the Shakespearean turn of phrase, it has also provided us with a labour code with various sub-clauses. Question: with an English crew, if you begin work at midnight, when is tea time? Question: how do you have a hot dinner at 3:30 a.m. in a country that can't manage to serve you lunch if you happen to be hungry at 3:30 p.m.? The problem was solved with a portable kitchen that cooked meals all night long in the Dean's Yard, not far from the tomb of the mad monk.

There is also the question of the ghost of Westminster Abbey. Now I must tell you that I do not believe in ghosts, or did not until then. If any setting rates one, certainly the Abbey, with its collection of passionate souls, has claim before many a place. Our visitor came the night of the big scene at the Browning grave. Siobhan was delivering her deeply felt lines, "How do I love thee." The crew was intense and involved. Tears were in her eyes.

Suddenly there was a creaking sound. Sound man Adrian Klein looked pained and puzzled. I shouted for silence, but none of us had moved. Then we noticed the giant oak door behind us, weighing about half a ton and leading to the ancient Saint Faith's Chapel. It had opened wide. We had not touched it. There was no draft. The door takes the strength of a young man to open. On two other occasions at about 3 a.m., our ghost's visiting hour, the door opened mysteriously. One of our group saw a flash of brilliant light in the room that was in total darkness. You explain it. I cannot.

Every attempt to film a magnificent marble figure of Death in the Abbey was thwarted. Each time we would pan on it the film fogged. One Abbey official later told me, "Oh, we've been trying to photograph it for years. The film always ghosts or fogs. No technician has yet been able to explain this." Then there was that cool wind that crept in behind when there was no place to have the wind come from.

I can recall reporting our adventures to W.R.J. Pullen, esquire, L.I.B., F.C.I.S. (I put in all those initials, even though I am not sure for what they stand, to show you that he is a serious sort of chap.) He was the receiver general and had his offices in the Dean's Yard. As he was a sober fellow, I thought he would laugh. Instead he said, "Oh yes, perhaps the mad monk. You know one of his problems is that he walks off the ground by about a foot, because the Abbey floor used to be higher by a foot. He seems to be harmless, though. No extra charge."

We didn't have to cook for our ghost. We hoped he wouldn't play too many pranks. Outside of a few shots turning green when he seemed to want to get into the picture, he presented few problems. But the tough electricians would not walk alone after the episode of the door.

Of course, Siobhan seemed to have with her all the spirits of Ireland. I really don't know who else could have pulled off the most complex bit of staging I tried, which was her playing Mary, Queen of Scots addressing the effigy of Queen Elizabeth. Would people accept a diologue between a flesh-and-blood actress and a stone statue?

> *(The camera tilts up from the stone face of Elizabeth I. Standing in the half light, part substance, part fancy is Miss McKenna as Mary, Queen of Scots. She pleads to Elizabeth. It is her finest hour.)*

ELIZABETH I:

> I did not think the Queen, my sister, would have consented to my death, who am not subject to your law, and jurisdiction; but, seeing her pleasure is so, death shall be to me most welcome.
>
> I will accuse no one; nay I pardon, with a sincere heart, everyone, even as I desire everyone may grant forgiveness to me, God the first, but I know that you, more than anyone, ought to feel at heart the honour and dishonour of your own blood, and that moreover, of a Queen and the daughter of a King.
>
> *(Gently the camera moves down to the stone face of Elizabeth I. Then in close-up her voice answers.)*

If I could but have preserved her life without giving my own.
But I was not at liberty to be cruel to myself. I know I have
but the body of a weak and feeble woman; but I have the heart
and stomach of a King, and a King of England too.
(The camera joins the music in this meeting which never
happened in life except by correspondence, and it captures the
mood of the figure of Mary, Queen of Scots.)

When the history of great theatrical moments is recorded, I hope
they find a small spot for Siobhan's acting the role of Charlotte Bronte.
We were scheduled to begin this particular rendition as usual at midnight.
The English technicians had checked that their hot tea would be ready.
Midnight passed with the famous gongs of Big Ben nearby, telling us
that London had survived another day and a new day was beginning. So
did 1 a.m. come and go, an echo across the Thames embankment. Then
1:30 a.m. passed. The technicians went for their tea and hot sausage.
Around 2 a.m. the great lady arrived. She looked a little, well, she
looked . . . let's say, strange.

She announced, "I have been preparing all day. And you know
what I think?"

"What?" I asked rather innocently.

"I think I should play her lying down here on the floor," Siobhan
proclaimed.

I gulped, a large 2 a.m. gulp. "Yes. Fine. A splendid idea.
But . . ."

"But what?" she asked in a demanding way, like Saint Joan
asking the infidels.

"But if you play her right there, you will be lying exactly on Mr.
Dickens, the best-read writer in the English language."

"All right," she said indignantly. "Then we'll do it your way."

And so just about dawn, as the first nuns were coming in for
morning prayer, with the great Abbey an echo chamber of flowing language, we recorded the perfect take of the perfect performance.

(Camera pans over from James Mason to reveal Siobhan again
in the corner of the Abbey close to the Bronte plaque. Once
again she is in that kind of half light to give the feeling that she
has stepped out from the covers of a book.)
CHARLOTTE BRONTE:
My sister, Emily, had a particular love for the moors, and there
is not a knoll of heather, not a branch of fern, not a young
bilberry leaf, not a fluttering lark or linnet, but reminds me of
her. The distant prospects were Anne's delight, and when I

look round she is in the blue tints, the pale mists, the waves
and shadows of the horizon. In the hill country silence their
poetry comes by lines and stanzas into my mind; once I loved
it; now I dare not read it:

Riches I hold in light esteem,
and love I laugh to scorn,
And lust of fame was but a dream
Then vanished with the morn.
And if I pray, the only prayer
That moved my lips for me
Is 'Leave the heart that now I bear,
and give me liberty!'
Yea, as my swift days near their goal
'tis all that I implore;
In life and death a chainless soul
With courage to endure.

*(With Siobhan speaking the last lines of the poem, camera now
pans gently to the plaque on the wall, which contains the
words "With courage to endure." Camera now comes back to
Mason who is standing beneath sculpture of Garrick, and
during next piece it pans up to statue, which shows a figure in
front of a parted curtain.)*

JAMES MASON (*on camera*):
There are those who made the words, and those who made
them come alive. When David Garrick died, his funeral train
stretched from London's theatrical district all the way to the
Abbey. Here the figure of the actor stares out from parted curtains
above the inscription: "As Shakespeare rose then to expand
his fame, wide o'er this breathing world, a Garrick came."
Oliver Goldsmith's pencil was less glowing. *(Dissolve through
to Garrick in various poses.)*
Like an ill-judging beauty, his colours he spread
And beplaister'd with rouge, his own natural red,
On the stage he was natural, simple, affecting,
'Twas only that, when he was off, he was acting.

When it comes to actors, they each have their moments when
performance takes them beyond the possible. There was such a moment
with lovely Lynn Redgrave. The idea was simple. We would find her
alone in the great Abbey hall, a solo figure, flesh among the rock and
stone and wood, and her lines would come from Queen Victoria at the
moment of her coronation. There were problems, of course. Queen Victoria, grandmother of the Empire, stood four foot nine when she stood

1.

2. My father and mother shortly after their arrival to Canada before my birth. Circa 1925.

3. Baba Bayla (centre) comes to visit. Circa 1930.

4. Left to right: I, my mother Perl, sister Dorothy, brother Ed. Circa 1940.

5. My parents and sister Dorothy in front of our St. Clair Avenue store. Circa 1935.

6. Young Harry (left) and brother Ed. Circa 1935.

7. Graduation from the University of
   Toronto, 1949, just before my mother's death.

8. A gathering of the Rasky clan. I'm third from right,
   back row. Circa 1940.

9. My father (right) in the McKay
   Street *schul*. Circa 1958.

10. My father visiting New York.
    1957.

11. Opening of the Stratford Festival. With Alec
    Guinness and the entire CBC film operation. 1953.

12. I begin my travels. Germany, 1955.

13. Young producer of "UN in Action" for CBS with announcer George
    Hicks and Larry LeSeuer. 1957.

14. Trying to be Hemingway. Panama, 1960.

15. In the jungles of Panama for NBC.

16. Fidel Castro with aide Dr. René Vallejo (far right). Havana, 1964.

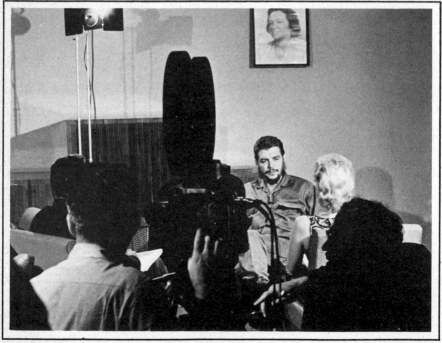

17. With Ché Guevara in his only filmed interview.

18. Outside the Carlos Marx School. Havana, 1964.
    Note the damage to the photograph.

19. Off the coast of Vietnam filming the shelling
    of a village by Americans. 1966.

20. Cruising the Mekong River with U.S. navy
    advisor. Vietnam, 1966.

21. Ready for action.
    Hall of Kings, 1966.

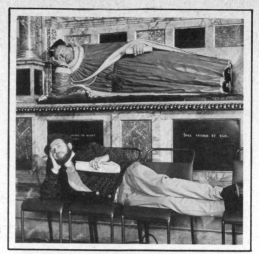

22. Posing with an adopted ancestor in
    Westminster Abbey.

23. With my wife Arlene
    receiving Emmy for
    Hall of Kings, 1967.

24. With Lynn Redgrave, preparing for
    Queen Victoria's coronation speech.

25. Selecting a shot of the altar at St. Peter's Basilica. *Upon this Rock*, 1970.

26. Everyone is Italian but me. Fifth from right is famous cameraman Aldo Tonti.

27. Checking Michelangelo's lines of the *Pieta*.

28. Orson and I.

29. Niagara-on-the-Lake for *The Wit and World of G. Bernard Shaw*, 1971, after my return to Canada.

30. Christopher Plummer and film crew at the home of Shaw in England.

31. Sam Jaffe as the prophet Isaiah in *Next Year in Jerusalem*, 1972.

32. Lorne Greene and I preparing for the ''destruction'' of Jerusalem.

33. Receiving the ''Nelly'' award for *Next Year in Jerusalem*, 1975.

34. My brother Tennessee and I touring New Orleans. 1973.

35. Opening of *Homage to Chagall*
    in New York, 1977.

36. Filming in Chagall's garden. France, 1976.

37. Arthur Miller on home ground. Connecticut, 1979.

38. With Arthur Miller.

39.

40.

41.

42. At home with my family: Arlene, Holly and Adam.

at all. Lynn was a foot or so taller. So we sat Lynn, with the baby fat
of young beauty on her, on the throne to recite the soliloquy. Here is the
way it went with Mason's introduction.

JAMES MASON (*on camera*):
>St. Edward's Chair has been used at every coronation since that
>of Edward II in 1308, built around the Stone of Scone, which
>Edward I captured from the Scots. The choice of wood, rather
>than metal, proved to be a dubious one, for during the
>seventeenth and eighteenth centuries the chair was not well
>protected. Visitors, seeking their own immortality, carved their
>names in the oak, and if you look closely, you will see on
>the seat itself the inscription of a small boy, proudly proclaiming,
>"Peter Abbott slept in this chair, July 5, 1800." So Peter
>Abbott's name is now in the company of kings.
>*(The trumpets sound and camera pulls back from the crown of
>the portrait of the young Queen Victoria.)*

JAMES MASON (*voice over*):
>It is the year 1838, the 28th of June. A 19-year-old girl is
>crowned Queen. Some say there was never a time like it. Queen
>Victoria herself remembered her very thoughts.
>*(We dissolve through a lone figure sitting in the spot exactly
>where the coronation chair would be placed for the coronation.
>She is dressed simply and begins her vivid account. There
>should be a marvellous feeling of wonder about this scene with
>this one figure against the impressive backdrop of the gold
>and glitter of tapestry of the high altar. She is in fact at that
>moment Victoria.)*

VICTORIA I:
>I reached the Abbey amid deafening cheers at a little after half
>past eleven. I was seated upon St. Edward's Chair where the
>Dalmatic robe was clasped round me by the Lord Great
>Chamberlain. Then followed all the various things; and last of
>those things the crown being placed upon my head which was,
>I must own, a most beautiful impressive moment; *all* the peers
>and peeresses put on their coronets at the same instant. My
>excellent Lord Melbourne who stood very close to me throughout
>the whole ceremony, was completely overcome at this moment
>and very much affected; he gave me such a kind, and I may
>say fatherly look. Later he said to me "You must be very
>tired." He spoke of the weight of the robes, etc., etc., the
>coronets and he turned round to me with tears in his eyes and
>said *so* kindly: "And you did it beautifully—every part of

it, with so much taste; it's a thing that you can't give a person
advice upon: it must be left to a person." When it was over,
the shouts, which were very great, the drums, the trumpets, the
firing of the guns all at the same instant rendered the spectacle
most imposing. The enthusiasm, affection, and loyalty were
really touching, and I shall ever remember this day as the
proudest of my life!
*(Camera zooms back: trumpets. Sound—actual recording of
coronation—"God save the Queen. God save the Queen. God
save the Queen." We fade to black to end act one.)*

But it was James Mason himself who gave the show its special
quality. Mason is one of those actors who does not act to you, does not
preach to you, does not perform to you. He talks to you. He has the
capacity to address the camera as if he is about to have tea or a friendly
drink with it. I know no other actor who has quite this capacity. I remember one small speech about the lesser known folks who happen to
be buried there.

JAMES MASON:
Not everyone here discovered a continent or changed the world.
Some are known to but a few. Like Thomas Parr, who died in
1635, honoured for having, as he claimed, lived to an age of
152. Albany Charles Wallis, drowned at thirteen "being his
father's only hope." Elizabeth Atkinson, body laundress to
Queen Anne. Philip Clark, plumber to the church, 1707. Jonas
Hanway, who earned his niche in history as the first
Englishman to carry an umbrella. A boxer, a painter, someone
called "Long Meg," dozens of notables, now noted for
nothing, resting forever with the great.

After 40 nights, the filming finally concluded. Was it a joy? No,
it was a misery. The dampness of the stone seeped into my bones. I had
been fortunate enough to rent a spacious house from Kay Searle, wife
of the famous cartoonist, which was located next to the public Porchester
Baths. Each dawn I would drive my rented Jaguar to the baths and soak
in the sauna till my blood returned. A couple of times when the Jaguar
broke down, I was so exhausted I just called the rental company and said,
"Send another Jag and don't disturb me. Just put the keys in the milk
box. I can't be bothered." And each night there would be cables from
New York executives second-guessing my camera moves. But in my
mind the film was finished whole, and I would take no second opinion.

I returned angry cables, understanding fully that each time I endangered my position, but I was determined to finish it my way.

It even affected my family life. I sent my wife and Holly home because I had to concentrate totally. It was then that I learned that a certain amount of madness must go with a man who steps over that delicate boundary when he strives to become an artist. It is a tortured crossing. You can never return. And no matter where you are and with whom, from then on you are alone, alone with God, the greatest artist of all.

The passion was in the film. I do not think I have ever seen such total unanimity in reviews, leading off with the unqualified raves of Jack Gould in the *New York Times*. My favourite headline of all came from Denver's *Rocky Mountain News: HALL OF KINGS* VINDICATES MEDIUM.

But the most fascinating interpretation came from the top broadcasting scholar of North America, Eric Barnouw. The difference between a film statement and art is that art allows for personal involvement. This is the way he saw it in his book *The Image Empire*:

> In 1967 every subject tended to become Vietnam. Networks, with a haunted intensity, looked for safe documentary topics that might lure a sponsor, and during the year they came up with "Venice," "Nurses," "The Pursuit of Pleasure" and other subjects. But some seemingly remote topics turned out to be, in the context of the day, Vietnam. On ABC-TV B.F. Goodrich sponsored a magnificent film shot in Westminster Abbey, entitled *Hall of Kings* and starring James Mason, Lynn Redgrave and Siobhan McKenna. The film was the work of the Canadian Harry Rasky. Turning to history, he found he could convey feelings he had not been able to express in *Operation Sea War—Vietnam*. The men and women whose words rolled out so magnificently were concerned with empire—its rise and decline. Many were words of warning. From the gloom of Westminster Abbey emerged William Pitt, Earl of Chatham, crippled and near death, but rising to demand an end to a war in America: "If I were an American, as I am an Englishman, while a foreign troop was landed in my country I never would lay down my arms. Never! Never! Never!"
>
> And there was Kipling, who had once urged Englishmen to take up the "white man's burden" to subdue and lead "the lesser breeds," but now pleaded—in the words of "Recessional"—for a humble and a contrite heart. And there, like an early voice in the cause of "love, not war," was

Elizabeth Barrett, with verses she had sent to the poet Robert
Browning:
"The face of all the world is changed. I think
Since first I heard the footsteps of thy soul
Move still, oh, still beside me . . ."

And then there was the night of the Emmy Awards. I knew, as
I knew the moment I first stepped into the Abbey, that the film would
be nominated. At the New York banquet hall I was sitting beside my old
colleague, Howard K. Smith. We had worked together several times. I
had long admired his work as a foreign correspondent when he was
Murrow's man in Germany during World War II. He is generally a polite
Virginia gentleman. Somehow the subject turned to Vietnam. My passions
against the war were so strong that it was the only time I ever came close
to a fist fight in a public place—in this case with a live TV hook-up.
Fortunately for both of us, our wives were wiser. They intervened and
physically separated us. I was so flustered that when my category was
called, as John Chancellor was reading the nominations, I stood up to
get my award before my name was spoken. When someone asked me
later what I would have done if I had not won, I replied, "I would have
casually gone to the men's room, and probably been quietly sick."

In my acceptance speech I was able to quote from one of my
heroes from the film, and comment on the state of U.S. broadcasting and
its war-torn wrangling of the moment. Disraeli said, "I believe that the
man who does not look up will look down; and that the spirit that does
not dare to soar is destined perhaps to grovel. Sir, life is too short to be
little."

In retrospect, I realize that it was the tradition of my childhood,
force-fed by my family behind the store in those Depression days of the
thirties, which sustained me in the making of the film. Hardship would
have won, if somehow my father had not believed that he had to sustain
tradition to help us preserve ourselves. It was our link with the race, our
bond with history, our understanding of life. Without tradition I knew
I could never have stood there in the Abbey, watched those great 10-
kilowatt lights rise, and made the film that put me in the company of the
kings of power and the princes of poetry. I had to be true to my own
faith and put it in the film.

So it was that a ceremony attended by the ABC correspondent in
London, Louis Rukeyser, marked the occasion at which *Hall of Kings*
was buried in what is called "the most holy vault" in the Abbey, to be
opened in the year 2066 when the Abbey will be 1,000 years old, so that
other generations will see what was said. That is how I came to be buried
there—my film, that is, which is me.

CHAPTER TWELVE

Upon This Rock:

Orson, don't breathe so hard on the Pieta

Bob Hope, Jack Benny, Snowflake the white gorilla, Michelangelo and Orson Welles were my creative company in the late sixties. How I came to be involved in this odd mix of characters is part of the nature of being a non-fiction film-maker. I do not believe that we ever have cause for complaint, because the work is more like play than anything I can think of. It takes a person to the most colourful places and adds a collection of individuals with whom he would most like to have dinner, if not breakfast. However, no amount of glory ever seems to make it easier to launch new creative expeditions.

After the enormous success of *Hall of Kings,* which went on to pick up a dozen international prizes, including the Cine Gold Eagle, I would have thought that ABC might anxiously offer me a life-long contract. I submitted several film ideas, including a film profile on a great man of the past, George Bernard Shaw, and one on a fascinating man of the moment, Bobby Kennedy. The Shaw film was announced, but vanished as culture became a cursed word in U.S. network television. As for Bobby, at that time no executive to whom I talked thought him worthy of a film.

Fortunately Walter Schwimmer had come up with a project which had a certain kind of merit. He had convinced the government of Illinois to take its entire budget for its 150th birthday celebration, and put it into a film which I would produce for American television. Since it would involve a number of celebrities who had been involved with the state, we decided to call it *I Remember Illinois*. I don't remember too much about *I Remember Illinois*, except that I did briefly get to work with a few legendary men of American entertainment. Perhaps a few words should be said about each.

Anyone saying an unkind word about Bob Hope will get the back of my hand. Of course, we all grew up on the *Road* pictures, and I don't think I ever did my geography homework from Oakwood Collegiate without having him turned in on the radio. The voice of Jerry Colona and the image of Canadian tundra are welded somehow in my mind. Walrus moustaches in the snow. Hope agreed to be in the film because he spent some of the more important moments of his life in Illinois. We picked him up at a state fair and followed him around for a day, and he ad-libbed some of the best local jokes imaginable.

Then there was the nightmare that every film-maker dreads. By the time the sound tape travelled from Illinois to New York, the sound itself had vanished. Maybe it was the magnetic waves of the airplane, or perhaps it was the ghost of the Abbey past, but it was gone. I was placed in the uncomfortable position of having to call Hope and apologize, and ask him to do it again. His reaction? "Sure, when do you want me?" I caught him some weeks later and found him as friendly as possible. "Look," he said, "I'm on the road all the time with film crews. Those things happen. You should have seen what happened with the troops in Korea!" I never heard the end of the story. But ever since, Bob Hope and I send each other Christmas cards.

To say that Jack Benny was a pro is not to simplify, but to try to give you an idea of a man of values. Of course, Jack had a special feeling about Illinois. Waukegan, where he was born, had become a legendary place because of its constant repetition in Benny scripts. We decided to take him home to Waukegan and film a skit in the Jack Benny High School, a shrine to the man who had never finished school.

Benny's humour was directed always at himself. For the occasion he wrote an original skit which was performed with the usual precision before an invited audience. His timing was flawless. And what did he talk about as we sat backstage and waited? He spoke of his one great disappointment: that his father, Mr. Kaplinsky, had not lived to see his success after those early, painful days in Illinois. Jack, the gentleman.

For the occasion, Benny Goodman put together his famous trio, with Gene Krupa on drums and Teddy Wilson on piano. When we arrived in the studio, he heard Teddy at the piano, and said quickly, "It won't do." I asked what he meant, and he said simply that he would not go on with the piano that had been rented for the occasion. I argued that it was fine, and anyway people really had come to hear his great clarinet. "Hold everything," he said. He walked around to where cameraman

Jerry Feil was preparing the shot. "That camera," he said, "what kind is it?" I explained that it was the best, of course, the Arriflex. "Well," Goodman said, "that piano is a Somer. You do not have a Somer camera." He made his point. Rehearsal was delayed and a proper Steinway was found. And he made almost mythical music. If you wonder why people still pay to hear Benny Goodman when most of the other jazz greats have been laid to rest, think of that piano.

There was something almost mournful about taking Dave Garroway back to the old studio in Chicago where his television career had begun with "Garroway at Large." Here was the pioneer of intimate broadcasting. He had been able to pass himself right through the wires and tubes to appear on the home receiver, as if he had just come in for a private discussion. Since he had left "The Today Show," which he had originated, he had sort of fallen apart. In his New York apartment he sat and peered through a telescope, as if waiting for the call to arms, the summons to return which never came. He philosophized, "You know, it's really not true that you have to be nice to people on the way up, because when you're on your way down, falling fast, peering in those corporate offices, there's a whole new group there and you don't know any of them."

I thought it was time to try Hollywood. Hollywood is an imaginary place where a great number of people go not to complete their fantasies. They are encouraged to do so, but it all turns to candy floss and is just as durable. Only those who never have to touch the ground can sustain themselves. The rest are destroyed or are dreamwalkers.

The idea was that the script I had written during long hours in New York might become a film. It was based on the beautiful, tender book called *The Children at the Gate* by Edward Lewis Wallant, who had also written a classic work, *The Pawnbroker*. Wallant's book had pursued me for some years. One way or another I found a way of obtaining an option on it. I considered it then, as now, one of the most important works of our time. I had sent copies of it and my script to a hundred places.

On a trip to Hollywood, I managed to see Gordon Stulberg, head of the CBS film division, Cinema Center. He read the book and said he thought it would make an important film. A deal was made and I headed west. Naturally I took a bungalow at the Beverly Hills Hotel. I soon realized that my entire advance would be gone in a week, so I rented a house—with a pool, of course—moved out my family and waited. And waited some more. Every day I went to a studio office, and parked my studio car in my studio spot. I discovered that all the men in the offices down the long studio corridor were also waiting to make films.

First my own script, which stayed very close to the beauty of Mr. Wallant's words, was discarded with the comment, "What we need is a film writer." I don't quite know what I was supposed to be. There were endless meetings with various poor souls who had come to Hollywood generations before, perhaps with a touch of originality now long gone. These empty, hollow faces greeted me almost daily. Each hoped this would be "the big one."

But from the hollow men came hollow words. And I began to live the Hollywood way, each day taking just a little more time in the pool and the sun. Sooner or later a writer or two turned out another film-script version of the book which basically needed no change. And my tan deepened and a certain blankness of mind began to overtake me. What can I remember? A ridiculous argument over the size of the offices; a cynical but accurate warning from a fellow director, Alex Singer, who told me to find something else; and from the fine writer of *A Fine Madness,* Elliot Baker, an even more accurate assessment: "You can't beat the system." Somewhere still they are all growing, aging, vegetating in the vegetation.

After six months my wife said, "We're leaving." I arranged anything I could find to make an exit. Someone was doing the National Georgraphic series out there, and I signed up to make the film *The Great Zoos of the World.* Those animals and birds carried me to far-off places away from the palm trees and celluloid minds. I still can't pass a camel without having a certain appreciation for its humpy kindness.

About the brief interlude into the animal world, I would like to observe that the men who run the various zoos are among the world's most interesting. Each is autocrat of his animal kingdom, keeper of his animal garden, king of his cages. The beginning of the film was quite beautiful, and it happened by accident while filming at the primitive Central Park Zoo in New York. A group of blind children were there that day. The expression on their faces as they touched an animal to find out what he was like is something I will never forget. If you are blind, what does a goat look like? I filmed them finding out.

A word must be said about the world's most fascinating creature. She is alive and well in the zoo in Barcelona. She is an albino, a pure white gorilla named Snowflake. As we filmed her, she reached behind her and threw dung at us. It missed me but landed on the camera. Snowflake reminded me a great deal of some of the people I had met in Hollywood, but she was certainly more honest.

I was unable to conclude the work on the zoo film because I received from Rome an offer I could not refuse.

The greatest *shul* of them all, the largest temple, the vast basilica of St. Peter's was to be my next subject. Stanley Abrams, a cheerful grey man from New York, who had spent a few fortunes in his time, had seen my *Hall of Kings* and wanted me to do the same for the immense Catholic shrine. In Rome he had befriended Archbishop William Carew, the Pope's English-speaking secretary.

To get permission, a little political intrigue had to be used. It was Carew's job to place before the Pope all the urgent matters of the Catholic world. Among them he placed a letter, signed by Abrams, requesting permission to bring our crew and actors into the holiest of holy places. The Pope initialled the letter, and a papal stamp was placed upon it. Now to this day no one knows if he was merely indicating that he had received the letter, or if he was indeed offering his blessing for filming to begin. We just assumed the blessing and so that was a start.

I remember my first reaction upon entering St. Peter's in Rome. I sank to my knees for meditation, as I would do in any house of God. But I must admit that while down there I started thinking about the lighting problems. How to translate the epic building to film? How to produce the feeling of awe that stuns you as you walk through the massive door, where the Roman daylight gives way to created eternity. I had some experience in this sort of undertaking with *Hall of Kings*. But St. Peter's was seven times the size of Westminster Abbey. It was as big as two football fields: 615 feet long and 434 feet high. Horace Greeley was not so far off when he called it ''a Niagara of a building''—all in need of light.

The plan was to dramatize the life and times of the building. The most imposing cast of actors was selected: Sir Ralph Richardson, Dame Edith Evans, Dirk Bogarde and Orson Welles. The key man, of course, was the cameraman. Perhaps the greatest of Italian cinematographers, Aldo Tonti, was selected. He had worked with and, in fact, had trained most of the top Italian directors. Being an Italian and a Roman, he felt that the assignment was an honour. Together with his son Luciano, Tonti selected special equipment and designed some as well: a giant crane with weights and balances which gave motion like music (an army of stage hands dragged it up the steps of St. Peter's), and a gadget for the 35 mm. camera which would allow for a 360 degree movement in a vertical position to embrace the texture of the immense dome.

For the most impressive scene, the opening of the centre doors to reveal the entire church, we engaged the help of the entire staff of technical people at St. Peter's—almost 100 technicians—and used enough power to light a small city. Somehow the fact that the entire crew was Italian seemed to help. They were inspired, wanting to show the world that this was their place and they understood it better than anyone.

And then there was the jewel of St. Peter's, the one part that seemed to defy all technical possibilities: Michelangelo's *Pieta*. In my opinion, it is the world's single most beautiful art object. Each night, night after night, Tonti and I would stop to admire it on our way to work. Each night for weeks we studied it, considered its challenge. Between us we had at one time or another filmed some of the greatest people of the world. But how to approach the master, Michelangelo? I had found some obscure writings by Michelangelo in my months of research at libraries in New York City and in the Vatican archives. In his deep poetry the secret of the *Pieta* emerged. Tonti read it in Italian to get the subtle meanings.

At last, we began. "How many lights?" I asked.

"One," Tonti said. "One shaft of light." One light. As if the sun had selected one special ray. All filming of the *Pieta* was done from above, the way Michelangelo had carved it. We saw it the way he made it, the way it has never been seen since. From the height of the crane, the special value of the relationship between mother and son can be seen: the face of Jesus, the face of Mary, forever in silent conversation.

A letter I had found also explains why the figures had the special look and age they had. Let Michelangelo tell you himself:

> Do you know that chaste women remain much more fresh than
> those who are not chaste? How much more, therefore, must
> this be true of the Virgin, who never entertained the least
> immodest thought which might have troubled her body. I would
> put this even more strongly. I believe that this freshness and
> flower of youth which she received in a natural manner was
> preserved for her in a supernatural one, so that the virginity
> and the eternal purity of the Mother of God could be
> demonstrated to the world. Such a miracle was not necessary
> for the Son. Quite the contrary, for it had to be shown that the
> Son of God was made incarnate in man and that he had
> suffered all that men suffer except sin. It was not necessary to
> make the human disappear behind the divine, but it was better
> rather to let the human follow its nature in such a way that he
> should appear to have the age that he really had.

Michelangelo seemed to speak to us himself as we filmed every detail of his masterpiece:

> The Living image
> Lasts longer in the hard Alpine stone
> When godlike art has, with superior thought,

The limbs and motions in idea conceived,
A simple form, in humble clay achieved,
Is the first offering into being brought:
Then stroke on stroke from out the living rock,
Its promised work the practised chisel brings,
And into life a form so graceful springs,
That none can fear for it—time's rudest shock.

For the recording of Michelangelo's exquisite poetry, I had Orson read it directly at the site of the *Pieta,* which at that time was uncovered. In fact, we could crawl all over it. The sound man stopped him. "Please Meester Welles, you are breathing so hard on the *Pieta*—a little less breath," he pleaded.

"I've been doing sound since before you were born, dear boy," said Welles, dismissing him. "Get on with it. I know exactly how to breathe."

Of course he did. Many people have asked how he was to work with. How does one direct the greatest epic director of them all? It was *getting* him that was complex. Orson likes to do his own deals. He lives high and mighty and always seems in need of ready cash. The genius of twenty is still in there somewhere among all the flab and bluff, and anyone who ever confronts a camera must salute his lasting achievement. There will never be anything quite like *Citizen Kane* again.

When we decided to go after him, he was in fact editing one of his own works at the same studio in Rome, the Rizzoli studio, which overlooks the Forum and the Coliseum and the eternity of it all. The script was delivered to him by Abrams, and Welles promised an answer by dinner time. Six o'clock passed, . . . then 7:00, then 8:00, then 8:30. I suggested to Stanley that he go to retrieve the script. He was quite nervous about confronting the great actor and his booming self. I went down and merely asked for the script. It was handed to me in a somewhat dumbfounded manner.

Fifteen minutes later Welles was upstairs in my office with an angry twinkle in his eyes. "Give me back that script. I never said what time I have dinner. With that cast and that setting, of course I'll do it." He laughed like a cigar-loving Santa Claus.

For each of his evenings with us, he was, as they say, a pussycat. He loved doing it and was as helpful as possible, always aware which lens was being used, how to move his great bulk with grace. While waiting for a shot one night, I thought I would make some between-the-scenes small talk. I said, "I don't suppose you ever heard of it but I began my career at CBS trying to do something similar to your famous *War of the Worlds*. It was a film called *The Day Called 'X'*."

"What do you mean I never heard of it. I sued CBS and it cost me $25,000 in legal fees and I lost." I suggested that his case was rather good, but I had never known until that moment that the suit had taken place. There in St. Peter's, in front of the *Pieta,* we became friends.

The cast was well, let's just say thrilling. Ralph Richardson, perhaps one of the half-dozen greatest living actors, acted as a guide and host. But he started badly. For several days Ralph was having trouble. He could not remember his lines and seemed to be speaking the words indifferently. I mentioned the problem to Abrams. One night Ralph arrived at 228 Apia Antiqua, the beautiful shrine of a house that I had been able to rent for my Roman winter. "I understand, old boy," he said, as if playing a British colonel at his club, "that you are unhappy with my services."

"That's not it, Ralph," I said. "You may be one of the greatest actors of all time. Maybe the greatest. But there is a problem in what you are doing."

"But, dear boy, don't you understand? You've asked me to do the most impossible role."

What do you mean?" I asked, somewhat stunned.

"You've asked me to play myself. And who am I? After spending my entire life on stage, how should I know who I am."

Next day and from then on, he was magnificent. Each time I gave him a new character to play. "Today, Ralph, you are one of those Italian guides who grabs you, trying to make a few lire from an innocent tourist." Ralph loved it, and I loved his performance.

When Dame Edith Evans arrived in Rome to play Queen Christina, she was like a schoolgirl off on a weekend of adventure. She was eighty, and like a bubbly, aged champagne of grace. Her scene was filmed over two nights. On the second night, when she invited me into her dressing lounge in a portable unit, I blushed a little because the wonderful old lady was in a flimsy slip. "Well, what do we play tonight?" she asked. I replied, "You look so young and full of excitement, suppose we do a scene of Juliet." She thought that would be just fine. But we filmed Christina, the crusty queen who gave up the crown for the cross.

During the early part of the filming, I came upon a painting of Bonnie Prince Charlie, one of the few notables buried in the church who is not a pope. I said, "It's amazing how much he looks like Dirk Bogarde." I was then advised that Dirk lived on the outskirts of Rome, and I convinced him to engage in a dramatic dialogue with Ralph at the tomb which reads, "They were the last of the Stuart race."

When it was his night to perform, Dirk joined us at the restaurant we reserved nightly. He would not eat. He admitted that he was too nervous. But his performance was full of the Bogarde magic. He was able to bring tears to the setting of stone. He explained later his device: "I learned to play the pauses." For a couple of weeks afterward, Dirk would call me at home, merely to find out how the film was progressing. He is truly a compassionate actor.

With this group of actors, and with St. Peter's as my set, I would have to rank the experience as one of the most satisfying of my career. Each night as the sun was setting, Salvatore, the driver of the Mercedes, would pass the great monuments of time and history as we worked our way to St. Peter's. Then when dawn came, we would make the journey home, the dew silver against the pine, the sky more a dream than a reality.

I think we found what was best about the place. Many a tyrant had ruled in those walls, but great artists had left their art there, and there was at least one saint, Pope John. I tried to recapture his spirit. The contemporary doors by Giocomo Manzu were dedicated to him. They are canvasses of bronze. John himself observed:

> How extraordinary is the artist's hand which can create a living
> work. What matters is that you seek. Also that you love
> humanity. Otherwise, you wouldn't spend a lifetime creating it
> with your hands and your heart.

There's an old Roman saying, "If you ask me what is St. Peter's, I will tell you I am St. Peter's and St. Peter's is me." Certainly after 40 nights fighting to commit the largest temple of Christian worship to film, I felt the same. Considering that I once had hated old churches, I began to accept as my own the words of Robert Louis Stevenson who said, "I never weary of great churches. It is my favourite kind of mountain scenery. Mankind was never so happily inspired as when it made a cathedral."

St. Peter's is mighty, of course. The current architect told me that the design of the spectacular dome is such that mathematically he cannot figure out how the weight is contained. Michelangelo, who had no training as an architect, made it stand. I have a sense, after living in his great building and knowing on a daily basis his Pieta, that I really have met Michelangelo. There's a verse of his that is with me still.

> . . . and if anyone remembers me,
> He seems to dream; so quick and greedy is death.
> That what has been seems never to have been.

Back in New York, my enthusiasm began to wane after a half-hearted effort was made to launch the film *Upon This Rock* in motion-picture theatres. It was decided to butcher it to television size. When it was offered to the Bell Telephone Company's agency, there was a protest about it being too Catholic. I responded, "We glow over only one pope, John, who was loved by everyone, and his only quoted speech in the film is in favour of peace." The reply came: "What makes you think the telephone company is against war?"

For this and other reasons, it seemed to be time to take leave of the city I loved, New York. Let's pause to consider the agony of America as the sixties ended: my agony and the events of "the chain."

PART II

CHAPTER THIRTEEN

The Chain

The black fist, out of the black New York jungle night, smashed against my cheekbone. And the darkness began the agony of destruction and recall.

I recalled Peter Christian and those snow-flooded Canadian Christmases. The only possible explanation for a tree inside was to keep it from freezing in the Canadian cold. The decorations obviously were so no one would notice it, as if it were part of the flowered wallpaper, growing with the house. And I kept my hand close to the fringe of my *tzitsus*, the Jewish ritual garment worn beneath my clothes to protect me from evil. Now I could enjoy the party among these strange people.

Mrs. Christian, a striking woman with dark eyes and very red lipstick, co-ordinated the activities. "Will the young man from St. Clair Avenue have cake?" I thought the question foolish as the cake was the reason for my being a guest. It was strangely hard with raisins and fruit, and not at all like the strudel my Aunt Minnie delivered to us for Rosh Hashonah. "God forgive me if it is not kosher," was a prayer uttered without moving the lips. The second piece was even better and I think I missed the prayer on the ice cream.

Pulling open the red and green surprises took the stiffness from the air. They exploded into noisemakers and jelly beans. And even Peter Christian seemed to take joy in the red, yellow and purple candies. He was a long-faced boy lost in only-child loneliness. He pulled on one end and I pulled on the other. When the bang came, it seemed that only one side of his face lit into a smile, as if he did not want to give too much at once. There was a tiny tin figure which, when wound, clicked across the rug and a monkey that somersaulted.

I relaxed until the double parlour door opened and *he* arrived. I think I began spurting Yiddish phrases. He was Mr. Christian. He zoomed across the room on an outsized skateboard, propelling himself with leather cups on his elbows. He rolled as far as the centre of the room, smiled intensely at me, and pushed his way out again. I choked on a jelly bean; Mr. Christian had neither arms nor legs, and without them he was no taller than I. After he had gone, I said I must hurry back home or my father would be angry. And I tried whistling all the way, past the store that made graveyard markers, in front of Doidge's candy store, not even thinking of his penny grab-bags, and not making my usual face at Waller's place.

The next several Christmases I made the same pilgrimage. The party with the Christians became a ritual. Each time Mr. Christian would wheel himself into the centre of the room for a brief look at the restrained joy, and vanish. Until one Christmas, after the distant wars in Ethiopia and Spain had passed, and he did not appear. By chance I spotted an item in the *Evening Telegram,* a photograph of Mr. Christian in a wheel-chair at a special commemorative ceremony marking the World War I battle of Vimy Ridge. The cutline said: "Edward George Christian, only Negro winner of Victoria Cross, dies."

All I knew was that they were not Jewish. I liked the cake. I was impressed with the Victoria Cross and I loved Peter Christian the one day a year I saw him. Now I recall him as my first Negro.

And now in New York the ache in my cheekbone throbs like a drumming pulse. I know there are no heartbeats in the face, but touch mine and you can hear my life as surely as if you had touched my breast. And it had been so casual.

Of course, the decade had been in the throes of its formal funeral. Any time that counts as its casual victims Martin Luther King and the brothers Kennedy could not seek its own end fast enough. Mourning does not become America. And like the Hebrew prayer, "Next year in Je-rusalem," there seemed to be a fantastic desire to cry out, "Next year in Innocence." If the temple of innocence were destroyed, burned, as-sasinated, could it be resurrected? "I am the Light." But where was the Light, where was He? The smog of falling expectations had clouded the Light. And if black was beautiful, where was beauty? Because the blacks were there, everywhere; the skyscraper could no longer hide them and Harlem could no longer contain them. They could no more be ignored. One at least was determined to say to me: look at me, study my face, know your enemy.

How did it happen? We had been on the West Side of New York, where the film laboratories had grown out of the pantry of Hell's Kitchen, at a screening of one of my films. Christmas was in my ear even though it was not yet November. And we had looked at filmed stills of World War I as a haunting harmonica had intoned the song which both the Germans and the English had sung in the trenches, with its message about the waste of war and the futility of brutality. Looking at a 50-year-old violence you could nod, shake a finger and sermonize with a superior air. Hard to get angry about the last generation's hate; it's so antique.

Of course, the streets had become meeting halls for dissent, charging groups with a damn-you-all-but-me anarchy. Who would run the schools? Have students the right to believe they know more than the professors? Where were we going with our Kafkaesque "we love a hate parade?" But it was not me. It was *them*. And I was forced to discover that no passenger can lounge in indifference if the entire carrier is sinking. When do you jump, when the water hits above or below the knees? I was surprised because any physical contact I had had since childhood was dedicated to romance or love, or at least, pleasure.

All disaster begins with innocence. Where would we have dinner? It was such an unimportant question, but it was the necessary link in the chain. Friday night and the film was over and there was reason to celebrate an early Christmas. My wife Arlene and I had to decide about dinner. Stay uptown or return to familiar haunts of Greenwich Village. "How about the fish place?" she said. The Captain's Table at Sixth Avenue and Eighth Street would do. It should have been so easy.

The cab headed down the greyness of Ninth Avenue. It was close to 8 p.m. and the tunnel traffic was getting sparse. It seemed an easy short-cut. Ninth Avenue is like a long truck stop. If you are a true New Yorker, you feel as if you've left the real city behind and are just holding on before falling off the end of the earth. And if you move quickly, without noticing too much, you have crossed various frontiers.

New York is a city of villages and societies. You can live a lifetime without crossing paths with old friends or new places. Now as the taxi bordered the meat-packing areas below 23rd Street, I had a feeling of being in another civilization. As we hit 15th, a sign caught my eye: "Old Homestead Restaurant, since 1868."

"If that place has been here a hundred years, it must be doing something right. How about we try it?" I said. How many evenings have you begun that way? Let's try it. What have we got to lose? Usually little.

The taxi made a left turn on 14th Street. We stopped on the south corner and I paid the fare. We crossed. It was an unspectacular night, not winter yet, but summer was a rumour with a year to wait. If there was dialogue between my wife and I, it was playful and pleasant, as was our relationship.

Coming toward us was a large Negro. I'd guess he was six foot one or two, about 250 pounds. Full across the chest in a short-sleeved blue polo shirt. He cruised rather gaily, I thought. Beneath the black curly hair a full grin, a wide grin. Trailing him against the side of the building were three other Negroes. They were lost in the shadows of the doorways. He looked as if he were going to pass a remark.

How many derelicts I had encountered from the closeness of the Bowery with their "how about money for a drink," or money for soup or subway. There were never pleas or pardons. It's an understanding; someone who has will give. They collect their nickels and dimes until there's enough for the cheapest wine, always cradled in a brown paper bag. And this man looked like he was about to make a verbal touch. Okay, I was fair game. I had a white shirt, a neat coat and a rather lovely wife. He continued, chest swaying, straight at me, all the time a pumpkin-lantern grin. He was going to comment, or so I thought.

Then . . . Recall the second! Even now in memory I cannot stand where I stood. I did not see his arm wind. I was smiling slightly, waiting for a word. Surely he would make a comment and we would pass, and never pass each other's way again. That's how we live—he in the world behind his skin, and I in mine.

"Ohhhhhh!" But I said nothing, shouted nothing. Not a sound nor gasp nor cry. His fist with the full impact of its cruising swing stoned against my face. One rock. A boulder of a blow. My glasses were wiped from my face and landed beside a post. I vibrated. I heard a sound like a steel pole being pounded with a hammer. Inside my head I could hear darkness. "Leave him alone." My wife's plea came from a great distance, even though she never left my side. Everything was distant. I could neither find nor feel myself. My feet could not move, but I felt myself flying into the night sky, into the men and boys who were me before that moment. Time past, time forward, but not time present.

The ache. "Ohhhhhh! Father, father! Oh God!" Recall . . .

I remember the second Negro of my childhood. It was summer and we watched the thermometer in front of McQuoid's Drug Store pop above the maximum line of 100 degrees. Despite the usual polio epidemic warnings, we boarded the free car daily for our hour in the cool water. We carried pouches of camphor around our necks like a primitive talisman to protect us. For all I know it was magic, because none of us ever became polio victims.

One noon, standing on the cement safety zone at Greenlaw Avenue, I saw Gilbert Levine reading a book, waiting for a streetcar. He wore a baggy tweed suit in heat that would have baked an apple. Beside him, also in an ill-fitting suit, was a dark, plump young boy whom I later discovered was Stanley Baldwin, named, of course, after the tough prime minister of England. Neither took any notice of me. I smiled. The idea of Gilbert Levine in a bathing suit seemed uniquely funny. When the noisy free car stopped, they boarded it with the solemnity of two short casket carriers at a Quaker funeral.

I sat across from them. Occasionally Gilbert Levine glanced up from his reading to mumble something to Stanley Baldwin. I had seen the myopic starch-white face of Gilbert many times. So it was Stanley who fascinated me. His skin was the colour of the chestnuts we used to play our game of chestnut-on-a-shoelace-string. When the streetcar turned the corner to head south on Ossington Avenue, the sun reflected against his skin, coloured it with the gloss of our handsome, genuine mahogany radio on which my sisters were making $5 weekly payments. At other times he looked as dark as Coca-Cola.

The streetcar lurched past 999 Queen Street, the "crazy house." The loud cheer which was our formal salute to the mentally disturbed inmates caused Gilbert to glance briefly from his reading with a look of disdain. Stanley managed a slight smile, and mopped his brow with a towel that carried the inscription "YMCA." His black curly hair was caked down as if it were in an oil painting. Not separate strands, but filled in by a careless artist. Neither he nor Gilbert joined in the songs. He averted my stare and seemed relieved when the car finally pulled up beside the beach. The children from a dozen other free cars, each carrying his own special paper bag, towel and suit, flew from the cars as if a stop watch were keeping time for the fastest to undress.

In the barracks-like changing rooms which had the distinct smell of Canadian maple and urine, clothes fell fast. Each boy became a bundle of running shoes, shirt and underwear. But Gilbert and Stanley undressed slowly, with Gilbert folding each item with the precision of a bank clerk. Stanley seemed in hiding as he removed his clothes, revealing the chocolate–coloured skin.

Halfway through the play period on the littered Sunnyside beach, Stanley stopped me. "How come you keep looking at me like some kind of freak?'' My words stumbled. "Just lookin'. That's all. Can't kill a kid for lookin'.''

"Looking at what?''

"Nuthin'. Just lookin' at your skin.''

"What about it?'' he asked angrily.

"Nuthin'. Just want to know why you are so burned. How come?''

"Very funny, indeed. You never seen a Negro before?'' Gilbert Levine looked up from his book to sneer. These were the first and last words I ever heard him say. The eyes behind the thick lenses accused me. "Sure, I been around. I seen all kinds of Negroes. Sure.'' I dug my toes in the sand and chewed on my knuckles. "See you 'round, you guys.''

Even then I did not associate the Christian family and my Christmases with something called "Negro.'' They were, I suppose now, more Lena Horne coloured. But Stanley was dark as a mahogany African mask. I felt peculiar and was too ashamed to ask my parents what a Negro was. Years later when I passed Stanley in the halls at the University of Toronto, I found myself avoiding him. The embarrassment lingered on.

How could a New York street be the same again? Once there was life; now there would be fear. The black man who had struck me made no effort to run. His arm lowered as if merely completing the necessary motion of walking. It had crushed my face on its way, but there was neither an "excuse me,'' nor an "I hate you,'' nor even a ridiculous "thank you.'' Three other Negroes trailed behind in the shadows and together they ambled away. Only the impossible grin of the man who dared hit stayed behind. I see it now still. Perhaps I could have hit back. But hit whom? Who was he who molested my body? Had he mistaken me for boss, slave-owner, bigot, millionaire, cop, crook, hater, who? It was Kafka in the New York night. The ache was much deeper than the drop of blood on the bridge of my nose. My mind was in pain.

Fifteen minutes later I was able to stop a police cruiser and explain the incident. The cop was named Daley. His partner was eating a hamburger at a nearby restaurant. Together we prowled along 14th Street. "There's a big one in a blue shirt,'' he said, pointing to a large Negro waiting for a bus at the corner of Eighth Avenue.

"That looks like him,'' my wife accused.

"No, not him.''

"We'll get him,'' charged Policeman Daley. The words had a vengeful urgency. Proverb three: envy thou not the oppressor, and choose none of his ways. Hardly a thought in a police car, but there it was. "I guess you're anxious to get even," said Policeman Daley.

"I must find him," I said.

We cruised for an hour, down the back alleys and the brooding empty avenues. Each dark face stood accused, huddled in doorways or walking in hunched-over shades and shadows. "If we find him, do you want to lay charges?" asked officer Daley.

"Yes, if it will stop someone else from being hit. But mostly I want to ask a question."

"What's that?"

"I want to ask him why." I suspect I knew. I suspect I know. I suspect myself.

Like the sidewalks and the buildings, the Negroes were there when I came to New York in the fifties. They were there as firmly and as unobtrusively. They chored by day in elevators and bathrooms and behind counters, the men lifting the heavy cases into trucks, smiling and bending, and vanishing by dusk into the subway kennels to the obscure firmament of Harlem. There were a few who passed, a dancer, a buck making it with a Sarah Lawrence graduate doing her PhD in free association. And the occasional "party spade" at Village and East Side parties, but never for dinner, darling. And the East-Siders soaked themselves in liberalism in speech and ivory tower writings, and went right on sending their children to private schools: white as letter paper, solid America locked into its compartments, with barriers as real as the Berlin Wall.

Once I invited a photographer of medium skill to a penthouse party, and in retaliation he asked, "Find me a rich lady, man, who wants a big Negro lover." He didn't say "black"; that was to come later. "Man, if I knew a rich lady, I'd find her a white lover—me." He thought me unfunny, and I suppose I was.

Once I had a date with a lovely caramel-coloured lady, lost and found in a pick-up bar, and discovered that she had to hide before we could get a cab home from Chinatown. She later went into the mistress business in Paris, where presumably cabs were easier to come by, unless you happened to be Algerian. And there was a particularly serious thin, coffee-coloured lady, who said she couldn't see me any more because she was Catholic. (Catholic, honey, *oy vay*, have you got your problems mixed.)

Perhaps in my profound innocence, the only fact that seemed odd was the glance. We were all face to face, we white and black, but never eye to eye. The eyes of the Negro inevitably were elsewhere when we chanced to pass in the street. We failed to recognize each other. He looked downward, sideways, within, but never at. If the fact registered, it did not punch in regularly in the time clock of my mind, which was off on other pursuits like money, pleasure, and the good morning of my soul. So, Brother Black, forgive my not yelling hello. You weren't really there.

How many years was it before I knew the surname of my cleaning lady? Where she went after Monday at 5 p.m. until the next Monday at 10 a.m. seemed oddly unrelated to her $12-a-day cleaning operation. She laundered on my day and perhaps wept the other six. Cheques were left and the washing deposited, and she was not on my mind. I wished her well each Christmas with an extra week's pay and liked her with a distant fondness. Forgive us, oh Lord, for we know what we do.

Did he comprehend what he had done, oh Lord, oh policeman. What was his reason? Officer Daley returned us to the scene of the crime, outside the Old Homestead Restaurant. "Describe your attacker, please." That seemed a simple request.

"Well, I think he was about six foot two. No, maybe, he was just six feet, or even less. You know . . . the impact. He was black. Very black. No, maybe brown. His shirt was short sleeved. No, maybe I just imagined hairy arms. Ape arms. No, maybe the sleeves were long. A full head of steel-wool black hair. Was there some grey in it? A beard, my wife thinks he had a tight beard round his chin. Black beard. No, I can't see a beard. Only one characteristic I'm sure of. That smile! It was an hysterical laugh without sound. Man, he enjoyed it. Physical relief. Like a sexual response, splat on my face. He let go a lot. The sock came from way back."

"You mean, he took a big wind-up?"

"No, I mean, from way back in the beginning. The origins of hate."

"Uh huh, I see. Well, I'll report it to the precinct. The punch came from way back."

Africa was a rainbow of darkness. The soil and the sky glared open and unafraid. And although every generalization has a counter-theory, it is obvious that the African people, when unmolested by the European, have a generosity and simplicity unknown to our cynical society. Softly, softly, the African nights embraced me, safe in the hammock of history, lulled to sleep in the mosquito netting of the past.

I can recall the drives at night in Kenya, where the wide-eyed wildebeest stared at trespassing automobiles and tons of rhino crashed at any moving thing. And a child of our time was taken away aboard a jet to the instant prejudice of some European or American city, and an entire village came out to moan a farewell. Where are they taking our boy? What good can come of it? And what can he be or who can he be when the Western education is piped into him to mix with the juices of centuries of jungle joy? They danced, pounded the concrete with open feet, shuffled off to buffalo rhythms. They are taking away our boy, the village cries. And the jet screams, and so do the animals, and who will be the winner?

I loved Africa but I did not know an African to love. No, there was one. Deep down in the pocket of Africa, in South Africa where the white rules with a pistol. I met the true Christian. It was a time when I needed kindness and found it. Chief Albert Luthuli gave me his hand and his hope and felt pain for the death of my father. He was my father at that moment. If my father art in heaven, like in the prayer books, there was the heaven of my father in him. He gave me that day.

"I feel no bitterness," he told me. "But I can tell you this country is being run by mad bullies, and in their madness they may destroy it." It was as if my father were talking. And I knew as we spoke that we find our parents in persons other than those who have given us birth. For it is those who offer us life who are our true parents. And even today when I recite the prayer of mourning on the Day of Atonement I sometimes see the face of Luthuli, who could not learn hate, along with the face of my father, who loved learning.

But 20 black countries I visited to start the decade, now a part of me, could never release the black man from my white self, not now.

Isaac Bligh, a Negro masseur at the Grand Central YMCA, suggested the chain first. "You can't be walkin' round with your face hangin' out like that. You want to see a man run? You come at him with a chain. And then he ain't goin' to bother you none, no more." He smashed his hand against my belly to indicate the gesture. Ike Bligh had been a boxer trainer and was full of the gossip of Harlem and the inside stories of the black *Who's Who*. Ike was convinced that Adam Clayton Powell was really a dark Greek in Negro drag. "Couple guys came at me couple weeks ago. Lucky I had a milk bottle," he said, snapping his gum fiercely as he made a splitting motion on my legs. "Took half a guy's face with that bottle. Get a chain." Ike Bligh had lately taken to wearing a black wig that sat on his head with the unconvincing reality of a Barbie doll. He twisted the last muscles on my back and warned. "Get a chain or don't come back with bruises and look for sympathy."

My skull was x-rayed and reluctantly I found myself at Mandel's Hardware on Eighth Street. "I didn't know you had a dog," Mr. Mandel said, while hustling through his shop.

"No," I confessed, "I want a chain as a weapon, as protection from mad dogs in the street—to help me." There were silver chains, dainty and obviously for a poodle. The brass chains were substantial.

"How much chain do you want?"

"Enough to stop a man with," I said.

"You have to tell me," he said nervously, as if selling an illegal gun.

"I guess maybe three feet," I said. "I have to carry it around in my pocket."

He snipped off three feet, anxious to have me leave before any other customers overheard our conversation. "That will be 75 cents plus sales tax." And now for 75 cents plus tax, for the first time in my law-abiding life, my anti-violent life, I was armed.

Non-violence does not come easily to a human being. I can recall my own childish experiments with it when I learned to run faster than any kid in the neighbourhood. If the shouts of "dirty Jew kid" followed me, I knew I could out-distance the nearest runner. My fast, thin legs meant more to my spirit than any thoughts of salvation. And if once I did pause to give battle to red-headed Terry Doidge, the Welsh bully with red pimply skin, the later thrashing by my father seemed well worth it. I mean, the Bible seemed full of that eye-for-an-eye stuff, and if God was just He also stared out of the Hebrew books of learning with a vengeful wrath, smiting Egyptians and others with plagues and chosen people armies. So what was so awful about a punch in the nose to Terry Doidge, who stopped his cussing promptly?

In later years, when I had cause to visit with Martin Luther King, I knew he was no runner. He was also no Chief Luthuli, despite the fact that both were awarded the Nobel Prize by the great neutralists, the Norwegians. When the news of King's death was flashed between commercials of the good life, I was at first strangely unmoved. He had said that he welcomed death in his cause. And there was violence, not love, just as there had been when the bullet hit Mahatma Gandhi in India and he cried, "*Ey Rama,*" oh God. But maybe that's how God comes to us.

Perhaps King wasn't talking to me because wherever he was, he was in His Tabernacle and there we can only understand, not talk to each other. King had said to me, "I came to see the greater power of the ethic of love."

They carried the Bible to the moon. How deep in us had King dug? And in me? "Judge me, O Lord; for I have walked in mine integrity: I have trusted also in the Lord; therefore I shall not slide."

The chain. The chain in my pocket. Warm in the sun. Cool to the touch in the freezing cold. It is now part of me. I test it on the brick wall—an upper cut, a downward slice, and pieces of pebble fall away. A slash against a metal grill. A beating of a cloth couch and it is indented. But against man? I walk in the streets, in sunshiny glare and in darkened shadows, and meet the stare of Negro men. Which will be my attacker and who my target? I study them. Those in white shirts and pressed pants and a hint of a shine on the shoes, and the chain is merely caressed. A buck with tattered coat and eyes hazed by noon moonshine, and the chain is held hard. The ones with strutting walk and drugged smile, and the chain is wrapped fiercely around my knuckles.

And the question: could I strike even if I were struck? And I try to imagine the sound, the links cutting into the flesh beneath the dark skin. Would there be blood, blood on the metal extension of me? Could I break a bone; is there that power in me? And who would it be? Who would I see: Peter Christian, Chief Luthuli, Martin Luther King . . . the man who struck, or all of them—which? This I know: while I possess it, it has made the jungle of New York real, and it is a chain that binds me. Only if I can let it go will I know my brother.

That is what I wrote to end the decade. Soon afterward I threw away the chain. I left to begin again at my place of beginning—Canada.

CHAPTER FOURTEEN

The Wit and World of G. Bernard Shaw

When I returned to Toronto at the beginning of the seventies, the echo of a New York mugging stayed with me for some time, like an aching bone. I searched for calm. One of the first people I met was the media maker-of-phrases, Marshall McLuhan, who pronounced, ''What we have here in Canada is instant nostalgia. We are America of the fifties, so you can be back in time.'' Not exactly. But it would do for the moment.

I found other truths. They were contained in the writings of George Bernard Shaw. I had been especially interested in him since the dean of Westminster had told me that he would never be buried there, at his own request. Shaw had observed so much for all of us. About his own home-coming he said:

> When I went to those great cities I saw wonders I had never
> seen in Ireland. But when I came back to Ireland I found all
> the wonders were waiting for me. You see, they had been there
> all the time; but my eyes had never been opened to them. I
> did not know what my house was like because I had never been
> outside it.

To challenge your past is to find a kind of knowledge. To find knowledge is to find memory. I was back in my house.

At the Canadian Broadcasting Corporation I found a sympathetic ear in a long-time friend and fellow survivor, the program director Thom

Benson, a man with a great deal of imagination. To him I proposed
making films in Toronto for international consumption, and perhaps admiration and acclaim, much on the lines of what Ken Russell had been
doing for the BBC before he disappeared in an orgy of self-indulgence
on the wide screen. It was agreed that I would begin with a film on
George Bernard Shaw. I had done the early research in New York, and
had been given approval by Shaw's literary estate because of the attention
that *Hall of Kings* had received. It was to be a four-way co-production,
involving the CBC, the BBC, PBS and Irish TV. For my part, I would
collect Canada's leading international stars to participate.

The central figure would be Shaw himself. When I did my film
on the Nobel Prize, I had been fascinated to find library footage on Shaw
and Einstein together. In it, Shaw had risen to toast the great scientist
with delicious and prophetic humour:

> You take the typical great man of our epoch. Suppose that I
> had to rise here tonight to propose a toast to Napoleon. Well,
> undoubtedly I could say many very flattering things about
> Napoleon, but the one thing which I should not be able to say
> about him would be, perhaps, the most important thing and that
> was that it would perhaps have been better for the human race
> if he had never been born.
> Napoleon and other great men of his time, they were
> makers of empires but there is an order of men who get beyond
> that. They are not makers of empires but they are makers of
> universes. And when they have made those universes, their
> hands are unstained by the blood of any human being on earth.
> Ptolemy made a universe which lasted 1,400 years. Newton
> also made a universe which has lasted 300 years; Einstein has
> made a universe and I can't tell you how long that will last.

How long would the universe of Shaw last? So much of his work
had been lost in frivolous productions, where actors bantered as if tossing
English softballs, trying to be so over-witty. What would he have to say
to our time and how could I help, given my own skill at film? He liked
to hide, of course, behind the mask of the exhibitionist egomaniac. He
would sweep out proclamations of his own status for all the world to
adore:

> I am no ordinary playwright in general practice. I am a specialist
> in immoral and heretical plays. My reputation has been gained
> by my persistent struggle to force the public to reconsider its
> morals. In particular, I regard much current morality as to

economic and sexual relations as disastrously wrong. I write
plays with the deliberate object of converting the nation to my
opinions in these matters.

Though my trade is that of playwright, my vocation is that of
prophet . . . Yours truly, George Bernard Shaw.

He liked to challenge all to come and try to find the real Shaw.
He said, "In some unaccountable way I seem to cast a spell on journalists
which makes them recklessly indifferent, not only to common veracity,
but to human possibility. The person they represent me to be not only
does not exist, but could not possibly exist." Find Shaw and you find
some of yourself. He may look larger, stretched out like an elastic band
of beard and forehead and brain. But he is us.

I needed locales, actors and imagination. Sitting in my rented
Rosedale home in Toronto with steady character actor Barry Morse, I
began to search for works to dramatize. We talked of his doing the Devil's
speech from *Man and Superman*. I didn't want to do it on a man-made
stage. I asked Barry as idle tea-time chatter, "Where is your idea of hell
on earth?"

"Well, I suppose really it would have to be the battlefields of
World War I, where men just died in the mud in a foolish war."

"Okay," I said, "We'll set hell there, somewhere in France or
Flanders Field. I used to have to memorize that poem at Regal Road
Public School. The poppies grow between the crosses row on row."

And indeed, when later we mounted an expedition to France, I
found the exact hill of hell. The fog sucked the grey sky to the earth, and
the wooden crosses neatly catalogued the endless dead, as if all men were
dead. Always, always, during those November 11th head-bowed days,
I had heard the pompous remembrances of such gallant battles as Vimy
Ridge. And that is where we filmed. And what was on the other side of
sermon-sanctified Vimy Ridge? Nothing but a slight slope going nowhere.
Mr. Shaw knew his human hell and helped me find it.

Shaw became an observer to battle in World War I. He risked his
personal popularity and criticized:

In both armies the soldiers should shoot their officers and go
home. I dislike war, not only for its dangers and inconveniences
but—as one who looks forward to a better world—because
of the loss of so many young men, any of whom may be a
Newton or an Einstein, a Beethoven, a Michelangelo, a
Shakespeare, or even a Shaw. Or he may be what is of much
more immediate importance, a good baker or a good weaver or
builder. War is not precise and economical. It is almost

inconceivably wasteful and extravagant. It burns the house to roast the pig, and even then seldom roasts him effectively. Calculation or no calculation, waste is the law of modern war; and nothing is cheap on the battlefield except the lives of men.

In passing, a small, technical point about my Shaw film. At the end of the endless dolly shot across the bleached crosses, as the camera pulled back to show that there was no hiding place from this man-made, institutionalized killing, we decided in the editing to add an operatic aria to the soundtrack, a female voice, keening for the folly of men. It was a highlight of my film decisions. It has always seemed like a personal mourning for indifferent death. Somehow only the artist can weep for the collective death.

In terms of the individual, Shaw appeared to rejoice in those who could defy all so-called normal authority, and those of super strength somehow seemed to be women. From Shaw's own description:

> Joan of Arc, a village girl from the Vosges, was born about 1412; burnt for heresy, witch-craft and sorcery in 1431; rehabilitated after a fashion in 1456; designated Venerable in 1904; declared Blessed in 1908; and finally canonized in 1920. She is the most notable Warrior Saint in the Christian calendar. She was also one of the first apostles of Nationalism. She was the pioneer of rational dressing for women. She had an unbounded and quite unconcealed contempt for official opinion, judgment, and authority. As her actual condition was pure upstart, there were only two opinions about her. One was that she was miraculous; the other that she was unbearable.

I needed an actress who could be all of that. She had to be part child, part woman, part innocent, part flirt, part bitch—a child to hold and comfort, a woman to adore. There was only one woman whom I felt had all these unusual qualities wrapped up in one small, frail, sinewy and sexy body. She was Genevieve Bujold. The daughter of a Montreal bus driver, she had steered her career with a precise certainty, and yet she was all contained in a boyish body behind a face that seemed to be asking for dimes and chewing gum in De Sica's *Open City*. I found her in Montreal and wooed her by phone for weeks to become part of the group I thought could do Shaw and the film justice. She was in the middle of an unfortunate affair after a difficult marriage, and my calls tended to come on like an interested psychologist. Finally she accepted, and the sequence was planned for the very cell in the very jail that had housed the Quebec liberationists after Canada's long night of insurrection, the

October Crisis. We moved out a dozen convicted murderers to film a Shaw saint.

Genevieve was dressed in a dark leotard. She was the timeless revolutionary caught in a mechanical, unconcerned hell. In Shaw's words was the theological argument that has always impressed me, not only about our own loneliness, but about the loneliness of God:

> There is no help, no counsel, in any of you. Yes, I am alone on earth: I have always been alone. My father told my brothers to drown me if I would not stay to mind his sheep while my country was bleeding to death: my country might perish if only our lambs were safe. I thought we would have friends at the court but I find only wolves fighting for pieces of her poor, torn body. I thought God would have friends everywhere, because He is the friend of everyone; and in my innocence I believed that you who now cast me out would be like strong towers to keep harm from me. But I am wiser now; and nobody is any the worse for being wiser. Do not think you can frighten me by telling me that I am alone. My country is alone; and God is alone; and what is my loneliness before the loneliness of my country and of my God? I see now that the loneliness of God is His strength.

Shaw, of course, wore many faces and faced many arguments. For his particular kind of humour I turned to actor Paxton Whitehead, as he was then directing the annual Shaw Festival at Niagara-on-the-Lake, Ontario. Paxton was able to talk and sound as if he were hanging onto an umbrella in a London tube: slightly too high pitched, pinched by a celluloid collar. He clucked out Shavian lines as if dropping warm eggs: "Every fool can get ill—but every fool can't be a good doctor."

Shaw labelled his very funny play *The Doctor's Dilemma* a tragedy, because he found human behaviour just too absurd:

> The absolute vegetarian said: "It is not the fault of our doctors that the medical service of the community, as at present provided for, is a murderous absurdity. That any sane nation, having observed that you could provide for the supply of bread by giving the bakers a pecuniary interest in baking for you, should go on to give a surgeon a pecuniary interest in cutting off your leg, is enough to make one despair of political humanity. But that is precisely what we have done. All that can be said for medical popularity is that until there is a practicable alternative

to blind trust in the doctor, the truth about the doctor is so terrible we dare not face it.''

For the more solemn Shaw I turned to John Colicos, who has a kind of darkness at noon about his performances. Colicos is an actor who has always been in an angry argument with himself about his life. His eyes are a little too narrow, his nose a little too flat, his lips perhaps too full to enable him to be one of the great matinee idols. But there is a great richness in the bluntness of his drive. He delivered one aspect of the Shaw sermon as Sir Andrew Undershaft, the tough, philosophical, lovable scoundrel of a millionaire in *Major Barbara*:

> My religion, well I'm a millionaire, that's my religion. Poverty, my friend, is not a thing to be proud of. Have you ever been in love with poverty like Saint Francis. Have you ever been in love with dirt like St. Simeon—such passions are not virtues but the most unnatural of all the vices. I've been a common man and a poor man and it has no romance for me. Leave it to the coward to make a religion of his cowardice by preaching humility—we know better than that. Poverty is the worst of crimes. All the other crimes are virtues beside it: all the other dishonours are chivalry itself by comparison. Poverty blights whole cities; spreads horrible pestilences; strikes dead the very souls of all who come within sight, sound or smell of it. What you call crime is nothing: a murder here and a theft there, a blow now and a curse then: what do they matter? They are only the accidents and illnesses of life; there are not fifty genuine professional criminals in London. But there are millions of poor people, abject people, dirty people, ill-fed, ill-clothed people. They poison us morally and physically; they kill the happiness of society; they force us to do away with our own liberties and to organize unnatural cruelties for fear they should rise against us and drag us down into their abyss. Only fools fear crime: we all fear poverty.

What was it that Shaw himself feared? There were footsteps, shadows, suggestions, long written descriptions as preludes to plays, and the inner areas of belief reflected in his creations, but I never did feel I knew for certain. When I arrived in Dublin with my film crew, provided by the BBC, I had a feeling that I was getting closer to the man and was less obscured by the legend. I was fortunate to have as my on-camera narrator Christopher Plummer, Canada's most exceptional actor. But who could be Shaw but Shaw himself.

On the doorstep of the home in which he lived, I recognized him well. Synge Street is an awful pile of grey sameness. Not a slum, not quite up to the level of any class, just drab and life-to-death existence with little hope of peaks of pleasure. The kind of street where you are born one morning at 7 a.m. and dead half a century later at dusk. The only indication of its once regal-of-mind tenant was a plaque erected by an admiring Dublin dustman. It says simply: "Bernard Shaw, author of many plays, was born in this house the 26th of July, 1856." It was a street not unlike my own St. Clair, where lives are lived in the time of a cosmic cough. The sameness that made me once want to swing high, swing away, swing off to the stars. Shaw's line by his own dustman, Mr. Doolittle, seemed baked into every identical stone of that street, my street, all streets like it: "Think what that means to a man. It means that he's up against middle class morality all the time."

Shaw's own wish to leap above the street of dread was expressed many times and in many ways.

> Ah, it's no use, me poor little friend. You can jump as high as
> a kangeroo, you can't jump away from your own heart and
> its punishment. You can only look at Heaven from here: you
> can't reach it.

In Dublin I felt closer too because there I found the essential man who loved to talk, who seemed to have endless time to answer callers, make proclamations. And if I went into a pub, as I often did to get a sense of place, there always seemed to be someone at the bar who was endlessly explaining, explaining anything, explaining everything. Out of this experience I got the notion of filming Shaw's great literary soliloquy about what it is to be Irish in a bar. The actor best equipped to handle it was Jack MacGowran, who had a face as Irish as the froth on a pint of Guinness stout. As it turned out, the filming had to be delayed until we reached New York, so it took place New Year's Day at the famous Whitehorse Tavern. There a lonely figure at the end of a bar declared profoundly what it is to be Irish:

> No, no: the climate is different. Here, if the life is dull, you
> can be dull too, and no great harm done. But your wits won't
> thicken in that soft moist air, on those white springy roads,
> in those misty rushes and brown bogs, on those hillsides of
> granite rocks and magenta heather. You've got no such colours
> in the sky, no such lure in the distances, no such sadness in
> the evenings. Oh, the dreaming! the dreaming! the self-torturing,
> never satisfying dreaming, dreaming, dreaming! No debauchery

that ever coarsened and brutalized an Englishman could take
the worth and usefulness out of him like that dreaming. An
Irishman's imagination never lets him alone, never convinces
him, never satisfies him; but it makes him that he can't deal
with reality nor face it nor conquer it: he can only sneer at
those that do and be "agreeable to strangers," like a good-for-
nothing woman on the road. It's all imagination, all dreaming.
It saves thinking. It saves working. It saves everything except
imagination, imagination, imagination; and imagination's such
a torture that you can't bear it without whisky. At last it comes
that you can face nothing real at all: you'd rather go shabby
and dirty than set your mind to looking after your clothes and
washing yourself; you nag and squabble at home because your
wife isn't an angel, and she despises you because you're not
a hero; and you hate the whole lot around you because they're
only poor senseless devils like yourself.

When you're young, you exchange drinks with other
young men; and you exchange vile stories with them, you chaff
and jive and jeer at them for not doing the things you daren't
do yourself.

Never mind my heart: an Irishman's heart is nothing but
his imagination.

Perhaps I never so much appreciated Mr. Shaw as in this comment
about the Irish madness. I married the final part of the narrative to a
newsreel clip of the Bloody Sunday riots of Northern Ireland. Of course,
Shaw's capacity to understand these countrymen of his was perfect; it
was if a reporter were doing an eloquent job of narrating the day's tragic
news. Use of devices such as this were part of my combined creative
work with film editor Arla Saare, who was the first film editor I had ever
worked with and was still by far one of the best. She helped make my
films musical portraits of vision.

In this film I especially liked mixing the man and his argument.
How he loved to argue! In a broken castle in a low mist outside Shaw's
English home, Chris Plummer performed the eloquent passage from *Man
and Superman:*

I, my friend, am as much a part of Nature as my own finger is
a part of me. If my finger is the organ by which I grasp the
sword and the mandoline, my brain is the organ by which Nature
strives to understand itself. My dog's brain serves only my
dog's purposes; but my own brain labours at a knowledge which
does nothing for me personally but make my body bitter to

me and my decay and death a calamity. Were I not possessed with a purpose beyond my own I had better be a ploughman than a philosopher; for the ploughman lives as long as the philosopher, eats more, sleeps better, rejoices in the wife of his bosom with less misgiving. This is because the philosopher is in the grip of the Life Force.

This Life Force says to him, I have done a thousand wonderful things unconsciously by merely willing to live and following the line of least resistance: now I want to know myself and my destination, and choose my path; so I have made a special brain—to grasp this knowledge for me as the husbandman's hand grasps the plough for me. And this, says the Life Force to the philosopher, must thou strive to do for me until thou diest, when I will make another brain and another philosopher to carry on the work.

Does a ship sail to its destination no better than a log drifts nowhither? The philosopher is Nature's pilot. And there you have our difference: to be in hell is to drift: to be in heaven is to steer. I can find my own way to heaven.

So Shaw was my teacher as well as my subject. But in the end it was Shaw himself who summed up his life best. There's a rusty bit of film that seemed to catch the old man in a playful, soulful mood. In it he said:

When I was young I simply didn't want to be a great writer at all. I wanted when I was a small boy to be a pirate and so on, then I wanted to be an operatic singer. Then I wanted above all to be a great painter. I wanted to be a great musician. The one thing I never wanted to be was a writer. And the reason was that I was a born writer. The thing was as natural to me as the taste of water in my mouth. It has no taste because it's always there. At least it's always in my mouth because I'm a teetotaler. However, don't imagine that being a teetotaler will make you great. It won't. I've known some people—and they've become great people and very distinguished great people, too—and their principal diet was whisky and big cigars.

The way to have a happy life is to be too busy doing what you like all the time. Having no time left to you to consider whether you're happy or not. And—oh look here, I'm getting talking. I must stop. Well it's very pleasant to have seen you all here and to think that you're my audience and all that

because I'm a born actor myself. I like an audience. I'm like a
child in that respect. Well, good-bye, good-bye. Good-bye.
Good-bye all of you.

When the film was finished it was a kind of wonderful entertainment, a mixture of Shavian joy and drama. The reviews were glowing.
But many questions had to be asked of it and myself. How deeply had
I been able to dig under all the words created for public consumption?
What did I really know of Shaw's heart-felt longings for love? I realized
that some day I should do films about living creators of his magnitude,
so that they could explain their deepest feelings, even if it were just with
a glance or in the way a question was left unanswered.

In Canada, the film proved to be a happy homecoming. In Britain,
the BBC, apparently convinced that only it understood Shaw, arbitrarily
cut out every fifth minute or so to compress the film into an hour slot,
thus butchering it beyond belief. In the U.S. after media consultant Mike
Dann declared it to be the best TV experience of his life, IBM considered
sponsoring it, but thought Shaw too against the Vietnam war. PBS mysteriously said it did not have the funds to run it.

But it was on the basis of seeing this film at a private screening
that John Leonard, senior cultural correspondent of the *New York Times*,
said that I was making better films than *everyone* in New York and
Hollywood. It was a turning point in the art of my life. I wanted to
believe about myself what Shaw had written:

> I believe in Michelangelo, Velasquez and Rembrandt, in the
> might of design, the mystery of colour, the redemption of all
> things by beauty everlasting, and the message of art that made
> these hands blessed.

I was to meet soon afterwards a living man who saw life and art
in a similar way—and that was Tennessee Williams.

CHAPTER FIFTEEN

My Brother Tennessee

I don't quite know how it started but you can verify the story if you pass by the Elysee Hotel in New York. Tennessee stayed there on a regular basis before he moved over to the West Side and his own place in town. Whenever I would stop by for a stuffed pepper lunch on Tuesdays, the doorman would tip his hat and say, "And how are you today, Mr. Tennessee Williams' brother?" I would reply, "I am very well, but I am not Tennessee's brother." And the doorman would chuckle and say, "Of course, Mr. Williams, anything you say. You'll find your brother in the restaurant."

I suppose he just thought it part of the family eccentricity and let it go at that. Maybe I should just accept it as such. Come to think of it, I really wasn't that fond of stuffed peppers, but somehow Tennessee had convinced me that I was, and I came to accept it in time. Served at the Monkey Bar, it all had a flavour of madness.

How did this brother thing begin? There are landmarks in a life, and my friendship with Tennessee has been one for me, as clearly as if I had crossed a bridge, inherited a fortune, or gone from being colour-blind to recognizing the richness of red or taking a bath in blue.

It began without question with my wife Arlene. We were visiting New York and she had been reading a lengthy *Esquire* article about him by Rex Reed, in which Tennessee made the famous statement that he felt that he had slept through the sixties, and Gore Vidal replied, "Well, you didn't miss anything." I had been searching for an idea to follow

up my successful Shaw film, and was anxious to extend the concept of
a life on film as seen through the words and creative thoughts of a
playwright. I had not been a student of Williams or even a fan, but I
recognized the quality of life he created on stage. It was Arlene who
insisted. She had originally come from Tennessee herself, and I even felt
that a film with him centred in the South might improve my understanding
of her. The journey I was to take was to go much further.

But first I had the usual problem of convincing everyone that this
was a good film idea. There was opposition on all sides. First the CBC,
with Canada going through its nationalistic needs. Why do an American?
Fortunately, the BBC in England said they would join in as co-producers,
giving the whole project international status. (The fact that the BBC
promise of support vanished, and that it later produced its own imitative
and unsuccessful film did not matter at that moment.)

There was the question of the author himself. Anytime I had seen
Tennessee on talk shows on television I had a feeling he became silly.
His interviews in the press also carried with them a nervous giggle of
self-deprecation. It was, as I found out later, his embarrassment at his
own vulnerability and his wish never to seem pompous. Unable to hide
behind any mask of ''mendacity''—I love that Big Daddy word of his—
if he involved himself there was no lying, no hiding. A bare soul was
revealed. The dramatic truth of human vulnerability is, in fact, the substance of his work.

I began with his new agent, who was helpful from the start. Bill
Barnes had recently taken on the job after Tennessee had had a feud with
his representative of many years, Audrey Wood. Bill liked the idea and
said he would try to arrange a meeting. I was in New York for a week,
and waited for the return call. Each day I would check the International
Creative Management office, but each day I got a negative response.
Suddenly it was Friday and I would have to return to Toronto without
a subject. I knew Tennessee swam every day, as I did. I finally suggested
with some desperation that I would even conduct my film proposal in the
steam room of the YMCA. Bill relayed the offer, which seemed to amuse
Tennessee, and he agreed to a first meeting at lunch.

We walked down from the Elysee Hotel to an East Side restaurant,
and I noticed even then that I was being studied. Years of people who
came on friendly, and who later abused him in print, left a visible emotional scar. I was honest and open and said simply, ''Look, I am Harry
Rasky. I want to try to do you justice on film. It is not a responsibility
I take lightly.'' I don't remember too much else about the lunch except
that it seemed relaxed, with some minor tensions. It was agreed that
Tennessee would take time to see my Shaw film, but it would have to

be in Los Angeles because he was heading there to present the Academy Award in the writing category.

When we arrived at the Beverly Hills Hotel, he suggested that we be joined at the screening by a long-time friend of his, Oliver Evans, a teacher at a small college in the San Fernando Valley. When it was over, Tennessee looked at Oliver, who gave an encouraging nod, and Tennessee said, "You've shown me a great deal about Shaw I did not know. Let's try, shall we?" There followed a long period of reading and study and word from Barnes that Tennessee would agree only if Oliver were retained as a consultant. Oliver had had a brain tumour operation and Tennessee wanted to finance a trip that Oliver wanted to make to the Orient. The $5,000 journey would be his fee. I agreed. And, in fact, Oliver's correspondence from distant places provided my first clues to the man.

Obviously there was something Williamsesque about having as my consultant someone we called "the professor," who was having his last wish before dying in a far away place granted by one of his oldest friends. Closely typed letters with intellectual insights would arrive from places postmarked Pattaya Beach, Thailand. The professor gave me the first deep understanding of Tennessee's compassion and his poetry:

Dear Harry,

Again shooting in the dark (for any letters you may presumably have written me have not as yet filtered through), I'm wondering if in your documentary you are planning to stress the fact that in so much of Williams' work the prevailing pattern turns out to be the gradual, but systematic and inevitable, disintegration of a person who originally was in some way distinguished—a definitely superior individual, in short. Indeed, so much is this the case that the title of one of his minor works, *Chronicle of a Demise,* might almost serve as a motto for the major body of his production . . .

The truth is that Tennessee delights in showing us people of both sexes who have reached the end of their respective ropes in various ways—people who are lonely, trapped and desperate. If he can be said to have a single major theme, it is surely this one. And it is true that the South, with its tragic history and its poverty, and the disorientation that, after all these years, still prevails there, makes an ideal setting for the depiction of individual catastrophes that mirror the general plight and the socio-cultural scene as a whole. I think this is something you might emphasize. Nor have I ever read, in any Williams criticism, this so-obvious relationship between the

locale of his plays and the predicaments in which their characters
so frequently find themselves . . .

   You may have noticed that one of Tennessee's most
characteristic obsessions concerns the plight of persons dependent
upon their—usually unwilling—relatives for their maintenance.
I suppose *Streetcar* is the first important play to reveal this
obsession, though it is present in several of the early one-acters.
He has always been particularly concerned about this type of
situation, which, of course, provides him with opportunity for
the compassion that is the hall-mark of his drama and—I've
always been convinced—that has also been a very large factor,
perhaps the largest, in his greatness. The defeated and the
mutilated are those characters whom we remember best, and I
think this holds true for the entire body of his work.

   After an informal "talk trip" to Key West with my family, Tennessee and I agreed that the filming would start in New Orleans. Final
approval to begin had not come from the CBC, but I was ready and so
was he. I discovered that a film crew and travel could be scheduled
without the necessary consent on other documents. So off I went and sent
back a telegram: "Tennessee Williams film shooting going great." In
fact, the film was made without ever being officially approved.
   Immediately Tennessee himself set the pace. I had labelled the
film *Tennessee Williams' South,* thinking that I would have some insights
into a real geographical locale, but the master molder of theatre turned
it all around with the first question. I asked him, as we sat in a park in
New Orleans, to describe his South. He pointed to his head and let out
one of his characteristic giggles: "You want to know about my South?
Sometimes I think my South is mostly right in here." I asked him innocently to describe it. "Can I describe it? Well, I think I've been working
at it for a long time, Harry, trying to describe it. I sometimes think I
inhabit my own country. It's where my head is, I guess." He laughed
again, and I knew I would have to find where his head was.
   And so my opening narrative began:

   Has it ever struck you that life is all memory except for the one
   present moment that goes by you so quick you hardly catch it
   going? In a sense this is a memory play about this man,
   Tennessee Williams. What he once called "the past, the present
   and the perhaps." Filmed over a year in the streets of New
   Orleans, at his home in Key West, in the South in general and
   his mind in particular.

The interviews and conversations that followed our first session were more personal than I had ever experienced. I felt like Alice who had stepped through the mirror. Once I was on the other side I had to become a part of that world beyond the glass in order to survive. And the family of Tennessee somehow became tangled up in my own. Each member was revealed, and in a way explained the man.

About the father: "My father had a great gift of phrase. All southerners have a great gift for idiom, it seems to me." I asked, "Where does that come from?" Tennessee answered, "Most of it comes from the blacks, you know. A great many of our idioms come from the blacks. The title *Cat on a Hot Tin Roof,* for instance, was a favourite phrase of my father's. When he would come home at night, after my mother would reprimand him for his drunken condition, he would say, 'Edwina, cut it out! You're making me nervous as a cat on a hot tin roof.' "

I asked, "Was, in fact, Big Daddy a portrait of your father?"

"More or less, except my father never owned very much of anything."

"Your mother, Edwina, is she the lady in *Glass Menagerie?*"

"She was, in a way. It was very amusing. When mother went to see the play in Chicago, she went backstage to Laurette Taylor's room. Laurette Taylor wore her hair in bangs, down to here. She said to my mother, who was staring at Laurette removing her makeup, 'Mrs. Williams, how did you like yourself?' And mother said, 'I don't know what you're talking about?' And she said, 'You didn't recognize yourself?' Mother said, 'Not at all. Was I supposed to?' And Laurette let that go by and continued removing her makeup, and then as an after comment she said, 'You know why I have to wear these bangs? Because I have a rather intellectual forehead and I'm playing such a fool.' " There was a loud laugh as if he had told a naughty joke.

"And Laura was patterned after your sister Rose to a certain extent?"

"You know, I think all of my characters are more or less created. I don't know. There was the fragility, the vulnerability—those qualities, yes. The delicacy, yeah, certainly those qualities. But I think characters undergo a great transmutation in the process of writing, even if they start from an original person, a true person, I mean."

Of course, all characters change when they move from life to the stage. But in Tennessee's work there is a person in a haunted house who contains the three chief elements of his own life: the father who fell in love with long distance and tripped the light fantastic out of town, the dominating mother who still sees herself as the belle, and the fragile sister.

Certainly Tennessee's sister is an obsession in all his literature, and I think in all his thoughts. He has cared for her in a way that few brothers are ever called on to do. Since an early, clumsy lobotomy, she has been more or less institutionalized, and he has used the profits of his art to be an attendant on her existence. Every meal and cigarette since she was a teenager has come from him. Her name is Rose and he keeps her like a fresh flower, visiting and loving a person who can never verbalize. The man who lives every day with words loves most a person who has not known any real use of words for 50 years.

I am sure this is part of the reason why Tennessee is so tuned in to all people around him. During the early filming in New Orleans, when we stopped for lunch, he was able to pick out something from every member of the crew to speak about: the eyes of the sound man or a question from the cameraman. He expressed a tenderness like none I have ever known.

Yet he could be incredibly, well, let's say eccentric. From the transcript, there is an interchange that took place as we had lunch at a sidewalk café. It is quoted in several volumes on his life. This is the way it went:

TENNESSEE:
This is called "Shadow Wood." It was written for a play called *The Milk Train Doesn't Stop Here Anymore:*

I once looked on a young green tree
that shattered darkness where it stood.
The name of it was tenderness
and where it grew was Shadow Wood.

The leaves of it were little hands
that scattered gold that had no weight,
and never dimmed to lesser gold:
it would have held me could I wait.

Somewhere it stays in grace of light
but I've forgotten where it stood,
and once abandoned, never twice
can it be found in Shadow Wood.

For tenderness I would lay down
the weapon that holds death away,
but little words of tenderness
are hard for shadow man to say.

Then in answer to a question:

TENNESSEE (*on camera*):
>The private lives of the people here are infinitely wilder than
>they appear to be on the surface, you know, in the open. Yes,
>I like to show the surface of their lives and then to show
>what's in back of the surface, you know—makes an interesting
>contrast.

RASKY (*off camera*):
>Do you think that that's why people everywhere can relate to
>your characters no matter where they come from?

TENNESSEE:
>I think of myself as being a very, very—an eccentric person,
>and I don't see, you know, how the majority of people could
>relate at all to the people I create. Do you think other people
>are eccentric as I?

RASKY:
>Perhaps it's more hidden in other people?

TENNESSEE (*laughing*):
>That's a relief to hear that. It's very encouraging. I shall continue
>with my eccentricity (*laugh*).

At this point he raised his glass to toast eccentrics everywhere,
no matter how hidden, and the laugh that went with the toast contained
the secret expression of a thought that was never put in words. I thought
as time passed in our mutual film that fewer words were needed between
us. Tennessee seems to have the capacity to know exactly what is being
thought, even before it is expressed.

Our walk through the old quarter of New Orleans produced insights into his most famous characters. Most of *A Streetcar Named Desire*
was written in New Orleans, and there were houses like the one in the
play on a street named Elysian Fields. This was part of our interchange.

TENNESSEE:
>"Desire" is also a real street. I was attracted to the name, you
>know.

RASKY:
>How would you describe your character, Blanche, in *Streetcar?*

TENNESSEE:
>Oh, Blanche, she was not a great intellect, would you think?
>(*laugh*) But she had great sensibility, I believe, great feeling. I
>think she was a neurotic, you know.

RASKY:

Could Blanche survive today?

TENNESSEE:

Could she survive today? I'm not sure she would even exist
today.

RASKY:

Why?

TENNESSEE:

Because the South has changed so very much. Well, maybe she
would. I have met many Southern ladies with all kinds of
romantic pretensions, but underneath Blanch's pretensions was
something genuinely sensitive and tender. And so many of
the Southern ladies that I meet nowadays with these Garden
District airs about them and the plantation niceties of behaviour
(*laugh*), you find them hard as nails underneath.

RASKY:

Didn't you say, though, that Blanche also was a tigress
underneath?

TENNESSEE:

Yes, she was. She was a strong weak person, a very strong
weak person. I don't mean that to be a totally nonsensical thing
to say. I would say she was strong, wouldn't you?
Predominantly strong. But with the odds in her disfavour, the
odds against her.

RASKY:

But why did she have to go mad?

TENNESSEE:

Because the odds were so very heavily weighted against her
and she had to expiate the death of her husband.

RASKY:

Which character is most you?

TENNESSEE:

I think that Blanche and Stanley Kowalski are the two sides of
every human nature. Stanley and Blanche were on a collision
course, and one had to break it, and it was Blanche. I feel I am
both Stanley and Blanche.

In our walk along Desire, Tennessee quoted from Blanche's most
important speech, which I was to stage later with the original Broadway
Blanche, Jessica Tandy. I thought it would take on more meaning if I
actually filmed it at Tennessee's home, which I did, in his garden court.
There was a moment of confusion when Jessica asked whom she was
addressing, because I had her direct her speech to the camera. She had

worked very hard on the scene with her husband, Hume Cronyn. This was to be the permanent record. I said, "Just imagine you are Blanche, 20 years after you have been committed to a rest home and someone asks you what happened."

Dressed in an organdy robe, bathed in the colours of the past, Jessica was magnificent. A small part of what she said:

BLANCHE:

> Maybe we are a long way from being made in God's image, but there has been some progress since then. Such things as art—as poetry and music—such kinds of new light have come into the world since then. In some kinds of people some tenderer feelings have had some little beginning that we have got to make grow. And cling to, and hold as our flag. In this dark march toward whatever it is we're approaching—don't, don't hang back with the brutes!

The professor had suggested that I read a poem by Tennessee about moths which seemed to suggest the character that Blanche was to become. I asked if Blanche were a moth. Tennessee said, "A very strong moth, a tiger moth." But why did he have this feeling about moths? "They represent delicacy, vulnerability."

This is Tennessee's poem, which I represented in my film with the faces of old, powerful, intense movie stars, dissolving in a symbolic burning flame:

> A plague has stricken the moths, the moths are dying,
> their bodies are flakes of bronze on the carpets lying.
> Enemies of the delicate everywhere
> have breathed a pestilent mist into the air.
>
> Lament for the velvety moths, for the moths were lovely.
> Often their tender thoughts, for they thought of me,
> cased the neurotic ills that haunt the day,
> Now an invisible evil takes them away.
>
> I move through the shadowy rooms, I cannot be still,
> I must find where the treacherous killer is concealed.
> Feverishly I search and still they fall
> as fragile as ashes broken against a wall.
>
> Now that the plague has taken the moths away,
> who will be cooler than curtains against the day,
> who will come early and softly to ease my lot
> as I move through the shadowy rooms with a troubled heart?

Give them, O mother of moths and mother of men,
strength to enter the heavy world again,
for delicate were the moths and badly wanted
here in a world by mammoth figures haunted!

Tennessee guided me through the world of the South with words.
I took a separate journey with cameraman Ken Gregg, in search of those
towns and villages that were his only home. They had a surface quiet as
calm as a cotton field on a dry July day at high noon, but there was an
undertow of expected violence.

Tennessee has many times explained the derivation of his own
name. This is the story I like the best:

TENNESSEE:

I was christened Thomas Lanier Williams. It is a nice enough
name, perhaps a little too nice. It sounds like it might belong to
the sort of writer who turns out sonnet sequences to spring.
As a matter of fact, my first literary award was $25 from a
woman's club for doing exactly that, three sonnets dedicated to
spring. I hasten to add that I was still pretty young. Under
that name I published a good deal of lyric poetry which was a
bad imitation of Edna Millay. When I grew up I realized this
poetry wasn't much good and I felt the name had been
compromised so I changed it to Tennessee Williams, the
justification being mainly that the Williamses had fought the
Indians for Tennessee, and I had already discovered that the
life of a young writer was going to be something similar to the
defense of a stockade against a band of savages.

I actually went to the Episcopal rectory in Columbus, Mississippi
and filmed his birth notice. There was a deep bond between Tennessee
and his grandparents. He called them "the gentle ones." I think the fact
that he spent his early years living in the back of churches tied him to
me, as the humble churches were not that different from the McKay
Street *shul*. His grandfather also gave him that early childhood relationship with God.

After my trip to his geographical past, I headed for Key West to
continue our conversation. When I told Tennessee that one of his early
church homes was in a state of demolition, he told me that he had fierce
nightmares about his dead grandparents. He seemed personally angry and
it was our only anxious time together.

During that trip he read to me a poem which further tied us together. It was the story of his relationship with his sister. I decided to illustrate it on film with my own children. They were the same age difference as Tennessee and his sister. The words were played out on splendid yellow-green lawns of childhood and empty beaches of space—a child's chase through space and time. Ever since then, Holly and Adam have felt Tennessee to be a kind of literary uncle.

> My sister was quicker at everything than I.
> At five she could say the multiplication
> tables
>> with barely a pause for breath,
>> while I was employed
> with frames of colored beads in Kindy Garden.
>
> At eight she could play
>> Idillio and The Scarf Dance
> while I was chopping at scales and exercises.
>
> At fifteen my sister
>> no longer waited for me,
> impatiently at the White Star Pharmacy corner
>> but plunged headlong
> into the discovery, Love!
>
> Then vanished completely—
>
> for love's explosion, defined as early madness,
> consumingly shone in her transparent
> heart for a season
> and burned it out, a tissue-paper lantern!
>
>> —torn from a string!
>> —tumbled across a pavilion!
>
> flickered three times, almost seeming
> to cry . . .
> My sister was quicker at everything than I.

Later when I met the "sister who was quicker" at a dinner Tennessee arranged for me and Arlene, I had a sense that he was revealing to me without words his most personal love and pain. We sat at a table in the Oak Room at the Plaza in New York, as Rose waved to imaginary passers-by. Normal conversation was impossible. Yet there was a look in their eyes. What did she know or expect or understand? How much of the past could she recall, as he sat there recalling all?

Of course, there is great tenderness in the character of Laura, the sister in *Glass Menagerie*. A dramatic sequence from the play became the longest I attempted in the film, and with mixed success. It was played out quickly for the cameras in a small suite at the Algonquin Hotel. I thrust Michael York into the role of the gentleman caller and fed him Southern rhythms of speech to recite. He did remarkably well. The mother, Amanda, was played by Maureen Stapleton, who is one of the greatest character actresses of our time. She arrived about midnight at the set, in a room crowded with camera lights and assorted persons, had a quick look around and said, "Oh my God, better get a bottle of wine ready. Here we go."

We filmed all night and Michael said politely that it was a "happening." The closing soliloquy was begun by actor James Naughton, but it was co-ordinated with a dramatic reading I had filmed with Tennessee himself in New Orleans. I think the blending of elements produced one of the most dramatic moments ever to appear in my films, as Tennessee acted and lived the words:

> I left Saint Louis. I descended the steps of this fire-escape for a
> last time and followed, from then on, in my father's footsteps,
> attempting to find in motion what was lost in space—
> I travelled around a great deal. The cities swept about me like
> dead leaves, leaves that were brightly colored but torn away
> from the branches.
> I would have stopped, but I was pursued by something.
> It always came upon me unawares, taking me altogether by
> surprise. Perhaps it was a familiar bit of music. Perhaps it was
> only a piece of transparent glass—
> Perhaps I am walking along a street at night, in some strange
> city, before I have found companions. I pass the lighted window
> of a shop where perfume is sold. The window is filled with
> pieces of colored glass, tiny transparent bottles in delicate colors
> like bits of a shattered rainbow.
> Then all at once my sister touches my shoulder. I turn around
> and look into her eyes . . .
> Oh, Laura, Laura, I tried to leave you behind me, but I am
> more faithful than I intended to be!
> I reach for a cigarette, I cross the street,
> I run into the movies or a bar, I buy a drink,
> I speak to the nearest stranger—anything that can blow your
> candles out!
> —for nowadays the world is lit by lightning!
> Blow out your candles, Laura—
> and so good-bye.

At this point in the film, the frail character of Laura blew out the candles as the shot dissolved to darkness on a real photo of Tennessee's father. Although this point was never mentioned in the script, I felt that the interweaving of life with the lyrical was what gave the scene its special quality.

When I wanted an actor to portray a Big Daddy-like person for a short one-actor called *The Last of My Solid Gold Watches*, I went to Burl Ives, who said he would travel anywhere to do anything for Tennessee. Burl has always seemed to have been created by Tennessee. And he was filmed in Key West, so the background of Tennessee's current life became a character in the film, just like Big Daddy.

For a sequence of *Night of the Iguana*, I could not afford to travel to Mexico, where the play and the feature film were set, so I decided on a more symbolic setting. I wanted very much to have Canadian-born Colleen Dewhurst co-star in the dramatic excerpt. She was vacationing on Block Island, and I decided to take my crew there with actor John Colicos. And there, on a tip of land, with a cliff and a foggy seashore behind, we filmed a most moving duet of Tennessee's version of God, "His Oblivious Majesty." It was a locale that suggested the end of the earth.

I asked Tennessee about this vision of life:

RASKY:

The priest in *Night of the Iguana*, do you relate to his feeling about God as he describes it?

TENNESSEE:

Oh, yes, very much, yeah. You mean that he connected him with the elements, yes, the naked elements, yes. I think back of existence there has to be a creative force, otherwise there could be no existence. Something has to have created existence. And just like the plainest kind of geometry, you know. Consequently there is a creative force or we couldn't exist. Nothing could exist. And so you may call him God. It's a good word, a short one.

At the time of our filming, Tennessee had a modest work running off-Broadway called *Small Craft Warning*. In it there is a speech that, as he says, "justifies the play." It is an eloquent soliloquy about the desperate loneliness of the homosexual. I had Bill Hutt, of the Canadian Shakespearean Festival, enact it with a background of modern paintings in tortured colours, an inner soul searching to express itself like the sad, agonized sound of a saxophone.

QUENTIN:

> What is the thing that you mustn't lose in this world before
> you're ready to leave it? The one thing you mustn't lose ever?
> The word that I had in mind is surprise, though. The capacity
> for being surprised. I've lost the capacity for being surprised,
> so completely lost it, that if I woke up in my bedroom late
> some night and saw that fantastic fish swimming right over my
> head, I wouldn't be really surprised. There's a coarseness, a
> deadening coarseness, in the experience of most homosexuals.
> The experiences are quick, and hard, and brutal, and the
> pattern of them is practically unchanging. Their act of love is
> like the jabbing of a hypodermic needle to which they're
> addicted but which is more and more empty of real interest and
> surprise. This lack of variation and surprise in their . . . "love
> life" (*he smiles harshly*) spreads into other areas of . . .
> "sensibility?" (*he smiles again*) Yes, once, quite a long while
> ago, I was often startled by the sense of being alive, of being
> *myself, living!* Present on earth, in the flesh, yes, for some
> completely mysterious reason, a single, separate, intensely
> conscious being, *myself, living!* Whenever I would feel this
> *feeling,* this shock of—what?—self-realization? I would be
> stunned, I would be thunderstruck by it. And by the existence
> of everything with astonishment. It would do more than
> astound me, it would give me a feeling of panic, the sudden
> sense of—I suppose it was like an epileptic seizure, except that
> I didn't fall to the ground in convulsions; no, I'd be more apt
> to try to lose myself in a crowd on a street until the seizure
> was finished. They were dangerous seizures.

Tennessee told me that in a way he was sorry that he had not
written an entire play about Quentin, whom he considered a truly tragic
figure.

Where Tennessee is at now is difficult to assess, except to say
that he is, as always, a man of intense feelings, vibrations, creativity.
He seems genuinely hurt that what he is working on currently is not better
accepted, for, in fact, who anywhere is writing anything better? I asked
about his current play of that time, *Small Craft Warning:*

RASKY:

> In that play we are all winners and losers. How do you rate
> yourself now at this stage of your life?

TENNESSEE:

> I think we're all winners and losers in rotation, you know. We
> go through periods of winning and through periods of losing.

I've gone through long periods of losing. A good ten years of it. It's a hard habit to break. But I still enjoy my work, even when other people don't, I enjoy doing it.

Like many things he said in the course of our hours of conversation, he seemed to be testing, always testing.

For me, some of his finest, rhythmic soulful sound came out of a recent work, much condemned—and I think much misunderstood—by the critics. It is called *Outcry*. The soliloquy about fear is the clearest human cry I have ever heard. He read it for me on film one late afternoon in Key West:

> To play with fear is to play with fire, no worse—much worse than playing with fire, fire has limits. It comes to river or sea and there it stops, it comes to stone or bare earth where it can't leap across, and there is stopped, having nothing more to consume. But fear—where did it begin? Where? When? This feeling of confusion, when— I can't think where. I try to conceal it, this confusion, but it's pretty obvious now that I showed enough evidence of it here. Fear—the fearless little man with the drum inside the rib cage, yes, compared to fear, prone to panic which has no—this feeling of confusion began when I can't think where I tried to conceal it this confusion, but it's pretty obvious now that I've shown some evidence of it, yes sometimes, I . . . it's ridiculous but I don't know where we last played (*laughs*). The fierce little man with the drum . . . the rib cage, yes, compared to fear grown to panic which has no limits, compared to that no other emotion a living, feeling creature is capable of having not even love or hate is comparable in force, magnitude, it should sit on a throne with crown and sceptre in the heart of the living creature. Not too rhetorical that, then what, oh yes, never catch hold of and cry out to a person you love or need as deeply as if you love—take care of me, I'm frightened, don't know the next step. The person so loved and needed would hold you in contempt of human law, and resisting arrest. Not quite like that but something like that. Work with that over, or maybe put it this way, in the heart of the person to whom you've cried out there is a little automatic sound apparatus. Yes, and it whispers to this person demand, blackmail, despicable, reject it. Yes, huh, and then the next morning you have to make your own coffee, your own phone call and go alone to the doctor . . .

say I'm afraid I'm dying.(*He paused, looked at me and laughed.*)
There should be a bravo now.

RASKY:

> The bravos have come in the form of honours. Pulitzer Prizes
> and the friendships of the famous. But the ultimate applause
> must come from you if you are to be a traveller in that distant,
> dark poetic place that is in all of us—Tennessee Williams'
> South—in feeling the emotion that is the last line of his human
> *Outcry,* that "magic is the habit of our existence."

And the bravos came for the film. It was called by the critic of
the *Toronto Star* "the best film ever made of a living person." The
reaction of Cecil Smith, dean of the U.S. drama and TV critics, was most
rewarding. It appeared in the *Los Angeles Times,* with the headline
"Raskymentaries: TV for Posterity."

> Harry Rasky's new documentary, *Tennessee Williams'*
> *South* was shown over the Canadian Broadcasting Corporation
> TV network on the playwright's 62nd birthday, March 26, to
> ringing acclaim. After which Rasky flew here from Toronto
> with the film under his arm to show it to the toughest critic of
> them all: Tennessee.
> Williams was here for the new production of *A Streetcar*
> *Named Desire* with Faye Dunaway and Jon Voight at the
> Ahmanson—he has since fled to the Orient. Rasky was
> apprehensive about him seeing it. He needn't have been.
> Tennessee loved it: "Let this be my epitaph."
> With reason, I might add. Not only is the film a definitive
> statement on the life, the work, the attitudes and beliefs of
> Williams, but in a documentary technique that has come to be
> known as a "Raskymentary," the film segues from the man
> into scenes from his plays, each complementing the other.

It is impossible to end a chapter on Tennessee Williams. Usually
when a film is over, the subject and the film-maker part and a distance
develops. In this case it was the opposite. At the screening that Cecil
Smith mentioned, after fortifying himself with friends such as Christopher
Isherwood and "the professor" and Faye Dunaway and Jon Voight,
Tennessee sat with a feeling of real wonder at the Beverly Hills Hotel
screening room. He smiled at first and said, "Why Harry, you have given
me the real MGM treatment." But we have talked many times about
many things since.

Perhaps his kindest answer was that he wrote a new work especially for me to direct, called *Stopped Rocking*, as yet not accepted by the U.S. television networks. Later, when he needed someone to direct the U.S. première of *Tiger Tail*, a theatrical version of *Baby Doll*, he asked me. It received glowing notices and we survived the mutual experience without one false word. But the most tender moment of all came when the film was finally carried on PBS. As it was telecast I sat in his suite at the Elysee Hotel in the presence of his sister Rose. The entire time she listened to the voice on the television set, but she stared at her brother in the room. Then, when it was over, she looked at me briefly. I think she smiled. No words were said.

I truly believe I had somehow become his brother. I think that God sends his messengers in the form of poets and artists. I believe that Tennessee is one of these. Their inner message is so direct that they might seem mad to us sometimes. But then which of us would seem mad to God?

CHAPTER SIXTEEN

Next Year in Jerusalem

I suppose it was a kind of homage to my father. It was a poem, a prayer I had to make. Probably it was a promise I had pledged myself, and therefore a bond with all the events that had made me. There is no way of talking of my film, *Next Year in Jerusalem,* without sounding mystical. Without belief it could never have been undertaken, and without faith it could never have been felt.

I remembered Jerusalem from those early years, from those haunting prayers of my father as cantor and leader at the McKay Street *schul* each Saturday morning and on the high holy days. If the *schul* was a tiny entrance to God's home, I was taught, before I knew of kings and queens and prime ministers and presidents, that the main residence for my King was a place called Jerusalem. In the cruel Toronto Januarys, that young boy who was me knew there was a warm city called Jerusalem. And on those frozen February mornings of my early teens when I could see the frost of my father's breath, I knew the echo of his song rose above the ice-covered roof and beyond the bleak, black trees into blue sky to the golden place on earth that was Jerusalem. If I half closed my eyes as I huddled within myself, I could carry myself with the sound.

And even before I understood the prayers or knew how to pray, I prayed.

By the rivers of Babylon, there we sat down,
yea, we wept, when we remembered Zion.
If I forget thee, O Jerusalem, let my
right hand forget her cunning.
If I do not remember three, let my tongue
cleave to the roof of my mouth; if I
prefer not Jerusalem above my chief joy.

The God of the Jews, said
"Rejoice with Jerusalem,
And be glad with her, all who love her;
Rejoice for joy with her
All who mourn for her . . .
Behold I will extend peace to her like a river . . .
As one whom his mother comforts,
So I will comfort you;
And you shall be comforted in Jerusalem.

I will not suggest to you that I had any grasp of phrases like "let my right hand forget her cunning," but as early as I knew anything I understood that there was "comfort in Jerusalem." So much for the beginning. Then when I travelled to great places and made films of stones and ideas, the name kept coming up. In Westminster Abbey the Anglicans sang the great Blake poem, "Jerusalem." And in Rome at St. Peter's Basilica, I filmed the great Bernini canopy that seemed squeezed out of a baroque tube, with its buxom bronze columns which, it is said, came from the design of the columns in Solomon's temple. All roads seemed to lead to Jerusalem.

Before I had left New York, I had tried for almost a year to mount a film expedition to Jerusalem. One friend, Steve Scheuer, had financed a brief exploratory trip, but I could find no financial backing. Thom Benson at the CBC agreed to my request to mount an expedition in 1973. I felt like a Canadian Crusader.

I chose as the host for the film my long-time colleague, Lorne Greene. Long before he had become the television cowboy and the dealer in dog food, Lorne had established himself as "the voice of doom," and I wanted a voice that sounded like the awe of the Bible. Lorne had had a Jewish past, and the idea of being the host flattered and pleased him. What I did not count on was his incredible instant recognizability which became something of a burden. Wherever we went, flashbulbs popped as people who had saved for a lifetime for their own pilgrimage stopped everything to take a shot of "Señor Bonanza." There were almost riots at the Church of the Holy Sepulchre, as people seemed to forget that they had come to see the site of the crucifixion, not the modern horseman. Suddenly it was the cavalry, not Calvary.

But Lorne was an imposing presence. He began walking up the steps of the Temple Mount as if about to lead a religious ritual. He passed under the sign that says "Notice and warning: entrance to the area of the Temple Mount is forbidden to everyone by Jewish law," apparently a reference to the geographical location of the Holy of Holies.

The Bible was my script and turned out to be an incredibly accurate guide to the past. Lorne intoned:

> In the beginning . . . in the beginning . . . in a way we all
> began here.
> It's even said that from the dust of Jerusalem God formed man
> and that Adam is buried here.
> Thus dust to dust.
> Some is fact, other is, well, let's say tradition. In this place is
> the history of war and wisdom, peace and power, kindness
> and cruelty, everything in short that is Man.
> Each of us in his own way lives in two cities—his own and
> Jerusalem.

I was trying to involve the viewer with a sense of his own presence in the city. I wanted so desperately, I think, to burst across the barriers, to have the viewer become a pilgrim with me, to do with film what Elie Wiesel, the poet of the Holocaust, had done with words:

> Jerusalem: the face visible yet hidden, the sap and blood of all
> that makes us live or renounce life. The spark flashing in the
> darkness, the murmur rustling through shouts of happiness and
> joy. A name, a secret. For the exiled, a prayer. For all others,
> a promise. Jerusalem: seventeen times destroyed yet never
> erased. The symbol of survival. Jerusalem: the city which
> miraculously transforms man into pilgrim; no one can enter it
> and go away unchanged.
>
>   This city of unshakable memory, I admit loving it, I
> even admit loving its hold over me. Distant lands no longer
> lure me. The seeker is weary of seeking, the explorer of self-
> excitement. Beneath this sky in which colors and faces clash,
> steps in the night reverberate to infinity; one listens, spellbound,
> overwhelmed. Follow them far enough and you will take by
> surprise a king lost in a dream, a prophet who reduces life and
> language to dust.

Out of the wilderness stone I wanted to make the patriarchs and prophets grow. Certainly when you leave Jerusalem to make your way down to the Dead Sea, you know they are there with you, perhaps praying just behind a stone, ready to be conjured up when the heat and mist embrace. The Judean Hills are the hills of home and to wander them is to be part of a psalm.

The only actor I have ever known who looked or sounded as if he could, indeed, be one of those living scribes of our mutual ancestors is Sam Jaffe. And if it is true that a man gets the face he deserves after he reaches forty, then Sam is truly the most rewarded of men. He has a smile like a flute note and a voice as rich as a cello. He re-created the story of Abraham ready to sacrifice his son to God, which in a way is also the beginning of the story of the New Testament. And he spoke the lines as if he were writing them, there at dawn in the wilderness, just on the edge of Jerusalem:

> And the angel of the Lord called unto
> Abraham out of heaven the second time.
> And said, by myself have I sworn,
> saith the Lord, But because thou hast
> done this thing, and hast not withheld
> they son, thine only son: That in
> blessing I will bless thee, and in
> multiplying I will multiply thy seed
> as the stars of the heaven, and as the
> sand which is upon the sea shore; and
> thy seed shall possess the gate of his enemies;
> And in thy seed shall all the nations
> of the earth be blessed; because thou
> hast obeyed my voice.

I was truly amazed to discover that the Bible is really an historical chronicle. You can begin at the beginning and chart on a calendar and map who did what, where and when. So that the promise begun on Mount Moriah to Abraham, and then passed on to Isaac and then to Jacob, can be seen as a direct connection. When Jacob calls on his sons and says, "Gather yourselves together that I may tell you that which shall befall you in the last days," we are ready to meet those who are to head the 12 tribes, our common ancestors.

Almost as an afterthought, I decided on a creative way to show the tribe leaders: by filming the Chagall windows. I allowed an afternoon on my schedule, and was so awed by the way his glass and the colours of the Jerusalem sky so perfectly blended that I had trouble leaving them. God, ᴏᴦ whoever wrote the Bible, had placed in his description of the 12 tribes virtually every human weakness and strength, and Chagall in his ancient wisdom had understood this fact so clearly that he needed no human form to express it. It could be done with colour, almost as if you had just stared at the sun and then tried to look at reality. It is there, but transformed.

In the Bible, there is always the promise of clear vision, but it is always just beyond reach, even of the most favoured, or especially of them. When the Lord recited the blessing and the curse to Moses, He said, "This is the land which I swore unto Abraham, unto Isaac, and unto Jacob. I have caused thee to see it with thine eyes but thou shalt not go over thither." Which of us who aspires ever does get to live in our private Jerusalem?

My film on Jerusalem was one of the few I have ever made where the script was completed before filming began. And among all the scholars I had to call on, the most efficient and accurate source turned out to be Ben-Ami Cohen, a Jewish driver who was assigned to me by the Israeli government tourist office. Ben-Ami had seen it all, and nothing confounded him. He could handle Jewish and gentile history alike. He merely began each sentence with "according to tradition." He showed me where David mounted his attack on Jerusalem through a water shaft "according to tradition."

The link between the Law and Jerusalem connected everything for me. The stories I was forced to study with my father on those long Saturday afternoons of my childhood on St. Clair, when I would much rather have been at the Royal George watching real heroes like Hopalong Cassidy, now all fitted into place. The stones of the Mount of Olives reminded me of real persons and adventures. When my friend Sam Jaffe, who came to Jerusalem with his warm wife, Bettye, and stood among the golden rocks and announced in the voice of Isaiah, I was listening to a relative.

> Many peoples shall go and say:
> Come, and let us go up to the mountain
> of the Lord.
> To the house of the God of Jacob;
> And he will teach us of His ways,
> And we shall walk in his paths.
> For out of Zion shall go forth Torah,
> And the word of the Lord from Jerusalem.
> He shall judge between many nations,
> And shall decide for many peoples;
> They shall beat their swords into plowshares,
> And their spears into pruning-hooks;
> Nation shall not lift up sword against nation,
> Neither shall they learn war any more.

The characters of the past were like people I had known. And in fact, in casting around, I gave the part of Mariamme, the wife of the tyrant Herod, to Toby Robins, a Canadian actress now living in London. I knew Toby when I was thirteen, and to my inexperienced eyes she gave the boys a difficult time because she was so pretty. She always seemed to be washing her hair on Saturday nights when I was a teenager looking for a date for the Junior B'nai B'rith dance. In the script she was about to give Herod the worst of times. Lord Byron expressed the rage and jealousy that seemed to be a part of my own early life, so it was not some distant cardboard heroine I was dealing with:

> Oh, Mariamme! now for thee
> the heart for which thou bled'st is bleeding;
> Revenge is lost in agony,
> And with wild remorse to rage succeeding.
> Oh, Mariamme! where are thou?
> Thou canst not hear my bitter pleading:
> Ah! could'st thou—thou would'st pardon now.
> Though Heaven were to my prayer unheeding.

And the day outside of Jericho we filmed Toby in blue robes with her blue eyes, she seemed, even then, just a little too flawless. Even the camels nearby had to be quieted down as the heat zoomed to about 110 degrees, but Toby seemed so cool. War, peace, time, destruction of empires—what were these compared with the memory of teenage love? Her speech began ironically: "For your compassion little need have I."

While we were down in the area of the Dead Sea we filmed the caves where the Dead Sea Scrolls and the ruins of the home of the Essenes were discovered. The leader of one sect "according to tradition" was a Galilean Jewish preacher, Jesus of Nazareth.

Since childhood I have always had trouble with the idea of Jesus. But there where the sun seemed to bake you right into the stone, at the Dead Sea as flat as eternity, I had no trouble conjuring up the events of the year 33 A.D. We followed the road through the wilderness, and I had no difficulty visualizing that final journey. The wilderness itself provided us with a tone poem of colour. Its bleakness took on dawn shades of orange-yellow and then the darkness of deep purple. It was a place for revelations.

At the Coenaculum on Mount Zion, directly above King David's tomb, I could imagine the Thursday night when they all gathered for the last supper of tradition:

And when the hour was come, he sat
down, and the twelve apostles with him.
And he said unto them, With desire I
have desired to eat this Passover with you before I suffer:
For I say unto you, I will not any more
eat thereof, until it be fulfilled in
the Kingdom of God.

Our camera moved with grace to the gardens of Gethsemane, where each twisted olive tree seemed to force itself into the final agony. And then we zoomed through the very walls of Jerusalem where no man can walk and dissolved through to the Stations of the Cross on the Via Dolorossa, ending at the Church of the Holy Sepulchre. But what gave this lofty sequence meaning were shots of agonized skies, lonely pine cones like winter death, and finally the choir singing the *St. Matthew Passion,* led by the rushing, river-like voice of Maureen Forrester. As orchestrated by Lou Applebaum, it was a film hymn.

The traditional site of the crucifixion is Calvary, or Golgotha which means a bald scalp because that's the way the hill looks. The Church of the Holy Sepulchre, which is constantly under repair at that site, became a particularly difficult location for filming, as we had to move our equipment up the tortuous streets by donkey. They were not wide enough for vehicles. Since the church is under the control of three sects, we had some difficulty inside. Every time we would begin to roll, another Christian priest would throw holy water on the lens, or start chanting when we called for *shekket,* silence. I couldn't help but contemplate how many wars have been fought as each side battled with the cry that God was on his side.

For most of us, the events of our theological history end with the time of Jesus, because that is more or less where the Bible leads us. But Ben-Ami Cohen, my all-knowing driver, had insisted that I read the works of Josephus, who tells us painful details of the Jewish Wars. It is fascinating reading. I was moved by the eloquence of an historical figure about whom I knew little, Agrippa II. His argument about the folly of going to war seemed to fit any time or place, but especially the Israeli situation, and I always felt his speech could have been part of a debate in the Knesset. Barry Morse flew in from London to act it out on the wall of the Citadel, an oration across time:

Whom will you find in the uninhabited wilds to be your allies
in this war? For in the inhabited world all are Romans. Not
even if you survive will you find a place of refuge. Again, the
danger that threatens is not only ourselves here but also those

in other cities; for there is not a region in the world without its Jewish colony. All these, if you go to war, will be massacred by your opponents, and through the folly of a few men every city will run with Jewish blood.

Pity your wives and children, or at least pity your mother city and her sacred precincts. Spare the Temple and preserve for your use the Sanctuary and its sacred treasures. I call to witness all that you hold sacred, the holy angels of God, the Fatherland which we all share, and tell you that I have held nothing back. If you make the right decision you will share with me the blessings of peace, but if you are carried away by your passions you will go without me to your doom.

War was delayed. But war came: five years of fighting. On the anniversary of the very day that the Babylonians destroyed the first temple of Solomon, the Romans destroyed the second temple. Josephus described the disaster:

There was no pity for age, no regard for rank; little children and old men, laymen and priests alike were butchered; every class was held in the iron embrace of war, whether they defended themselves or cried for mercy. Through the roar of the flames as they swept relentlessly on could be heard the groans of the falling: such were the height of the hill and the vastness of the blazing edifice that the entire city seemed to be on fire, while as for the noise, nothing could be imagined more shattering or more horrifying. There was the war cry of the Roman legions as they converged; the yells of the partisans encircled with fire and sword; the panic flight into the arms of the enemy of the people cut off above, their shrieks as the end approached.

Eyewitnesses said before the sunset there were to be seen in the sky over the whole country chariots and regiments in arms speeding through the clouds and encircling the towns. One man stood in the ashes of the Temple and shouted: "A voice from the east, a voice from the west, a voice from the four winds, a voice against Jerusalem and the Sanctuary, a voice against Bridegrooms and Brides, a voice against the whole people."

Josephus was truly one of the great war correspondents of all time. Although some critics have said he exaggerated, as he was not personally present, I have seldom read such violent descriptions of an event. It should have been horrifying enough to prevent all future wars. But then you know what happened.

Filming at Masada, the place of final refuge and ultimate defeat for the Jews, we were at a locale without escape—high on a mountain, barren ruins, complete isolation save for the modern cable car. If hell is that hot, then all those child's world pictures of the devil dancing are exaggerated. Movement of any kind was impossible. If *we* had to decide whether to give in to the Romans in order to escape, I really wonder what I would have done. But there, that blistering August Day, I filmed Israeli actor Joseph Yadin, whose brother had conducted the excavations and whose father had been the identifier of the Dead Sea Scrolls. Now in the halo of hell, he was the leader Eleasar, exhorting his followers to die for a cause:

> We chose death rather than slavery. Where is the mighty city Jerusalem, the mother-city of the whole Jewish race. If only we had died before seeing the Sacred City utterly destroyed by enemy hands, the Holy Sanctuary so impiously uprooted! Let us at once choose death with honour and do the kindest thing we can for ourselves, our wives and children.
>
> Is anyone too blind to see how furious they will be if they take us alive? Pity the young whose bodies are strong enough to survive prolonged torture; pity the not-so-young whose old frames would break under such ill-usage. A man will see his wife violently carried off; he will hear the voice of his child crying "Father" when his own hands are bound.

And so they killed each other in order not to be taken as slaves: 960 people died that day at Masada. Two old women and five children lived to tell the tale, and to see what was left of Jerusalem's temple.

The camera followed a lone sparrow hopping in the fierce heat of the sun at the west wall, the Wailing Wall. As the camera panned from scarlet prayer platform to platform, the gold-embroidered star of David caught the brilliant rays. In a shadowed corner some old Jewish men were praying. Out of the cracks of the stones, there was sparse, desperate growth. The ornate temple is not there, except in memory. And in memory it is more glorious than any building that has ever been created by human hands, for each man can see it as he will in his mind. The temple of the mind is the most magnificent.

Despite the passion of the Jewish hold on Jerusalem, I wanted to show that it had great meaning for Arabs as well. I sought out an Islamic expert in Jerusalem and another one in Canada to explain to me the Moslem mystique.

It was clear that they were the last of the builders. There was to rise in golden splendour the Dome of the Rock, where Moslems believed Mohammed made his mystic flight to heaven. If you accept tradition, it is the same place where Abraham was commanded to sacrifice his son Isaac, Mount Moriah, and the same place where the two temples stood. And the Arabs call it Haramesh-Sharif, the noble sanctuary. In Jerusalem, history is a layer cake.

To gain permission to film inside the Dome of the Rock in colour, which had never been done, I had to make a visitation to the Waqf, the keeper of the most holy places. The introduction had been made by the dynamic mayor of Jerusalem, Teddy Kollek, who had gained the respect of the various Arab leaders. Up in the back of the great gold building, I entered a small office which housed a small wooden desk and a low couch. With me was the Israeli secretary, Leihe, who had been working on permissions. Leihe was one of those Sabra girls who claim to have had ancestors all the way back to the burning temple and who have never left the land of Israel. She looked as if she could be playing Wonder Woman in Hebrew. She was fluent in Arabic and she interpreted my plea.

The Waqf studied me. He offered a cup of thick Turkish coffee and said, "The third most holy place of Islam cannot be the setting for an actress. No, it is forbidden."

"Your excellency," I replied, "our great respect for your holy place would not allow me to bring in an actress." I was sure he had conjured up belly dancers in scanty costumes on the prayer rugs. Another cup of syrupy Turkish coffee was called for. Leihe indicated to me that this was a good sign. Progress.

"But I'm afraid even an actor could not be allowed in. This is the holy ground you must know where, from which place, Mohammed made his ride to heaven." I had, in fact, hoped to stage a dramatic reading there. But I quickly retreated. I knew that no arm twisting would have any effect. However, a little ego massaging might be in order.

"Your grand, great holiness," I began, magnifying the title as I went, "let me put it to you this way. When I filmed in St. Peter's in Rome, the most holy of holy places for all those Christians (slurring the word 'Christian' a bit for his benefit), it was the Most Holy Father, Pope of all the Catholics, who personally signed my petition to film there, as it was the Dean of Westminster, head of all those Anglicans, who gave his permission in London. Here in Jerusalem, most honoured master of these holy shrines, only you have that grand power."

He tried not to smile with pleasure. Another pot of coffee was summoned. There was one of those long pauses which are pregnant with meaning. He swayed a little, as if in semi-prayer as he answered: "Given

the fact you have dealt with the Christian Holy Father, we are willing
to make a concession to have you place your camera in the Holy Shrine,
but you must observe all our rules and never interfere with prayer.'' With
that he waved his arm and seemed to slip into meditation with Allah.
And so we bowed slightly and salaamed our way out.

And so I was back in church, a Moslem one this time. Everyone
hopes for a chunk of eternity. It is interesting that an iron grill surrounds
Mohammed's rock, because apparently when the place was inhabited by
the Crusaders they chipped away at it. Had the Christian salvation of
Jerusalem lasted longer during the time of the Crusades, only a pebble
would have been left. In filming the interior, the Israeli technicians walked
on stocking feet carrying huge ''brute'' lights to make the Moslem shrine
glow. One small detail the Waqf never told us: our pass was good for
only one day at a time. A ritual had to be observed to gain a new one
daily, and it depended on the mood of co-operation of the day. But the
golden glory of the mosque was filmed.

The scene that I had hoped to film inside I moved to the wilderness.
It was a dialogue between two great historical figures of the past, the
brilliant Salah-ad-Din, known to us as Saladin, and King Richard the
Lion Hearted of England.

Two flags hung in the baking sands, symbols of the two armies,
and the echoes of the great warriors seemed to sweep all the way to
Galilee. What was filmed was an imaginary meeting, for the two opponents never met in life. For Richard, I had to manufacture dialogue
along the lines of the chronicles of the crusades, because even though
he reached the edge of Jerusalem, there is not one line written about what
he thought or felt. As for Saladin, there were actual letters, and his
language had the richness of a flowing robe:

> This is a joyous day: Only God can know the measureless delight
> of both peoples. I was ready for battle. But I knew the power
> of the winter and the glory of my God. I told my generals who
> were prepared to die: the land, the lives, the children of all
> Moslems rest upon you. If you fail, which God forfend, they
> will roll up the land like a scroll. The Moslems over all the
> country rest upon your valour. Wa-s Selam.

The awkward co-existence of religions went on for centuries.
There were a few more crusades, not all successful. St. Francis started
out and did not arrive. There was the pitiful Children's Crusade. And
then there were the individual pilgrims who made journeys to Jerusalem
almost as casually as we do today. Chaucer's Wife of Bath made three
journeys, thus, presumably, being thrice blessed. Marco Polo came by

to take oil from the lamp of the Holy Sepulchre to Kublai Khan. But Jerusalem would not be in Christian hands for seven centuries. After Saladin there was a great deal of rivalry. The Egyptians came and the Turks took Jerusalem in 1516. Suleiman the Great restored the walls, built the Damascus Gate, and gave the Old City the look it has today.

Napoleon expressed an interest; the German Kaiser came. Strange pilgrims came like Chinese Gordon, soldier and scholar, who had his own theory about the location of the real hill of Golgotha where Christ is said to have been crucified. The Jewish population grew during all that time. But events were taking place elsewhere that would significantly alter the life of Jerusalem.

Far away in the Hotel de Castille in Paris, an Austrian Jewish journalist watched the public degradation of a French Jewish army captain, Alfred Dreyfus. He heard the cries: "Death to the traitor! Death to the Jews!" They said of him that he had "a countenance lit with the glance of the Messiah." He looked like a Hebrew prophet. Theodor Herzl began a dream:

> Imagine: the promised Land, where we can have hooked noses,
> black or red beards, and bandy legs, without being despised
> for it. Where at last we can live as free men on our own soil,
> and die tranquilly in our own homeland. Where we can expect
> the reward of honour for great deeds; where we shall live at
> peace with all the world, which we have freed through our own
> freedom, enriched by our wealth, and made greater by our
> greatness. So that the derisive cry of "Jew!" may become an
> honourable appellation, like Englishman, Frenchman—in short,
> like that of all civilized peoples. God would not have kept us
> alive so long if there were not left for us a role to play in
> the history of mankind.
>
> What is it the Italian king once said to me. Oh yes. "I
> like this love for Jerusalem. It shows the love for an idea. I
> myself have seen the Jews at the Wailing Wall. I used to think
> it was a farce until I saw it with my own eyes. No beggars,
> but men like yourself were weeping."
>
> And the Pope. I remember our meeting. He told me,
> "The Jewish faith was the foundation of our own, but it has
> been superseded by the teachings of Christ. The Jews who
> should have been the first to acknowledge Jesus Christ, have
> not done so to this day." It was on the tip of my tongue to
> remark, "It happens in every family: no one believes in his
> own relatives."

On July 3, 1904, at the age of forty-four, the modern Moses was dead. In his will, Theodor Herzl asked that his body be buried in Vienna, next to that of his father, "to remain there," he wrote, "until the Jewish people will carry my remains to Palestine." On August 16, 1949, his coffin was carried to the State of Israel and the next day laid to rest on a ridge facing Jerusalem from the west. It is called Mount Herzl. The prophet was in the Promised Land.

I dramatized the Herzl speech in the museum in Jerusalem set up to his memory. But then the question was how to portray the unthinkable, how to tell the unspeakable, how to show the unviewable, the Holocaust. The Israelis had gathered remnants there in Jerusalem at Yad Vashem, a museum of death. With matchless taste they mounted the most powerful photos of those awful days. On the day it was closed, I filmed there. I recall bringing my children along, so they would not forget. It was a mistake. For months, Adam, just five, cried out in the night at the images, beyond nightmare.

At Yad Vashem, there were nameplates in stone from synagogues that had been destroyed by the Germans. These were mounted on a wall outside the building at Mount Zion. They were like tombstones for ideals that had burned. A few tattered scrolls of the law had been saved and encased, the name of God parched on His parchment. I filmed these, moving the camera in a kind of rhythm that was to allow for painful time and aching silence. Later, in the post-production of the film, I added the voice of Maureen Forrester singing the most sacred of Hebrew prayers, *Kol Nidre*. It became a massive prayer for the dead. I cannot listen to it now without tears, and whenever this part of the film is run I try to leave the screening room. I fear that for a moment I almost looked at the embarrassed face of God, and like Moses, I had to be punished. But I did the best I knew how.

In terms of the life of the film, in Canada it caused a quiet sensation. People across the country called me to say they felt they had had a religious experience watching the program. A priest told me it was like a mass. A Baptist said she saw Jesus. An Egyptian expressed envy. Later it was selected by the Association of Canadian Radio and Television Artists as the best film of the year, for which I was grateful. It was purchased for broadcast by both PBS and the BBC. Neither ever ran it. One theory is that there was "oil" pressure not to do it. It can't be proven. But it was curious.

In Canada, the combined Arab delegates in Ottawa held a meeting to protest the film, and later recommended to the president of the CBC that the negative be burned—just like a third temple, I thought. He did not give in to the pressure and I have always honoured Laurent Picard for that. Although I felt I had tried to cast an even-eyed look at the holy but worn city, I received threatening phone calls. So much for my universal message of peace.

But later it all came together for me. On the Jewish New Year, I was asked to give the sermon at the McKay Street *shul*, on the site where my father had delivered his songs to God. I told the poor congregation which had never been able to afford a rabbi that each man lives in two cities, his own and Jerusalem. And most especially, since the destruction of the temple, that anywhere God is loved is a part of the new temple, ongoing forever. It was just in time. Soon, the *shul* that once was our home and had had continuous services every Saturday for every Sabbath of the twentieth century was sold to the Grace Tabernacle, a black church. Only a few Jews were left on St. Clair Avenue West. But I prayed that day that a part of Jerusalem, a part of my grandfather and father, a part of my children who attended the service, and a part of me would always be there.

All his life my father dreamed of realizing the prayer "Next Year in Jerusalem." He was never to be able to go there. I think I brought some of Jerusalem home with me—for him.

CHAPTER SEVENTEEN

Marc Chagall:

This film will help me live longer, not less

Y ou say it's not possible, but it's a fact: the glass danced. In Canada and the United States, I had seen prints of the 12 stained-glass windows designed by Chagall for the Hadassah Hebrew University Medical Centre. They were often decorations in Jewish homes, in the same way as Italian Catholics exhibit nativity scenes. They were official announcements in middle-class homes of art appreciation. But all those reproductions did not allow for the miracle of colour that confronted me and my crew that day in Jerusalem when, as part of *Next Year in Jerusalem,* we came to film the windows that had made Chagall's name a legend.

The first lesson was as clear as the Jerusalem sky when I entered the Hadassah Synagogue. Stained glass must be lit from the back to provide the translucent quality that gives the art form its strength.

I had heard that Chagall himself had not been too happy with the setting for the windows, and the reason why became obvious. The windows are jammed together in a building that without them could be a bunker. They are not allowed to soar. Thrust together, they are like overlapping paragraphs, like musical notes pounded out on a keyboard all at the same time.

It seemed to me that my job was simple. As I was not an art specialist, I had to take each window and explain its components, to treat each window like the work of art it was. I had pre-recorded the commentary, narrated by Lorne Greene directly from the Bible. While cameraman Ken Gregg filmed, I played the audiotape. The poetry of the Bible became a camera direction. The fish swam in a red sea, and the boats moved and ancient Israel was alive. Each window became the leader of his tribe, the persona. Suddenly they were so simple—the candles and the lambs and the Hebrew script. But even in the simplicity there was mystery. The colours were like no other colours I had ever seen. The mind, the creative hand that had constructed God in glass, that person had to be extraordinary.

But I did not think too much more about Chagall for some time to come. We left Israel just before the '73 war came that tested the nation. I returned to the safety of Canada and spent some time in London putting together a rather ordinary film honouring the wedding of Princess Anne. My misery was increased by the fact that I had to follow the progress of the Israeli-Arab war on the BBC, which seemed to lean over backwards to honour its long pro-Arab tradition.

Back in Canada, my wife bought a Chagall print, a section of the Paris Opera ceiling, as an anniversary gift. She hung the poster over our diningroom table and said, "How about Chagall?" That is where the project began. Each Friday at Sabbath dinner, I would look up at the green paper canvas and see those people flying through the air, and I would think about the glass that danced in the Jerusalem sun. We were somehow linked. But still I did not quite see it as a film for me.

Then my wife brought home a volume from the Holy Blossom Temple library called *My Life,* the autobiography of Chagall. It began, "First of all, I was born dead." My God, I thought, he writes like he paints. What kind of man is he?

> I did not want to live. Imagine a white bubble that does not
> want to live. As if it had been stuffed with Chagall pictures.
> They pricked that bubble with needles, they plunged it into
> a pail of water. At last it emitted a feeble whimper. But the
> main thing was, I was born dead.

The volume lit my soul: page after page of a man shooting through pink clouds and dazzling colours of human expression. It concluded:

> These pages have the same meaning as a painted surface. . . . If
> there were a hiding place in my pictures, I would slip into
> them . . . . I am certain Rembrandt loves me . . . . Moscow
> 1922.

I wanted to call back to the book, "I love you. Don't go away Mr. Chagall, I love you. Let me film you to show my love. Let me make your portrait on a screen of images and music and motion. Hold out for me. Don't pass from this world yet.'' Anyone who could conclude an autobiography in 1922 and still be going strong half a century later, would perhaps wait, would perhaps understand. A film about Chagall and his life became an obsession. The question was where and how to begin.

It's possible that God plants his angels in strange places. While tracking down Chagall, I began to accept revelations as if they were as certain as snow in a Canadian winter. On the wall of Thom Benson's office was a framed print of a Chagall rabbi. When I presented the idea to my old friend Thom, instead of saying, ''Why should a Canadian broadcasting corporation involve itself in a film on a French painter,'' he said simply, ''I wonder why Chagall can't paint fingers? Maybe we should find out.'' If Thom Benson had never made another statement in his life, that would have been enough. How wonderfully cavalier. Not why do Chagall creatures fly? Or why such flashing colours? No. Simply, why does he paint the fingers that way? I'll always love Thom Benson for that.

The Chagall hunt began. I had tried writing to an address supplied by the French government to request an interview. There was no reply. It was agreed that I would attend an upcoming film festival in Monte Carlo, where my film *Next Year in Jerusalem* was scheduled to lead off the event attended by Princess Grace. It was reasoned that this film, which had been selected as the best of the year by the Association of Canadian Radio and Television Artists, would have a huge reception in France, and Chagall would welcome me when I went to call.

I was wrong twice. But not in the final analysis. The Chagall angels merely prodded me in different directions. The Jerusalem film did not make any official impact at Monte Carlo. The eastern European judges treated it as if it had leprosy on its sprocket holes. Because it made a passionate case for Jewish Jerusalem, I was viewed as the enemy.

As for Chagall, when I went to see him, I travelled all morning by bus and then by taxi to St. Paul de Vence. The driver warned me that to arrive without an appointment would be uncomfortable. To say the least. From the gate to the entrance, we were chased by a growling dog. Just to leave the cab seemed to be a risk. I took it. I presented my card at the door. The angry maid was very specific: ''Mr. Chagall, never, never receives anyone without an appointment.'' It was a long, lonely trip back along the coast to Monte Carlo. The festival took on a gloomy air with my mission unaccomplished, and it began to seem that I would not win even the honorary religious prize. How could the Pope's deputy turn down Jerusalem? Easy I found.

Back in Toronto I was licking my wounds when I got a call from my next Chagall angel. Amnon Gil-ad was the head of the Israeli government tourist office. He had reasoned that the success of my film *Next Year in Jerusalem* had kept the Canadian tourists flowing to Israel after the '73 war when they had slowed down from all other western nations. We had become friends. "Teddy will be here," he said. "Let Teddy help." He was referring to Teddy Kollek, mayor of Jerusalem. I had met him briefly when I first planned the Jerusalem film, and he had sent me a telegram congratulating me on the ACTRA prize. He has often been described as a bull of a man with excess energy. He is that. There is also about him the feeling of a person who knows he is destiny's servant. He tries not to reveal this too much, preferring the tough calling card of the world's most famous mayor. I think his sense of mission is something that never leaves him.

I was given the code name of the place to find him. He was staying at the Inn on the Park on the outskirts of the city. He was not registered. I left word for the "Mr. X." I was told to call. I waited nervously all morning and into the early evening. The phone rang. "This is Teddy. I am here for one night only. I leave after breakfast tomorrow." The tone was flat and unemotional. I thought it would be followed by, "I don't have time to talk to you." Teddy Kollek is known as the man who never sleeps, who handles every problem personally. "What do you have for breakfast?" I found myself giving the mayor of Jerusalem my breakfast order. There was silence for a moment. "Be here at 6 a.m."

It was not quite dawn when I made the long drive to what I presumed would be a useless rendezvous between the world's busiest mayor and me, a man with an obsession. The situation seemed unlikely that cold morning as I knocked on his door. I was greeted by a huge man who must have weighed 300 pounds or more. He was obviously the bodyguard and had been sleeping in the outer room to guard the door. Bodyguards, I thought! How can I bother him with my small problem?

Teddy Kollek stared at the wall as I quickly ran through the events at Monte Carlo and the unanswered request. He didn't pause for long. He seemed to be drawing on his Solomon connections. "Eat the breakfast. I have to leave for the airport." Was that it? He yawned the huge yawn of a man who has been on too many airplanes, who has listened to too many problems. "Rasky has been good to Jerusalem. Jerusalem will try for Rasky." It was almost Shakespearean. "You draw up a letter, send it to me in Jerusalem. I will send it to Chagall. It will be done." He looked at his watch, yawned again. The guard indicated that our morning rendezvous was over. They had to be moving on to some other secret meeting in another city.

There was no mention in the local paper that the mayor had been in town. And indeed as the days passed and then the weeks I began to wonder if I had really had the meeting, or whether I was letting all that angel dust get in my brain. But then it arrived—a letter from Madame Chagall which said that she would welcome a visit. Thom Benson cast the dice. "Take a film crew along," he said. Yes, we would find out about those fingers in the painting.

I returned to Europe with a film crew. This time when I arrived at La Colline in St. Paul de Vence, I was greeted by a tail-wagging friendly dog, the maid offered fresh tonic water, and Madame Vava Chagall smiled. "Teddy says such nice things about you." Who says there are no angels? Now, the adventure began. The house, La Colline, is extraordinarily modern, and the reception area is almost cold, except for the fact that giant Chagall oil paintings decorate the walls. They are hung in such a way as to make the whole room seem to float.

Chagall entered. I must say that his short rapid movements made him seem like a boxer in training. His blue corduroy pants and open blue polo shirt set off his gray halo of hair. Immediately I felt something of Ben Gurion in him, something of my father, something of a playful boy. His quick smile was, in fact, so complete that it seemed to project actual light. "So, what is this all about?" he asked in French.

"I told you. You know. This gentleman, recommended by Teddy, has come to make a film." Madame Chagall was firm and in total control.

"Let him make a film if he wishes. But I will not be in it." *Oh!* I can still feel the pain. I had waited all those months, gambled on bringing a film crew; my own reputation was at risk.

"But . . ." Madame Chagall caught the expression of absolute agony and leaned forward confidently. "Slowly, slowly," she said. "It will be all right."

Chagall began a kind of play. He poked his head at me. "Listen, how do I know what the script will be?" I was ready. In one hand I had a copy of his book, *My Life*. In the other I held a copy of the Holy Bible, borrowed from some hotel room.

"Here is the text. Your own words and the words of God."

He seemed to like that relationship. "All right. Very good. But what will it look like?" When scared to death, fight back, I thought. If I lost Chagall now, my entire year's work would be gone.

"Monsieur Chagall," I said with surprising calm, "tonight when the sun sets and tomorrow when it rises, it will look a certain way to me. Only when you paint it, will I know how you see it."

His face lit up like the burning bush. "You have seen a Chagall, yes." He gestured to his walls clothed with his brilliant works. "I must see a Rasky, before one begins. Is that possible?"

He thought he had me. "I happen to have with me"—I gestured very magnanimously in my fear of going too far—"I happen to have with me a print of my film *Next Year in Jerusalem,* which has in it your own windows.''

"Come back tomorrow with a projector to show it and we will see. Meantime you can begin the filming without me.'' He seemed to jog out of the room, he was gone so quickly. Madame Chagall, who spoke perfect English, calmed me. "You will see. It will be all right.''

Next afternoon, with a borrowed projector and bent nerves, I arrived back with my CBC crew. We set up the projector to show the film on the wall. The butler moved two wing chairs into position for the Chagalls and a smaller one for me. They entered, took positions as if for a command performance. Madame Chagall leaned over to ask, "How long is it?''

"Ninety minutes,'' I said.

"He'll never sit through it,'' she said matter-of-factly.

He gestured to begin. Then he asked that the sound be lowered a bit. I watched his face and not the screen. At first he was in repose, but when the Chagall window section came on, he pointed at each image as the camera travelled over the glass that danced. He was like a child for a time. When that section passed, he was calm again. The first 30 minutes passed by. As the reel ran out I asked, "Shall I go on?'' He gestured, "Yes, yes.''

Then the second reel began, images of ancient Israel, dramatic re-enactments in English which he would not understand, various views of the crucifixion, with the music of Bach and the lofty sound of Maureen Forrester. And the second reel was done. He rose. I asked, "Is that it?''

"No, I merely am going to the bathroom. Prepare the rest.''

Then the third reel rolled on, reaching its climax at Yad Vashem with the photos of the Holocaust and the piercing cry of *Kol Nidre* sung to perfection by Maureen. Chagall wanted to avert his eyes. He couldn't quite look, but still he did, appearing to suffer pain with each changing photo.

It was finished. He was silent for minutes. "Do you wish to know what I think?'' he asked.

"Of course. Of course. That's why I'm here.'' Then quietly he offered the greatest compliment I have ever had. "Your film, this film will help me live longer, not less.'' I had tears in my eyes. He rose to go and added, "Maybe I will walk in your film, but I won't talk.''

There was one more advance session. I had prepared a script outline, and Jeannette Bertrand, the French-Canadian script assistant, worked all night to translate. I was summoned back. This time Chagall with some warmth said, "I like your outline and filming can begin. Maybe I will talk a little.'' He went back to his studio and Madame

Chagall explained that the interview would take place on film after a few days. They would be away for, as she put it, "a weekend or so."

Meantime I began to hunt the colours of the sky, to see them as Chagall might. Each dawn and dusk we tried for God's play with the horizon. We made our own mechanical sky-watching device. Ken Gregg and I devised a lens attachment which broke down the colours into blocks of green and red and blue. We experimented with all kinds of natural backgrounds to see if we could find a dream look to the world. Test film was flown to Paris for quick and exact processing. I summoned the head of the lab to Nice, so each frame's colours could be studied. We filmed each canvas and print in the Chagall Museum in Nice. And waited.

The weekend turned out to be two weeks. They had gone to Switzerland. Finally I phoned Madame Chagall again and she said, "Come Wednesday, after lunch."

Lunch that day was something I will never forget. We had found the most charming spot in St. Paul, overlooking the walled city. But I could not eat. I kept focussing on the sky, which had been threatening all morning. Would it be too hot to walk, too rainy to talk, too muggy to appear at all? What would happen? My laconic cameraman, Ken Gregg, sniffed the air: "It could rain." The trout I was trying to eat seemed to smile knowingly from my plate. I did not risk a digestive encounter with him.

We drove back to the Chagall house, which was five miles or so from the walled part of the city. We parked in the circular driveway, and I rang the bell. For a couple of long minutes there was no answer. Could it be that no one was home? Eventually the maid did answer. Her expression was non-commital. "Around the back," she said. It was more or less an order. The sky was close to tears. Me too. Chagall appeared suddenly. He looked up at the sky. "It's too hot to walk," he said. "I'll talk." He smiled. "Ask me anything."

I had come armed with half a dozen written questions, not knowing what to expect. The camera crew moved with precision. We were ready to go. The questions and the answers poured out of him, as if he had been waiting for someone to ask. There was no delay. His face deep in thought, always amused, always playful, always wise. No question about it. He was playing with me. But he was also projecting important concepts. He was not one to suffer fools lightly nor did he use his precious time frivolously. Each breathing moment seemed to have its place in his scheme of things.

It was a kind of mental dance into his past and present ideas. At first the questions were somewhat formal:

"Has your place of birth, Vitebsk, haunted your work?" A note of impatience. The question had been asked many times. "Louder," he said. "Speak louder." And so I asked the question again louder. He smiled at my discomfort. "Ah, you know, the place of your birth is fixed in your mind for your whole lifetime. You can go to the north pole if you like, but you always carry with you your birthplace. At least, that's how I feel."

I tried to show I was prepared for anything. "Some of the many books I have read talked about Paris being a second place of birth to you. Is that correct?"

"Ah, yes, it's true. In the twentieth century when the artists came to France, they surely experienced a second birth. As in past times when artists went to Italy, they were born a second time. Possibly later, in a hundred years, they will go to America to be born a second time. That's the way it goes."

"How have world events affected your work?"

A sigh. "The same as everyone else. You become the events of the world. As you are wounded you become an invalid. If you are talented, it changes your talent. It is absolutely reflected in your work. Exterior events cause all humanity to change, artists included." Much later I thought of that essential answer: "You become the events of the world." I challenge you to reflect on that for a day and see how it changes your own attitudes.

I wanted to talk about his new museum, for that was his passion of the moment. "Are the persons we see in the pictures real people?"

"If you are talking about my biblical messages, they are real biblical people, of course. But I introduced people from another era. Parents. Your parents. My parents. All parents. I have reflected in the biblical sphere some that reflect our era as well, so that it won't be just a personal thing but a world-wide thing."

"I notice in your paintings so many acrobats and clowns. What is their role in what you're trying to say?"

The question gathered a certain smile. His eyes darted with enthusiasm. All his clowns seemed to be dancing before him. "Ah, but listen. Don't you know? There are a lot of acrobatics in many characters. There are clown things, clown acts. Certain wars have been proclaimed by clown-type persons, if you want. It's not something extraordinary. It's a normal thing. In life, there are clowns, acrobats. There are all these types."

I imagined the sound of the merry-go-round. He seemed most content with his thoughts. Maybe, I thought, I could try the big question. "Everyone has a private image of God. What is your concept of God?"

"Of God? Listen, you talk to me, ask me a question to which even Einstein had no answer. And I am but an ordinary man. Ah, no. It is given to nobody to know what is God. For me God is love. The divine. It's love. I often say that it is through love that we manage to live our poor lives. An ideal life can possibly be achieved only through the methods of love. It is through love that you find the best social life, the best politics, the best art. You know, all through the Bible there is talk of love. But even after thousands of years, there are no big results.''

He now seemed totally submerged in the expression of his ideas. Now, I thought, I could pose a little controversy. ''I notice that even in the pictures you have done of the creation there is a picture of the crucifixion. Why does the crucifixion play such a role in your work?''

He seemed pleased to be able to answer this question which had been thrust at him by many Jewish scholars, always with the suggestion that he had crossed some religious barrier that for them offended. ''I have often been asked this question. For me, the crucifixion . . . those who were crucified are the martyrs. Everything that was happening not too long ago in those terrible wars—they are the crucified, the martyrs. That's what it is. It's not strictly religious. It's a human thing. Of course, then it was a sublime cause for which they were crucified. For me, a certain ideal.''

The eyes of old men often run with tears. Now the expressive face heaved forth tears. I thought I would shift the direction of the questioning. ''May I ask the question that many people have asked a hundred times. Why are so many people flying in your pictures?''

He seemed almost to levitate. His eyebrows were like trapezes swinging across his mobile face. ''It's surely the way I see it. Because there was a great need to find a certain ideal thing, which was not on earth, which was beyond our everyday life. So I, as a boy, as a small boy I used to think that there must surely be this ideal we are looking for, which is completely beyond the world of our home and street. That is why that hope, to be able to fly, to find that ideal.''

I began to phrase a second question, but now his enthusiasm had been sparked. He wanted to add something. ''I must tell you that I painted my flying characters before Sputnik was put in orbit. I used to be asked, 'Why do you look up to the sky? Nobody can walk there.' And now you see later, they have nevertheless walked in the sky.''

I thought that perhaps the interview was drawing to a conclusion, so I threw in a general question. ''Having lived through so much, having created so much, do you remain an optimist?''

''Ah yes, I am never pessimistic. Except, I am pessimistic when I think that life, our earthly life, must come to an end. Then I am caught for words. But I'm not pessimistic because my motto has always been to look for love. Only love interests me and I am only in contact with things that revolve around love. So, I am never pessimistic.''

His thoughts trailed off and the film ran out and I waited. "Hurry," he said. "Ask me anything. I will talk." Cameraman Ken Gregg and his assistant, Johnny Maxwell, jammed in another roll of film.

While waiting, Chagall asked for the small volume of his works, which I carried. He thumbed through it, and was able to say where each work was located. He was like a kid announcing all the great museums in all the great cities that had honoured poor Marc Chagall of Vitebsk.

"Do you have a favourite among your paintings, Monsieur Chagall?"

"Ah, I don't have any. No."

"Which of the other great painters who have lived do you have a great respect for?"

"I like all the great artists, Michelangelo, Rembrandt, and so on." No one alive or recently dead was mentioned, I noted.

"What do you still hope to do? You are now eighty-nine. Do you still have one great aspiration?"

"Indeed. I shall do a few more paintings which interest me, but I cannot talk about my paintings. You know, I cannot talk about myself. For that you must ask the specialist, who may scold me. Perhaps criticize. It's not up to me to talk about that."

I thought it best to return to the past, to return to Vitebsk, the magical village of his birth. "Do you see it vividly in your mind or has it become an imaginary place."

The memory of Vitebsk brought a new flowing smile to his face. "Yes, yes. I think unfortunately I incorporate its scenery too often in my paintings. It is perhaps a fault. It proves that something has entered my being too deeply, like a microbe. And it is difficult to get rid of it. I am too intimately linked with that place where I was born. Since you come out of the womb of your mother, you think about your mother. These are human beings. If I were born at the north pole, I would remember the north pole. If I were born in Canada, I would be a Canadian. There is no miracle in that. It is a very natural thing."

I wondered if, indeed, he felt rootless after the constant upheavals in his life. For a moment he seemed a little desperate, looking about for his wife. Then the sun came through a cloud and he could feel the new warmth on his face. "No, indeed. Good heavens, I love France. I am French. Look at that. (He pointed to trees and flowers in his garden.) It is unbelievable. If I were not in France I would not be who I am. Oh, if you could see my paintings before I arrived in France, in the early part of the century. The paintings were of a certain kind. Not too bad. But France is a country which has contributed enormously to the artists of the twentieth century. For me, France is an incredible country."

"Oh I know there are other countries. I like America, for example. I also like Israel, because it is the country of the Bible. If I had not been there, the biblical museum would not exist. I am religious because I adore the Bible—as a political student. That is how I am religious. Because the Bible is the highest form of poetry. I like Israel. Unfortunately, I do not live there. But I go there once in a while."

The interview went on to specific works, such as the great stained-glass window at the United Nations. "I was asked after the death of Hammarskjold to make a memorial to him and the others who died with him. I did a stained-glass window after the prophet Isaiah and it was placed there by the new secretary general. I was there when it was unveiled. I also did a large work at the Metropolitan Opera House. I like America a great deal. I think of America and Canada as being together, as great countries which, it is hoped, will play a great role in the world later."

There was the question of the theatre, the mixture of theatre and art. "Do you have a great love for the theatre?"

"Ah yes, the theatre! The first thing I did for the theatre was for the Yiddish Theatre in Moscow in 1919. It was a mural. Later the theatre was closed in the days of Stalin. The paintings were saved and are at the Tretiakov Gallery in Moscow. They are rolled up and hidden at the moment, but when I went there not too long ago I saw them.

"Later when I returned to America I did the ballet with the choreographer Massine, first the *Allegro* by the poet Pushkin. Later I did the ballet for Stravinsky, *The Firebird*. Then, *The Magic Flute* by Mozart for the new Metropolitan Opera. I hope they will repeat it if the American public likes Mozart. I really don't know because they seem to be mad for Verdi, unfortunately. But I think *The Magic Flute* is a fantastic thing. Then, of course, there's the Paris Opera Ceiling I did for Malraux. Also a ballet for Ravel in Paris. These are things I did for the theatre."

There was a pause of relief for Chagall. His wife had arrived back from shopping in town. She joined him in the garden to act as his translator and comforter. I decided to ask him about Moses. I had spent days studying his works while waiting for the interview, and was struck by the power of the figure of Moses.

"For me you can say that the role of Moses is enormous. He is a grandiose personage who wanted to proclaim the human values of the first order. He was so powerful that he never even entered Jerusalem. God was jealous of him. He told Moses that he would die, that he would never enter, because he had a few doubts. Like every genius he was punished by God." He laughed. I wondered if the fact that some of the world's cooler art critics had not taken Chagall seriously bothered him, and hence whether he would not find his total Jerusalem on earth—if, in fact, he felt he and Moses had something in common. He seemed stunned and amused and irritated at the suggestion. He made a vast, grand gesture, talking to God as well as to me and the camera. "One mustn't exaggerate."

He now seemed full of humour and ready for anything. I asked about the secret of his long life. Each of us is always looking for the secret, in order to push death back as long as we can. No matter what I expected, his answer took me by surprise.

"I have a secret. I think I was influenced by my mother in a very special way because of her great love for me. It struck me so much that I told myself that I must justify her love for me. I wanted to justify it so that she would not be disappointed in me. I saw in her a first-rate symbol, yes, that is like poetry.

"That is not all. My mother was an illiterate woman but I believe that she gave to me all the love she possessed in her because she had not been spoiled by her environment in life at all. But I felt that she expected great things, almost miraculous things from me."

Now his face and manner and the colours of the day seemed to blend into the very air. I asked, "Where do the colours come from?"

"You know, the destiny of the Jewish people affected me greatly in life. And I saw throughout the Bible, I saw an unbelievable source of colour—of its people, in its history. In the Bible, I saw such unparalleled sources of colour that I did not need to look for them in nature. It is supernatural-like . . ." The phrase hung and blended with the air. I found myself smiling and rejoicing.

Madame Chagall excused herself with a laugh: "Voila, j'ai fait mon devoir."

"It is now a nice day," he said. "Now I will walk." The camera followed him across the garden. Although strong in spirit, his body seemed to bend with the slight breeze. He pointed to trees and a mosaic of the sun he did for his wife. I thought he would now vanish. He had exploded his thoughts on me that day and the camera recorded them. But he stayed to go page by page through the book of photos, making comments as he leafed through as if he were leafing through marks of his life. "That one is in Moscow. One must go to London for that. Leningrad . . . this one in Geneva. This was my first wife, yes, a very happy time . . . my daughter. Yes, that is Chaplin. He is a genius but he knows very little about art . . ."

As he moved through, page by page, I caught sight of a few lines of poetry. I commented that I thought he was a very good poet. He said that he wrote for himself, but he added something that struck me then and fortunately still haunts me. Chagall said, "Ah yes, it's the soul, created in my soul. Yes. Life!"

I say it was fortunate because as the months went by after that warm French afternoon, I was able to track down his poems and find more of his soul, indeed of life. But for the moment, the day was ending. I had to leave. It was like leaving part of my soul, part of my life. He embraced me. I sighed. I knew my own life had reached some kind of new level which I did not understand. I would never be the same. A secret had been exchanged from soul to soul.

Our filming concluded in the area of the South of France. Each sunrise, each sunset. Over and over I contemplated what he had said about seeing colours more vividly than they were in nature. We filmed his great tableau at the Maeght Gallery and the mosaic at the university at Nice, and all living things that seemed to relate.

Then on to Paris. My map of Paris was his book, *My Life*. I had to find the settings, and most especially the light that had inspired him. Since Paris is itself a monument to art, there was no problem finding the settings that he had described. The problem was to retrace his steps and thoughts to make time stand still. Paris is like a giant parking lot and raceway 23 hours of the day. The one hour that you can find the old Paris is just as darkness gives way to dawn, before the heavy trucks spill black fumes into the air. Then you can feel what Chagall felt: "I was struck by the Paris light. I felt airborne. Then I began to understand colour. What glorious freedom." We raced the sun to find its morning light before the trailer trucks blurred it.

There was the question of the controversial ceiling of the Paris Opera House. We were advised that to light it we would have to bring in power from the suburbs at great cost. How to film it? We decided that, since we could not bring in lights, we would try natural light by undercranking the camera. Since we could not build a scaffolding to reach the ceiling to test the light intensity, we would have to film every shot three times at different experimental speeds. So we lay on our backs all night, half in dreams, filming Chagall's dream of music. As I lay there, I suddenly burst into laughter.

"What's got into you?" Ken Gregg asked, somewhat annoyed as his neck ached.

"I've suddenly realized what Chagall has done. Some of the critics say that the painting doesn't fit the ornate surroundings. If you think about it, Chagall has turned the entire opera house into a gilt picture frame for his painting."

And so as we lay there on our backs we all began to laugh. The guards eyed us suspiciously.

At the Paris Museum of Modern Art, we filmed the works at hand and caught the humour and love of his "Double Portrait with Wine Glass." Obviously there is no gravity when you are in love. On to London and the Tate Gallery, and then back to Toronto and New York. Constantly filming every work I could find, 1,000 works in all.

Two things I had to understand and they did not come easily. First, what it was to be a mystic. I studied the texts of Martin Buber and from them I journeyed back to the Caballa. They were a maze that would not provide the way out. Second, Chagall's poems, and in them I came to a fuller understanding of the man. His soul seemed to shine through with more form:

> There was a time when I had two heads
> There was a time when these two faces
> Were covered in a loving dew
> Just now it seems to me
> That even as I draw back
> I moved forward
> Towards a high gate
> Behind which walls stretch out
> Where spent thunder sleeps
> And lightning shatters
> Mine alone is the land
> That exists in my soul.

As the editing proceeded, I knew that I needed a voice for the narrative that was itself a musical instrument. My first choice was James Mason, with whom I had shared an Emmy for *Hall of Kings*. I tracked him down in Switzerland and he agreed to perform, and perform he did in superb style. The entire recording was done before lunch in Geneva without him ever seeing the film. Only once was there a problem, when he could not seem to get the right tone for the poem about the crucifixions. We must have tried it ten times. At last I said, "James, pretend you are at an Irish wake and you are keening with the women."

> They are calling me . . . they beckon me . . .
> The innocent . . . the guilty . . . to their grave . . .
> The last spark goes out
> The last body extinguished
> Silence takes over
> As before a new torrent
> I stand up . . . I take leave of you . . .
> I walk toward the new temple
> And down there I light a candle
> Before your painting.

When Mason had finished, I flew back. I almost felt I could make the trip without a plane. He was perfect.

In New York I recorded the fine character actor Joseph Wiseman, who has a voice like a Jewish violin, doing the Chagall translation. When the time came to add music, I worked closely with composer Lou Applebaum, the skilled man who had worked on all my films in the past eight years. Mozart turned out to be our best friend, with assistance from Christoph Gluck.

My obsession about purity of effect gained momentum. When the soundtrack was being recorded by leading members of the Toronto Symphony, I felt that the sound was dragging. "Stop everything," I shouted. I dashed to my home where I had a collection of Chagall prints. I returned to the studio, where I hung them around the room. "Now," I said, "if Chagall can listen to Mozart while he paints, you can look at Chagall paintings while you play." It worked. The music soared like a Chagall lamb in flight.

Now came the trauma. I held a preliminary screening for the CBC official who was directly responsible at the time. He said, "Cut the film down from 90 to 60 minutes." I weighed many alternatives because I knew that this work was more important than any I had tried before. I studied my Bible at night and there was a psalm about not having man strike down what had been created. I decided that I would steal the negative if necessary. I prayed and just in case, planned.

I arranged a second screening and just happened to have in attendance three "impartial" viewers: the very astute Helen James, a veteran and sensitive TV executive, Claude Bissel, the gentle, scholarly former president of the University of Toronto and Amnon Gil-ad of the Israeli government. At the end of the screening, all three jumped up and said, "Was that really 90 minutes? It went so quickly." The CBC executive smiled and said, "Yes, the length seems right." I confessed to him later that if he had insisted on a cut I would have killed him. He told me he knew that.

Normally when a film is completed for television it is, in fact, finished. But *Homage to Chagall—The Colours of Love* gained a life that transcended itself. All the mystic passion that had gone into it would not allow it to rest. Thanks to the generous support of Marvelle and Murray Koffler, my local benefactors, the film went to commercial movie theatres around the world, received exceptionally good reviews and won many international awards. But perhaps the most important tribute for me was Chagall's final reaction to the completed film.

I arranged a second visit to Chagall and his wife at St. Paul de Vence, this time to show the film. The same projector was borrowed from the Chagall Museum, and a very nervous projectionist accompanied me to the great house on the hill. When Chagall entered the room, he looked even younger than when I had first seen him. His face was open and he stared at me curiously. "So what are you doing now?" he asked. I answered, "Monsieur Chagall, I am still working on your film. It will not be finished until I have found its proper audience." He smiled. "Wonderful. Wonderful. You are possessed by it. An obsession is wonderful. It will keep you young."

And so we began the screening. The Chagalls were mounted on their throne-like easy chairs for this private adventure into his life. Each time one of the paintings that hung in the room was seen on film, Chagall jumped up and down, pointing from one to the other, exclaiming, "Look, the colour, it is perfect. Perfect." The 90 minutes rolled by and I looked only at his face, never at the screen. His face was a screen of comment, perhaps the most beautiful I have ever seen.

Then, it was over. He stood. He took my hand. Then he hugged me. "You have made a work of great love," he said. And then he nodded, "Yes, great love." I was pleased and proud but thought I should ask, "Any mistakes? Any changes?"

"No mistakes," he said happily. "But perhaps . . ."

"Perhaps?"

"Perhaps it is a little long. Maybe you should cut it a bit here or there."

"Monsieur, if you had to cut that beautiful Chagall painting on your wall, which corner would you cut off?" It was a huge work of two lovers over the Eiffel Tower.

He smiled. "I have thought about it for a long time. You must cut nothing. It is perfect. It is like a Chagall painting, full of little secrets. A work of love." He grasped my hand again. He took one of the Chagall posters that had been made to advertise the film, and at the top right-hand corner he signed his name. He looked at it for a while, then added the word *merci*, and pointed an arrow to my name. "Now I must go back to work." He vanished in a smile.

It was the last time I saw him. Since then I have seen the film about 300 times. And you know, it is full of secrets. I am still enjoying them. This film will help me live longer, not less.

CHAPTER
EIGHTEEN

Arthur Miller on
Home Ground

A man's home ground is where he feels most free. For Arthur Miller, now in his mid-sixties, winner of a Pulitzer Prize, author of nine plays, a novel, short stories, essays of observation, his home is a Connecticut farm 95 miles north of New York City, 350 open acres of land which he works. With his wife, professional photographer Inge Morath, and his daughter, Rebecca, a 16-year-old, long-legged beauty of soft, gentle colouring, he lives in a 200-year-old house. Here he writes daily, carves furniture with a Lincolnesque love of working with his hands, and views the world as a kind of lawyer-judge in the court of human affairs.

It seemed inevitable that Miller would become the subject of one of my films ever since I had concluded *Tennessee Williams' South*. These two men are like bookends in the library of the living stage. They emerged at the same time and had their classic plays on Broadway in the same year. And I'm not certain that anything has come close to *A Streetcar Named Desire* and *Death of a Salesman* in importance since. In America's rush for fast and disposable foods and entertainment, Williams and Miller have been overlooked as current playwrights by critics and the public, though they are both still prolific. Both are tough and tender spirits, combining hope and despair. Let me say, having searched the fabric of their lives, that I feel that these men should be honoured daily as epic poets of our times.

I wrote to Miller at the end of 1977 and, ironically, received the reply while I was in Atlanta directing the world premiere of Tennessee

Williams' *Tiger Tail* in February of 1978. The theatre giants were relegated to opening in American cities of secondary cultural importance. After the play was successfully launched, Miller agreed to meet me. The play had opened to mostly superb local reviews, and I was feeling strong when I first encountered Miller in a New York apartment on the East Side, which he was renting for the winter.

His shyness was immediately obvious. He shares with many important people the quality of vulnerability. I have always thought that it is the giants who are the easy targets. Miller's limbs seemed to fold around him as he sat on a straight-back chair that was too small for his frame. He looked most uncomfortable. "I don't know," he said. "I don't know if I want to start all that again." Of course, what he meant by "all that" was the kind of brutal publicity he had endured during his marriage to Marilyn Monroe. He studied me to see whether I would reveal my intentions.

I suggested that viewing *Tennessee William's South* would show my approach. Not once in a year of interviews, I pointed out, had I asked Tennessee the inevitable question about his homosexuality. Miller provided his first smile. "You can ask me that question. No problem." The initial tension eased and his wife entered, carrying a shopping bag. Inge Morath is one of those women who seem remarkably in control of themselves and the world in general. She has a European elegance and quick warmth.

We travelled across town to the offices of International Creative Management and screened the film about Williams. Both Millers sat fascinated, watching Tennessee reveal himself in his way. "You must do it, Arthur," said Inge. "You must have it done. Look what we have just learned about Tennessee."

Tennessee Williams and Arthur Miller are not friends. Their lifestyles are so divergent that their only common link is the theatre. Each knows that the other is a giant. However, there is also a certain reluctance to be totally forthright in mutual praise. Miller stared at me, obviously examining the perils of an exercise that stirs the inner pain of the past. "Okay, if you really want to, let's go."

And so we began. Plans were set for me to spend time at the Miller house in Connecticut. A few weeks later, I met Inge on the steps of the Metropolitan Museum in New York. As we drove north in her Mercedes, the talk inevitably came around to the previous Mrs. Miller—Marilyn. It was good to have it out of the way and not haunt my intentions.

"How did you meet Arthur?"

"It was actually on the set of *The Misfits*. I was taking stills for Magnum. But we hardly said hello. No one can blame me for his separation from Marilyn."

"Was it complicated moving into the farmhouse where she had lived?"

"No, it was only taking down the mirrors. There were mirrors everywhere. You ask Arthur about Marilyn."

The rest of the drive seemed easier. The comment about the mirrors stayed with me. Later I was to feel in that house that Marilyn must have had a constant desire to prove that she was there, that she existed. The daytime nightmares of her life would perhaps vanish in mirrors.

Inge told me of her life in Europe. *Holocaust* had been on TV the week before and she said it was impossible to watch "a show" about those times. Even now she remains thin because her digestion has never recovered from her terrible experiences. I could see that a woman who had survived a Nazi camp could handle the relatively trivial problem of the afterglow of the presence of Marilyn. Marilyn was created by myth-makers like Mailer. But Inge gave off strength.

The house is humble enough. Low ceilinged and unpretentious, but linked to the earth around it by great beams and wide windows. The land is wooded, and gave me the feeling of Big Daddy's phrase: "the greatest acres this side of the river Nile." Arthur took me on a tour. "The pond is the centre of all life. We grow shade trees to sell sometimes, but I'm not much of a salesman. All the pines I planted so many years ago, look at them now. I'm trying for strawberries this year. In my barn I make the furniture and do some carving."

Miller is a man who is always pulling slivers out of his hard hands. His connection with the land is not for show. He walks it with a kind of grace, like a proud captain of a ship. "Ever since Brooklyn, when I planted my first pear tree, I have wanted to make things grow." To grow and to create.

That night we had dinner cooked by Inge's mother, a jolly, solid woman who is a leading chemist in Austria. The fried chicken had a special tang about it. Inge and her mother retired about 10 p.m., and Arthur and I stayed up past midnight drinking wine and brandy. Our conversation covered Canadian politics, our mutual friend, Edgar Snow, the depressing state of theatre in America, the even more depressing state of television in America. I was totally impressed with his openness and his quality, yes, his quality. He seemed a full 350 acres of substance.

I slept comfortably that night in the Miller home, secure that I was embarking on another adventure into a life that would alter my own life and perhaps others. In the morning, Arthur drove me into town, Roxbury, pointing to the side angle of the property, continuing the discussion that swung from the territory of his farm to his mind.

Some weeks later, I returned with a full film crew for a first discussion that was to last all day. It helped that my cameraman was a Japanese-American, Koby, who had the confidence of a hunter stalking a prey. Miller started somewhat stiffly, almost as if performing a ritual. But as the day moved on, he opened up more and more. What you cannot find in the interview that follows is the nuance of humour, the slight shrug, the powerful gesture. Miller became, before my eyes, a giant oak, rooted, yet blossoming, tied to the land and the landscape of provocative thought, yet capable of the terrible inner suffering of the true poet. He was both boy and man, defender and accuser.

RASKY:

>Okay, okay. Well, sitting here in lovely Connecticut countryside near your house seems so far away from where you were born. Could you talk about those early days? I mean the absolute contrast of those early days from where we are now.
>
>(*The sun and a spotlight made Miller squint slightly.*)

MILLER:

>Well, in the first place, I always had, from the earliest times of my life, I always wanted to live in the country for some reason. It may be a throwback to ancient generations or something. I don't know where I got it from, because nobody else wanted to do that in my family. But it is a contrast, in the sense that I lived and was brought up in Harlem and in Brooklyn, New York. And in a way it was my ambition always to get out of there.
>
>In another sense though, I love the city. And I was saying to somebody the other day, it's like a village to me. It may be a sign of having been around a long time, but I can hardly walk down a street in New York anymore without running into somebody who either knows me or who I know. I ran into a man ten days ago on Madison Avenue. He waved to me from a very elegant grocery store and came running out. I recognized him at once. The last time I had seen him was in 1933. He's the man who was responsible for me going to the University of Michigan. His father owned a grocery store and he had been at Michigan, flunked out, came back, thought it was great, told me all about the literary awards that they gave there, which was incredible news.

RASKY:

>Is this a kind of an escape, though, in a way? I mean, to be here rather than in the city?

MILLER:

> I've written most of what I've written in the country. When I
> got out of college, I had no money and I was on the WPA
> for a while. And I was making $22.77 a week and rented a
> house out on Long Island for $80 a summer, which had no
> plumbing or nothing. And I started writing out there. I don't
> know what it was. I always connected expanding and creating
> something with the country, not with the city. I've written
> in the city. I wrote *A View From the Bridge* in Brooklyn. I
> wrote a lot of radio plays in Brooklyn and stories.

It was obvious that this was going to be a full and revealing day.
The only sound was an occasional tractor that hummed up the road. I
could feel the peace he felt, and wanted to know more about his roots.

MILLER:

> My father was for most of his adult life in the coat and suit
> business. He was a manufacturer for 25 years. He was born in
> what was then the Austro-Hungarian Empire, part of what
> was actually Poland. My mother was born here in New York
> and they were middle-class people, finally. He came over, like
> most of those immigrants, ready to work, and it was possible
> to prosper in a relatively short time, like a decade. And they
> were both, their parents were both from the same tiny village,
> near Cracow, Poland. And he never had any education; she
> did. They were nominally orthodox people but they really never
> saw the inside of a synagogue, excepting on the high holidays,
> which was standard operating procedure for a lot of them too.

RASKY:

> In your plays, there seems to be a very heavy moral tone,
> religious moral tone perhaps. Where would that have come
> from? Do you have a grandfather or anybody like that who was
> very religious?

MILLER:

> No, my grandfather was a businessman. There were no
> intellectuals in the family, and no moralists. They were
> primarily doers and makers.

RASKY:

> Where do you think that came from?

MILLER:

> I have no idea. I really don't know. I didn't start reading very
> much until I was in my really late teens. I read earlier on but it
> was mostly for fun.

RASKY:

What sort of reading would you have done in those early years?

MILLER:

Well, I would have read the British classics when I was in my early teens; that is, stories by Kipling and maybe Dickens. That was the standard fare in the schools. They basically taught British English in those days, and it was fundamentally an English literature education. We had Brett Hart and Mark Twain, but that was not regarded really as serious literature, I don't think. But I was not, I didn't regard myself as a big reader or anything. My mother read enormously. She could read a book in an evening but it didn't catch.

RASKY:

Well, how about the theatre? Did you get to the theatre in your early days?

MILLER:

My mother and father went to the theatre. They saw all the big hits of the twenties and brought back the sheet music, because most of what they saw were musicals, and some of the great ones. And she'd play them on the piano Sunday morning after they'd been out there Saturday night, and we'd sing. I had a good voice and I could follow the music quickly. But the theatre, I never was taken to the theatre much or at all until—I don't know—I guess about eleven or twelve she took me up, you know, in Harlem on Lennox Avenue and Seventh Avenue.

In the course of a long day we moved from play to play, from one moment of his life to another. It is impossible to state everything here, but his comment about *Death of a Salesman* was so rich, I would like to include it. I had watched an interview with Elia Kazan just a few days earlier. And the question of the character of Willy Loman, the salesman, had come up. Kazan said that *Death of a Salesman* was the only play he directed in which men in the audience wept openly. I asked Arthur if that was because the men were, in fact, seeing themselves.

MILLER:

Oh sure, sure. But why? You see, they were seeing themselves, not because limitless facets of Willy Loman were revealed in the play—a lot of him is revealed—but because the situation in which he stood, and to which he was reacting, and which was reacting against him was probably the central situation of contemporary civilization. It is that we are struggling with forces that are far greater than anything we can handle, and with no

equipment to make anything mean anything. Willy Loman
is trying to write his name on ice on a hot July day.
       And it's tough not to feel that one is simply vanishing
in smoke. That there is no value left behind. That anything one
does has any real meaning. He's trying to create meaning.
And I think that struggle is what creates a high anxiety in people.
The fear that whatever they have accomplished is really gone
with the wind, or that they haven't done what they thought they
would do. It asks ultimate questions, the play does. And that's
as important, if not more so, than the fact that Willy Loman
is such and such a character. If he were in a different play, I
assure you, they wouldn't be weeping. They're weeping because
the central matrix of that play is—I say this modestly because I
didn't engineer it that way—but it just happens to have been
the central one of what most people are up against in their real
lives.

Miller without Marilyn is subject enough for any film or book.
Nonetheless, since he had married the ruling sex symbol of our time,
there was no way I could feel that I had fulfilled my commitment to my
viewers without talking about her. But Miller's visual dignity is a kind
of oppressive exterior. It's something like approaching the president or
prime minister and asking what breakfast cereal he prefers. I think the
reasons for his marrying her became clearer to me later on as I related
more and more to his past. We began speaking about her through his
script of *The Misfits,* a classic film. He began by speaking of the two
main characters. It was interesting that when he spoke of Clark Gable
he had no trouble referring to him by name, but with the character played
by Marilyn it was as if mention of her name would restore living ghosts.

MILLER:
       She wants stability. She wants things not to change. She wants
       to rely on people. While at the same time, she is terribly
       suspicious of them and will probe until she discovers that point
       at which they will turn against her. That point of unreliability.
       His viewpoint is, yes indeed, that's true, that is life. Life is
       unreliable, but in order to live, you have to accept and even
       embrace the tensions between expectations, which must never
       be lost, and their disappointment, which is inevitable.
             She is saying that everybody disappoints you. But there's
       always somebody in the offing who won't. It is interesting
       that Gable and she, off film and on, exemplified both these
       positions. Because he certainly lived the life of enormous vigour

and expectation, at the same time that he was almost totally
sceptical about practically everything.

RASKY:

And she wasn't?

(*He thought, hesitated, and then replied carefully.*)

MILLER:

Well, that's the contradiction. She was. She couldn't believe in
anything. She believed in everything.

I commented that it was strange how the film was a kind of fortune
teller. Three great stars—Gable, Monroe and Montgomery Clift—were
to die premature deaths after its completion. It was to break up his
marriage as well, a turning point in his life. I asked about her death,
which he had first heard about in Connecticut.

MILLER:

I was here, of course. I hadn't seen her in a long time. And I
didn't know anything about the way she was feeling, or what
she was doing, and it just seemed to me such a monstrous
waste, that she should be gone that way. 'Cause she was, she
was in a terrific struggle for herself. I always felt it was an
accident. I really didn't think she—she was always playing with
suicide, of course, she was getting as close to the edge as
she could—but I can't believe she really went over voluntarily.
    She needed a little luck, not even a lot, just a little, to
keep it at bay 'cause she didn't have it. I guess she was the
original of all the ones who declared a kind of free soul and at
the same time, ironically enough, were suffering a kind of
depression within even as they were declaring that freedom.
And acting it out. And she was literally herself, for all the good
and bad that she felt that she was acting it out. She was being
up front, what she really felt like. And that was a new style.
She was bound down by innumerable weights and possessions
she wanted to get rid of, but couldn't. I mean that things
possessed her that she couldn't disengage from. She was quite
the opposite of a free soul.
    It was inevitable, obviously, because it happened. But a
little blessing would have deflected it maybe.

Of course, as he spoke, there was much unspoken. But I felt that
he had revealed as much as he could, and I felt that I had dared as much
as I was able. The death of Marilyn was a public trauma. Since she died
young, memories of her were frozen in most people's minds. She had

a public sexual vitality of which each viewer felt part owner. She was the cotton-candy dream girl. Fantasies die hard.

In the course of our conversation, Miller said at one point, "The production of a new play, I've often thought, is like another chance in life. A chance to emerge cleansed of one's imperfections." There is little question that the production of *After the Fall* may have served this purpose for him. At the time it opened in New York, many thought it a thinly disguised account of the turbulence of his marriage to Marilyn. When I asked him if it were more autobiographical than other works, he turned rather testy for awhile, but it was a question I had to ask. He replied: "Well, it's neither more or less than any of my other works. That's the only answer I can give you. I can think of innumerable terrific subjects, but I didn't live them. Somebody else lived them and it's not my business to write about them."

Our discussion drifted off to human responsibility for guilt. And Miller quoted Camus' *The Fall*. I've often thought since about this question of how responsible we are for the life and love of others, for the life and death of others. It haunts Miller's works and it haunts most of us, I think.

Perhaps the most poignant moment in the film was the long soliloquy that ends *After the Fall*, which he read on his Connecticut porch, while we dissolved through to shots of his wife Inge and his tall, beautiful daughter Rebecca. A new love had sustained him and the speech is a tribute to Inge and his new life:

> But love, is love enough? When you know how to kill. Or is it possible that this is not bizarre and I'm not alone, that no one lives who would not rather be the sole survivor of this place and all its finest victims. Who can be innocent again on this mountain of skulls?
>
> But what will defend her? That woman hopes. Or is that exactly why she hopes, because she knows what burning cities taught her and the death of love taught me. That we are very dangerous. And that, that's why I wake each morning like a boy, even now. Even now I swear to you there's something in me that could bear to love this world again. Is the knowing all? To know and even happily that we meet unblessed, not in some garden of wax-fruit and painted trees. That lie of Eden, but after, after the fall, after many, many deaths. Is the knowing all? And the wish to kill is never killed. But with some gift of courage, one may look into its face when it appears and with a stroke of love as to an idiot in the house, forgive it, again and again, forever.

In some ways Miller is a man waiting in the wings for a new triumph. If it never comes he has, as the saying goes, paid his dues. I asked him to tell whether Arthur Miller had paid a price.

MILLER:

> Yeah. The price that you are stuck at a task which never leaves you. You're never satisfied. And a lot of people are satisfied. They feel they've accomplished great things. I never do. And I don't know the writer who really does. A real one. It's always, you're always renewing your resolution. To do something really good. And I suppose that goes on to the last minute. But, so that's a price you pay. This endless, endless frustration with a few moments of immense pleasure at a structure that has stood instead of collapsing. But then, if you count them, you can count them. In a lifetime there aren't that many. So that's a price I think you pay.

Somewhere in our conversations Miller had mentioned his short story, "I Don't Need You Anymore." It struck my imagination and I filmed it as if I were filming my own childhood. It was simply the story of a young boy on the Jewish high holidays, commanding his world to take notice, for he was preparing to take over as the conscience of mankind. Miller had done that in a way, and with memories of the *shul* on McKay Street, I tried too. It commanded, in turn, a price. This question of price. We have all paid it, our price. No life is free. But what was it that motivated Miller? Why did I share so many views with him? Yet, of course, we were not the same.

It was that day, that day in Brooklyn. We had gone to look at his street. And what I found was that his street was my street. It was also the street of George Bernard Shaw in Dublin, the street of Martin Luther King in Atlanta. It was the street of striving, the street of sameness, the street of continuity. It was the street from which we all dreamed of distant places. It was called Avenue M and Third Street, the all-common street, the heartland of America, Canada, Ireland, England. The neighbourhood. The better life. The ordinary life. Not a slum. Not luxury. Compartmentalized lives. Neatly filed days. Beginnings . . . endings. On such a street one could dream of marriage to sex symbols, movie stars on giant screens, larger than life. On such a street I could imagine myself as a boy wanting to fly like Chagall or wishing to lead many lives, which I did, and all of them would somehow become my own.

My daughter Holly, now a teenager, wrote as the opening line of a poem, "The world turns 'round without a sound." And so, it seemed to me, time turned all the way round, and I was where I began—back on St. Clair Avenue West.

After Words

To conclude. No, *to continue*—for this must be the 11th commandment.

Late in July, 1979, on a hot Sunday afternoon, my universe was squeezed down to size, and the consequence was that I knew I had to get on with this volume quickly. What was it? A hornet. And I was almost dead. A family of hornets had come to plant a hive in my Toronto garden. I decided to cut them off. Wearing tennis shorts in preparation for an afternoon swim, I walked over and casually dropped a brick on their home. I walked away. As I left, suddenly there was a sharp sting on my left foot. Damn, what a nuisance, I thought. I'll be late for my swim.

I walked into the kitchen and with no concern dabbed the invisible wound with a little vinegar (an old-fashioned remedy), added some vitamin E ointment for good luck (a new-fashioned remedy, and sat for a few minutes on the porch. Heat. My head was getting warm. I walked upstairs to lie down. Perhaps the air conditioner would cool me off. Now lying on the bed alone, my breath, my breathing going . . . going . . . gasping. Clinging to what air I could swallow, unable to talk, unable to call for help, unable to stand. Finally with every muscle, pushing the sound, a call: "Help, oh God, oh help!" In a few minutes, I was being transported in time back through the events of these pages, and in place to the Mount Sinai Hospital, where a double dose of adrenalin restored my heartbeat, my life.

Now came the meaning. Suddenly the colours of understanding, the link of all life. Like Chagall's vision of all life being holy. My life now connected to the hornet, to a stinger too small to see yet large enough to topple me, large enough to end me. Revolutions in Latin America, grenades in Vietnam, wild bullets in Gaza, spears in the Congo. None were so potent as the tiny stinger of an angry hornet protecting his home on my home ground.

Our lives were connected. *All life is connected*. Once this is understood then it is perhaps the beginning of understanding. All the lives I have written about are mine, as mine is theirs. Each film has asked a question and each question suggests another, and they are all endlessly connected. That is why there is no end.

It was Sunday, November 11th, the 11th day of the 11th month, a time of remembrance. My father died that day, too. I went again to the cemetery, that Sunday in 1979, to say my private *Kaddish* for Leib, my father, and Perl, my mother. Adam, who was eleven, said he would join me in the pilgrimage.

We drove north in Toronto on Bathurst Street, where once I had pushed that bicycle laden with dead chickens for Sabbath suppers. I can never drive that road without seeing myself in the rear-view mirror of memory, struggling up the hill, just on the edge of the Holy Blossom Temple. And north beyond that, where Jewish homes cling to both sides of the road, huddled against past generations of prejudice. Once it was farmland. Now it all blurs in the frost of time. West along Wilson Avenue, alongside a superhighway that bisects like a granite axe.

Where is it exactly? I always miss the cemetery which once seemed so grand, and now is surrounded by cement factories. And the road has been newly widened and passes it by without any special ceremony. We turn and find our way back. We park, the only car on a small hill called Mount Sinai. (And where, where is Moses?) The first frost is in the November ground. How lonely is the frozen earth! The sky is the colour of the Bulldog steelwool I stacked in my father's store, the grey bulging over to touch the crust of ground. Where does it begin and where does it end?

We trip over stones in search of my parents . . . *Wagman* . . . *Wilkes* . . . *Feldman*. And for a moment there is panic. Am I in the wrong graveyard? We circle around. And they are not lost. New graves have changed the skyline of stone slabs. Here, here they are, side by side. *Beloved mother and wife, beloved father*, says the inscription. Remembered and respected, say I. We scout around for pebbles. It is the tradition to place small chips of stone on the headstones to indicate that there were callers. We are callers connected forever and ever.

It is Sunday. How far really do we ever swing away from our past? No matter how far we push. No matter what we do with our bodies. No matter how far we try to remove our minds. The umbilicus has been cut but not broken. The chain that binds us is on a hinge like a swing, and so we swing up and out, then back, and repeat again and again.

There are tears, involuntary. I try to hear my father's song, but there is silence and the Canadian wind. On the edge of the cemetery, we hear the Ontario Northland Railroad, its diesel mourning, as it heads north as once I did to Kirkland Lake. Silence again.

"Dad," says Adam, "if we move from here, will we take them with us?"

"Sure, in a way, we always have them with us."

I try to say the *Kaddish*, but the words seem too impersonal.

"There should be a prayer," I say to Adam.

"I know one," he says, wanting to help.

"What is your prayer, Adam?"

"Sweet dreams," he says.

Amen!   *To continue . . .*

Acknowledgments

"My way of joking is to tell the truth. It's the funniest joke in the world." George Bernard Shaw said that. I wish I had. But I list him here among those who helped with this volume, this life.

From the past, I would add Michelangelo and Disraeli and the unknown scribes of the Bible. From the present, the gifted writers Tennessee Williams, Arthur Miller, the Durants, the simple love of Chagall, the dancing genius of Baryshnikov, the song and friendship of Leonard Cohen, the mystery of Christopher Janus—all of whom have been subjects and friends.

Actors and their wives who have helped bring words to drama, Claris and James Mason, Lorne Greene, Elaine and Christopher Plummer, Bettye and Sam Jaffe who also adopted my family as theirs.

The various members of the Rasky clan who have been patient with my daydreams over the years, especially my brother Frank, who encouraged me not to become a lawyer or God-knows-what. My own kids, Adam and Holly, with their constant "earth-to-dad" as I dreamed some of these lines, and Arlene who has had the patience and love to deal with the creative and sometimes absent mind. And don't forget best-man Gerry Morris.

The CBC has been especially kind in allowing me each of the past ten years to offer "something-from-Harry" without complaint or criticism, especially Laurent Picard, Al Johnston, Peter Herndorff, Thom Benson and John Barnes.

Critics along the way have been especially kind, starting with my old-time friend Gordon Sinclair, Bob Blackburn, Jack Miller, Blake Kirby, Wes Hicks and Joan Irwin in Canada. In the U.S. Cecil Smith and Dan Sullivan of the *Los Angeles Times*, Judith Crist, Jeff Lyons, Eric Barnouw, Michael Arlen of the *New Yorker*, and John Leonard of the *New York Times* and Judson Hand of the *New York Daily News* who also became my favourite intellectual drinking companion. Emily Genauer, the great art critic, first saw the love in *The Colours of Love* and Marvelle and Murray Koffler kindly found a way to share it with thousands all over the world, helped by lawyer Martin O'Brien. And wise Walter and Fay Schwimmer in Chicago, bless you.

This volume began with a chance conversation with Eric Koch and then was pushed lovingly by literary agent extraordinary Lucinda Vardey, typed with wise comment by Claire Guinn, assisted by my smiling associate Aili Suurallik and combatively edited by patient Sarah Swartz. To all I am grateful.

The films it deals with were joined in creation with my faithful

262 Nobody Swings on Sunday

crew: Ken Gregg, Arla Saare, Geoff Cheesbrough, Johnny Maxwell, Erik Hoppe, Erik Kristensen, with music of course by Lou Applebaum. Thank you all. In the past there was Tonti in Rome and Koby in New York with editing by marvelous Mavis, and a thousand others.

To the people of Canada and the U.S. who have responded with kindness and warmth to my film works and passion, who have allowed me to swing my heart out on film, I am forever grateful.

Credits